# REAWAKENING

*The New, Broader Middle East*

**Jerry M. Rosenberg**

**University Press of America,® Inc.**
Lanham · Boulder · New York · Toronto · Plymouth, UK

**Copyright © 2007 by**
**University Press of America,® Inc.**
4501 Forbes Boulevard
Suite 200
Lanham, Maryland 20706
UPA Acquisitions Department (301) 459-3366

Estover Road
Plymouth PL6 7PY
United Kingdom

Library of Congress Control Number: 2007929247
ISBN-13: 978-0-7618-3850-0 (paperback : alk. paper)
ISBN-10: 0-7618-3850-3 (paperback : alk. paper)

"I like dreams of the future better than the history of the past."

Thomas Jefferson writing to John Adams, August 1, 1816

\* \* \* \* \* \* \* \* \* \* \* \*

This Volume is Dedicated to

*RITA ROSENBERG CHILD*

Her sparkle brings joy to all in her presence. Her future promises to be both challenging and exciting.

# TABLE OF CONTENTS

# PREFACE

"To Jerry M. Rosenberg – With much respect for your attempt to organize a great dream…..I believe you have addressed yourself to the very foundations which will lie at the heart of the future of the region and I hope indeed that the day is not far off when the plan will be brought to realization."

**Shimon Peres**

The post-Intifada II era could arguably be closely identified with the re-election of George W. Bush for a second four-years in November 2004, and Yasir Arafat, the symbol of Palestinian nationalism and a future state of Palestine, lying comatose and dying in a Paris hospital, both significantly impacting on the future direction of events in the Middle East.

Then, in January 2005, Mahmoud Abbas was elected President of the Palestinian Authority, and the first pluralist election in 50 years was held in Iraq where 275 members of the national assembly were chosen to draft a permanent constitution. Abbas had inherited a bankrupt, powerless and divided PA. (The next few years would continue to show the curse of these internal divisions; Fatah and Hamas would remain in conflict.)

In August, Israeli settlers were evicted from the Gaza Strip, leaving the territory to its 1.3 million Gazans anxious to combine with the West Bank and form the future Palestinian state.

On January 4, 2006, Ariel Sharon, the Prime Minister of Israel suffered a massive stroke; his political career suddenly came to an end. A mere few weeks later, on January 26th, Hamas won an impressive, and yes, democratic election to gain control of the Palestinian parliament. Their victory was a blow to PA Prime Minister Abbas and, perhaps more critically to the goals of President George W. Bush.

As heir to Ariel Sharon, Ehud Olmert took over the office of Prime Minister following the March 28th election in Israel. Within a short time period huge shifts in the Middle East landscape have occurred. (Olmert would have a brief political honeymoon until the summer 2006 invasion of Lebanon.)

One day later, Hamas' prime minister and his cabinet were sworn in, putting them in control of the Palestinian Authority. It appears that both sides of the Israeli/Palestinian conflict have sworn to deal as little as possible with each other.

In July 2006, Israeli troops pursued Hamas militants in Gaza and Hezbollah terrorists into Lebanon. Kidnappings of Israeli soldiers were given as the reason for the intrusions across borders. The international community protested, while the U.S. continued its support of Olmert's decision. After 34 days of killings, a truce agreement was implemented. November 2006 mid-term U.S. elections saw the Democrats regaining control of Congress, the replacement of Secretary of State Rumsfeld with Robert Gates, followed by a determination to disengage U.S. troops from Iraq prior to the 2008 presidential campaign.

--------------------------------------------------

How to reconcile a failed U.S. policy in the Middle East - from the Quartet's stumbling and fading Road-Map, designed to overcome the Israeli/Palestinian conflict, to reform and democracy in Iraq, to containing the nuclear ambitions of Iran, and beyond.

Then there is the challenge of a declining and dismal attitude by a significant portion of the world's population towards the U.S. Throughout my life, the U.S. was looked upon as a glowing model of what might be, a projection of freedom, independent thought and economic opportunity. The poor and the developing nations modeled themselves as best as they could on the miracle of U.S. accomplishment; our constitution, our might, our governing principles, and our growing, affluent life style.

Since 9/11, many of us shudder at what our children and grandchildren will inherit. We bear witness to a rapid deterioration in our nation's prestige and clout, both political and economic. We are less and less listened to, and perhaps more importantly, less and less cared about. We, at the same time, are often demoralized and puzzled by six years of attempting to answer: "Why Do They Hate Us?"

Our naivite and gullibility have become our burdens and reality is now setting in. President George W. Bush, despite and because of his reasons of national security and global determination to spread "democracy", has put the U.S. in harm's way since the invasion of Iraq.

The Administration's clear support for Israel's 34 days war against Hezbollah in Lebanon further weakens how neutral the U.S. is The President has perpetuated a series of dismal decisions that continue to make all of us slide down a path of inadequacy, with the threat of future attacks on our shores.

In a short time, voters will weigh the pros and cons of the past years. Blame will become a political sledgehammer. Democrats and Republicans will not be shy this time around to finger-point the inadequacies of our past foreign policies. No longer will global affairs be relegated to the bottom of the pile as polls of the past years have shown. Moving up the scale, overseas aspirations and decisions will no longer place last, but will compete for attention with jobs, unemployment, crime, and quality of education. In other words, these past few years have pushed all Americans into a more sophisticated awareness of the world around us. Hopefully, we will never turn our attention away again.

Assuredly, there are alternatives to present day dealings with the nations of the broader Middle East. This volume communicates several of them, based on historical proof that a reinvented Marshall Plan for the region, followed by a carefully organized regional economic community, of a potential 28 nations can be the harbinger of future stability and prosperity in a neighborhood of one-half a billion people.

For more than a decade, ever since the signing of the 1993 Oslo Accord on the White House lawn, I have researched and studied (at times been tormented) about a Middle Eastern regional prosperity that would take us beyond the present day stalemate.

Avoiding the principle axiom, that with peace (simply defined as the lack of war) a raised living standard and greater prosperity was possible. Along with others deeply involved in the area's crises, I forced myself to accept and tried to convince contemporaries at all levels that economics and cross-border trade could be the glue keeping the peace on a steady and improving course. Now I see how wrong I was. Thirteen years of developing and then restructuring models were based on creating instruments for the laboratory. I now believe these concepts and designs are required. They need to be ready to "go," and they must be in "place," even though they must await the end of the battles. That is exactly what happened more than a half-century ago with the launch of the Marshall Plan in 1948, three years after the end of World War II. Today, the principles are the same, though the cast varies as do the issues, but devastation and fear remain. In 1945 there was destruction, unemployment and lowered living standards throughout Western Europe, and a perceived threat from an aggressive Soviet Union. In 2006, there is destruction, unemployment and lowered living standards in nations throughout the Middle East, and a threat, not from the dismantled Soviet Union, but from terrorism, extremism, and militant fundamentalism.

In the spring of 1958, while studying in Paris on a French Government Bourse and a Fulbright Scholarship, I heard Jean Monnet (arguably the father of the European Union) speak at the American Church, where he repeatedly praised the historic contributions of the famed World War II U.S. general, and later Secretary of State, George C. Marshall. European recovery and reconstruction was made possible, he argued, thanks to the generosity of the American people and to the 1948 Marshall Plan.

Monnet was the architect of the European Coal and Steel Community, a union initially between former enemies France and Germany. In 1958, the Common Market would lead the way towards an astounding European Economic Community. Now called the European Union, it includes 25 nations with a population of 450 million people who consume ¼ of all worldly manufactured goods. The EU is a vital entity pursuing the addition of more member nations, including Turkey.

I mistakenly believed that the economic integration of the founding six nations of the EU from Western Europe was part of a grand strategy of rehabilitation following the destruction of the Second World War. Monnet and his handful of supporters solely promoted the concept of raising living standards by creating jobs and industrial growth as a means to keep the Soviet Union at bay. Only later did I begin to understand the importance not only of the United States' vast financial contributions to the Marshall Plan but, more importantly, its crucial role as conductor of the finely tuned orchestration of both confidence- and nation-building.

The Marshall Plan provided aid for 16 nations at a cost to the U.S. of $13.3 billion (the Congressionally approved amount was $17 billion) in today's dollars about $100 billion. (President Bush has already committed more than this for Iraq alone, and the figure continues to rise. Funds for Afghanistan, Lebanon, Palestine, and other countries of the Middle East add to the growing drain on our Treasury and taxpayers.)

Spreading assistance throughout the region of 28 nations, including Iraq, Afghanistan, Lebanon, the future Palestine, Israel, etc., I expect that a purse of at least $1 trillion will be required.

No longer will it be feasible for unilateral monetary contributions from the EU, other Arab nations, from Japan, the U.S., or any other lone country/union to work.

# Preface

Henceforth, a unified approach with institutional structure and governance to oversee the disbursement of funds as well as to monitor the region's countries as they move, over time, toward economic co-dependence will be required.

*     *     *     *     *     *     *     *     *

Following the signing of the Oslo Agreement in 1993 between the Israelis and Palestinians, a global commitment was made to move the peace process forward. Economic assistance was the glue to keep things on track. As a specialist in regional economic cooperation, I was asked to design models for economic integration in the Middle East that extended throughout the Arab-Muslim world of North Africa (Central Asia, though Muslim, was not considered in the peace process in the mid-1990s).

Former President Bill Clinton, in a letter to me, wrote "as you point out, there is an opportunity to define the future of the Middle East in terms of reconciliation and co-existence rather than confrontation and violence. There are no limit to what can be done if the region's energy and talents can be channeled into creating new opportunities and building a land as bountiful and peaceful as it is holy."

Ariel Sharon was a newly elected Prime Minister when he examined a copy of my book "Arafat's Palestinian State and JIPTA: The Best Hope for Lasting Peace in the Middle East" and together we discussed the feasibility and likelihood of it ever being realized.

His presence was as formidable as his winning smile. It was difficult for me to connect this gentle communicator with his history of military leadership. The man who some claim began Intifada II by boldly and deliberately visiting the Al-Aksa mosque on September 28, 2000, now in our conversation projected genuine interest in my recommendations.

Taking the forty-nine year old success story of the originally named European Economic Community and eliminating the non-functioning, inappropriate, impractical approaches, while retaining the unique qualities of the present day Union, I would apply this information to interact with other attempts at regional cross-border arrangements around the globe. It seemed a rather straightforward, simple, obvious, and easy transfer.

At the Middle East/North Africa Economic Summits held in Casablanca (1994), Amman (1995), Cairo (1996) and, finally, in Doha (1997), I addressed small groups on a model for regional economic integration that would help sustain the region's peace.

Conversations were held with U.S. Secretary of State Warren Christopher and Secretary of State Madeleine Albright, Israel's former Prime Ministers Ariel Sharon, Itzhak Rabin, Shimon Peres, Bibi Netanyahu, Ehud Barak, current prime minister Ehud Olmert; Palestinian Authority Chairman Yasir Arafat, King Hussein of Jordan, King Abdullah II-the present King of Jordan, Andre Azoulay-Senior Advisor to King Hassan and King Mohammad of Morocco, Turkey's former Prime Minister B. Ecevit, President I. Karimov of Uzbekistan, and many others.

They all convinced me that successful regional economic cooperation would be the primary means for long-term stability and prosperity.

Jordan's King Hussein, sorely missed today, acknowledged both the legitimacy and possibilities of my initial model for an economic community of Arab nations working in harmony with Israel. The Executive Secretariat of the Middle East North Africa Economic Summit (based in Rabat, Morocco) asked me to write a book in time for the

Preface

1996 Cairo conference, describing my model of regional economic integration accompanied by the flow of financial assistance.

What followed were meetings with dozens of prominent leaders from the Middle East and North Africa. Additional sessions were held with experts at The World Bank, The International Monetary Fund, the U.S. Department of State, and at several U.S. Embassies.

Initially, this volume was confined only to nations of the Middle East and North Africa. With the attacks of September 11, 2001 and its aftermath, and an awareness of the inter-relationships throughout the region following invited briefings at the U.S. Department of State, it seemed essential to add the Muslim, non-Arab, countries of Central Asia, Afghanistan, and Pakistan as potential partners.

\*    \*    \*    \*    \*    \*    \*    \*    \*

This book, is based on more than thirteen years of pursuing the dream of a stable, and more prosperous Middle East, North Africa and Central Asia. With gradual, monitored, and transparent cross-border economic integration (rather than antagonistic isolation) based on the model of the Marshall Plan, that dream can be realized. Never in modern history has such a Middle East Recovery Program (MERP) been so timely.

And just as India and China have become the engines of lower cost labor for the world, the broader Middle Eastern nations can also be participants in the global manufacturing economy.

Natan Sharansky, Deputy Prime Minister of Israel during Prime Minister Sharon's first term in office, wrote to me on May 9, 2001 "As you know, I believe a recovery program for the countries of our region is of utmost importance. This program must bring not only economic growth, but also democracy, transparency in government and human rights to these countries, some of which are less than fully familiar with these concepts. I hope, by drawing on the 'Marshall Plan', you are able to formulate a blueprint that can succeed in the Middle East. I further hope that you are able to use the 'Marshall Plan' to illustrate to others how such plans have been successful in the past, and how, despite the daunting odds, such a plan could create economic growth, democracy, and peace in our region. I wish you much success in your important work."

President Bush was infatuated with Sharansky's 2004 book, "The Case for Democracy: The Power of Freedom to Overcome Tyranny and Terror." He has often been quoted telling reporters to read it so that they can get "a sense of what I'm talking about " vis-à-vis the Middle East. In "The Case for Democracy" Sharansky makes three primary points: first, that realpolitik is bankrupt; second, that democracy is the best insurance against terrorism; and, third, the world truly is divided between good and evil.

In this book, I hope to illustrate the pros and cons of MERP; to address the huge costs for funding it; and to transfer tenets of the Marshall Plan to a corner of the world which has been long sunk in poverty and lost to hatred.

The Marshall Plan was set to run from 1948 through 1952. Its end was the coming war in Korea, which shifted the emphasis from nation-building to defense against the oncoming Communists. Importantly, as one of its conditions, it gave birth to what we now call the European Union. The parallels are powerfully apparent. My three-track proposal for the Middle East rehabilitation and aid would commence with Palestinians in the West Bank and Gaza, then broaden to other nations of the Middle East, and finally embrace all nations of the Middle East, eventually adding other Arab-Muslim and non-Arab Muslim nations.

Ideally, all eligible Middle East, North Africa, and Central Asia countries would hopefully participate in the formation of MERP.

This volume has been years in preparation, commenced long before the World Trade Towers and Pentagon attacks of September 11, 2001; before the September 2000 (Al-Aqsa) Aksa-Intifida crisis facing the peoples of Israel, the West Bank and the Gaza Strip; before Saudi Arabia's Crown Prince Abdullah's call for a 22 nation-Arab League plan for a permanent peace with Israel; before President Bush's June 2002 pronouncements regarding Chairman Arafat and economic development for the Palestinians; before the campaign against Saadam Hussein, before the release of the United Nations "Arab Human Development Reports"; before the election of George W. Bush as president, before the death of Yasir Arafat; before the end of Ariel Sharon's tenure as Prime Minister; and before the summer 2006, 34 day invasion of Lebanon.

Valuable information has been gleaned from recent news releases, and, most critically, from feedback following several briefings at the U.S. Department of State, The World Bank, the International Monetary Fund, and U.S. embassies where regional experts patiently sat with me during my attempts to explain my models. Comments were fair, genuine, and most helpful.

In addition, travels to conferences and research centers in Morocco, Egypt, Israel, Jordan, Qatar, United Arab Emirates, Turkey, and Uzbekistan, have provided me with a critical insight into the region's potential should peace and stability take hold.

I am thankful to Ellen, my exciting, beautiful, loving, and accomplished wife of 46 years, to my children Lauren, Bob, Liz, and Jon, all who remain supportive of my interests and ongoing projects, and to my four granddaughters-Bess, Ella, Celia, and Rita - who in their innocence, remain my hope for the future.

To write this book, I relied on many sources, including four of my earlier books on the Middle East. In particular, I have utilized a considerable portion of "Nation-Building: A Middle East Recovery Program", published by University Press of America in 2003.

This volume should not be considered a work of historical scholarship. If it has made a contribution, it is with new models for a future Middle East of stability. It has been written for an informed general audience, and therefore I have avoided including excessive citations and references as usually found in scholarly publications.

In early February 2006, the Marshall Foundation and the U.S. Department of State held a meeting to explore lessons of the Marshall Plan for today's hot-spots. The combination of historians sharing ideas with practitioners was a great learning experience for me. Some of the "lessons" from this 3-day meeting in Washington, D.C. were applied throughout this volume.

I also extend my appreciation to Dr. Larry Bland and others at the Marshall Foundation for their 2006 Marshall-Baruch Fellowship enabling me to gather last-minute materials for this volume and to ready the manuscript for publication.

And to two of my brightest, charming, and dedicated graduate students, Gregory Henderson and Nathan Betancourt, who carefully reviewed the final manuscript and came up with numerous brilliant suggestions, I extend a warm appreciation.

The genius of those who, in 1947, wrote and argued for passage before the U.S. Congress of the European Recovery Program have largely been forgotten and unsung. In applying significant portions of their plan, with twists, I acknowledge their skills, tenacity, and dedication as they created a policy masterpiece of historical proportion.

Tomorrow's events will assuredly alter these proposals which are mine alone, to be defended by me. If or where I am found in error, I alone am responsible and apologize in advance for any shortcomings.

**Jerry M. Rosenberg**                                   **May 5, 2007**
**E-mail: rosenbrg@andromeda.rutgers.edu**

# *REAWAKENING*

## *1945-1951*          *WESTERN EUROPE*

## FLOW CHART IN SEQUENCE

*END OF WORLD WAR II*

*DESTRUCTION*

*POVERTY*

*NATION-BUILDING*

*COMMUNIST THREAT*

*U.S. CONGRESS*

*THE MARSHALL PLAN-16 NATIONS*

*EUROPEAN RECOVERY PROGRAM*

*EUROPEAN UNION-27 NATIONS*

*STABILITY AND PROSPERITY*

# *REAWAKENING*

## *2000-20??*      *BROADER MIDDLE EAST*

## FLOW CHART IN SEQUENCE

*NO END TO KILLINGS*

*SUICIDE BOMBINGS*

*INSURGENCY*

*POVERTY*

*NATION-BUILDING*

*TERRORISM THREAT*

*U.S.CONGRESS/UNITED NATIONS*

*MIDDLE EAST RECOVERY PROGRAM*

*MIDDLE EAST COMMUNITY-28 NATIONS*

*STABILITY AND PROSPERITY*

# CHAPTER I

## INTRODUCTION

**"The Middle East has always needed active American engagement for there to be progress, and we will provide it, just as we have for over half a century."**

**Colin Powell**

"Stuff happens," said the nonchalant, now former Secretary of Defense Donald Rumsfeld as looters stripped Bagdad. It is "the birth pangs of a new Middle East," claimed Secretary of State Condoleezza Rice as Hezbollah rockets fell on northern Israel and Israel's Air Force bombarded Lebanon.

By the end of 2006, President Bush's Middle East Road-Map was in near total disarray and the majority of Americans were calling to bring the troops home from Iraq. The long awaited Iraq Study Group report was released.

The costs, both human and economic, are staggering. Figures of $1 trillion, and more, are projected to be needed to cover military and rebuilding costs for the return of normalcy, just for Iraq.

The National Priorities Project, a nonpartisan education and advocacy organization, breaks down U.S. expenses for Iraq by state and town. For example, their figures assume an average cost of $2,844 for every household, or $1,075 for every American.

In 2006 alone, the U.S. will spend approximately $100 billion for the war effort. That amounts to four times what the government will spend on all science, space, and technology projects and three times what will be spent on caring for natural resources and the environment. That figure is also more than twice what the federal government will spend on U.S. elementary, secondary, and vocational education.

This was the war that promised to be short-lived; perhaps several months with a price-tag of $50 billion, and few if any people would die. By mid-summer 2006, over 2,800 coalition force casualties, including 2,600 Americans, and between 40,000 and 45,000 Iraqi civilians had been killed.

Then, by August's end in 2006, the destruction in Lebanon and Israel demanded a minimum of $3-4 billion to rebuild their infrastructure, housing, adequate food and medical facilities, and to invigorate the economy.

(Anticipating a mini-Marshall Plan, about 60 governments and aid organizations met in Stockholm to raise funds for the Middle East. On September 1$^{st}$ they pledged $940 million in early reconstruction aid for Lebanon. The following day, in a spirit of unity, they then pledged nearly $500 million in aid for the Palestinian people in the West Bank and Gaza. The process had now begun.)

As the Middle East ruptures, the subsequent political debates call for new solutions. Alternative plans must now be put on the table that include multilateral efforts to bring stability and prosperity to the region. The 2008 presidential election will assuredly become the platform for condemnation, accusation, and programs for a rapid resolution of a growing U.S. involvement.

This volume presents both a short and long-term set of models for a reborn Middle East. Once the killings cease, will the region be able to recapture the glories of its past? Can living standards be raised along with the cultural richness it once possessed? While Europe slumbered towards its own renaissance, the Middle East - North Africa, the Levant (the traditional Middle East), and Central Asia - was spirited and prosperous, the leader in trade and science. Its future may suggest a revival of its golden and remarkable history – its reawakening.

-----------------------------------------------------------------

Taskent, Bukhara, and Samarkand - the jewel of Central Asia's Islamic world, were unfamiliar places during a recent trip to Uzbekistan. The serene beauty of its mountains rivals that of the Himalayas. Its deserts are as dry as any on earth. Fertile valleys and visible oases dot the landscape.

In the ancient past, there was abundance, bountiful tables of food were ever-present, and suggested glory and prosperity. Today, poverty, and especially drought, are the most devastating causes of daily strife in this overwhelmingly Muslim nation of 26 million people.

Throughout Central Asia's history, water and trade have been dominant forces. The ancient "Silk Routes" linked China and Afghanistan with the West. Alexander the Great passed through the region in the 4th Century B.C., as did the warlord Genghis Khan eight centuries later. Marco Polo arrived at the end of the 13th century, followed by Tamerlane-the Uzbek national hero who, by the 14th century, had reached the western Afghan city of Herat.

Commanded by the Koran to seek knowledge and read nature for signs of the Creator and inspired by a treasure trove of ancient learning, Muslims evolved a society that, in the Middle Ages was the scientific center of the world. The Arabic language was synonymous with learning and science for 5 centuries; a golden age that introduced the modern university, algebra, the names of the stars and even the notion of science as an empirical form of inquiry.

Muhammad made his impressive trek from Mecca to Medina in 622 A.D. His soldiers swept out from the Arabian Peninsula in the seventh and eighth centuries, annexing territories from Spain to Persia. In the process, they rediscovered the works of Plato, Aristotle, Democritus, Pythagoras, Archimedes, Hippocrates, and other Greek innovators and philosphers.

And then, around 1600 A.D. the decline began. The void was to be filled by Western Europe as its Renaissance. Islamic scholars that had once led the world in science, lost it at that time. Centuries of extensive neglect and conquest continued.

For four hundred years the Muslim world was in the shadow of the West. And for four hundred years, the West didn't pay Central Asia (and the Middle East) much attention – unless it was to secure the region's oil at the cheapest prices.

In 1991 all that began to change. The Soviet Union collapsed and suddenly the West again took an interest in the 60 million people living in the five ex-Soviet Central Asian countries of Central Asia – Uzbekistan, Kazakhstan, Kyrgyzstan, Turkmenistan, and Tajikistan.

The terrorist attacks on September 11, 2001 forced the United States to reevaluate its involvement in the region. The U.S. bombed Afghanistan and in 2003 attacked Iraq. The American presence in this neighborhood, in all likelihood, may never wane again.

---------------------------------------

With a broad sweep of the brush, the Middle East as a geopolitical map has been permanently redefined. From Morocco on the westernmost end of the Mediterranean Sea, across North Africa, past Turkey and eastward into the heart of the Middle East, then swinging northeast to Central Asia, Pakistan and Afghanistan, half of the world's one billion Muslims surround the land of 6.5 million Israelis.

Israel remains embroiled by her neighbors, Hamas in Gaza, Hezbollah in Lebanon, all consumed by the challenge of a still-to-be born Palestinian country, a fresh reemergence of Intifada uprisings, and a nearly successful, but nevertheless failed, attempt at resolution. Following Israel's Ariel Sharon's passing from the political scene, Prime Minister Ehud Olmert is facing new threats and opportunities.

Indeed, someday, yes someday, there will be stability and peace in the so-called Triangle, with the creation of Palestine as a state coexisting alongside Israel. Whether it results from exhaustion, or deliberate

negotiations, Israel's unilateral action will give way to hard
won tests. "I believe that in four years' time Israel will be
disengaged from the vast majority of the Palestinian
population within new borders...." Olmert argued during
his campaign. Sooner or later, level headed leaders will find
a resolution to the prolonged existing conflict.

History books will remind us how apparently simple
it was back in the year 2000 when former President
Clinton, meeting with Israel's Prime Minister Barak and
PLO Chairman Arafat, nearly concluded a peace agreement
at Camp David.

Yasir Arafat and Ariel Sharon did the unthinkable.
Arafat recognized Israel's right to exist and Sharon gave up
the Gaza Strip. Together, but certainly independently, they
both made so much history, and now history is waiting for
them. Palestinians and Israelis are having to adjust to life
without larger-than-life leaders.

Born a year apart, both Arafat and Sharon changed
history in ways that many people see as irreversible: Arafat
by recognizing Israel in 1993, laid the groundwork for an
eventual state of Palestine. Sharon by withdrawing from
Gaza and building a barrier in the West Bank, effectively
killed the dream of a Greater Israel incorporating captured
Arab territories.

Arguably, Arafat squandered a great historical
opportunity, while Sharon was in the process of seizing one
before his stroke stilled him.

The inheritors in 2006, Olmert, Abbas and Hamas
now control the region's destiny. In this post-Sharon/Arafat
era new faces dominate with Hamas' January 25th victory in
the Palestinian parliamentary election and Prime Minister
Ehud Olmert taking center stage as the voice of Israel.
(While a two-state solution remains the most viable

alternative, there is growing talk of a possible three state solution, with the West Bank and Gaza Strip transformed into two separate entities. The West Bank would be controlled by Fatah and the Gaza Strip by Hamas.)

Within two days, events solidified. Ehud Olmert came out ahead in the Israeli election of March 28, 2006. He then claimed, that he would define Israel's borders over the next four years. The following day, the new Palestinian prime minister Ismail Haniya and his cabinet were sworn in, formally putting the Islamic movement Hamas in charge of the Palestinian Authority and marking an almost total break in the government's contact with Israel.

To the north, Israel's Lebanon border was attacked and the 34 day war in the summer of 2006 with Hezbollah took its toll on both citizens and soldiers. Complicating matters, Syria and Iran were accused by Israel and the United States of direct involvement.

Today, that tiny corner of Israel's immediate neighborhood of 11 million, is now having its destiny geographically redefined by a wider expansion of countries into what we might call MENACA – the Middle East, North Africa and Central Asia. Meanwhile, President Bush now talks of a "broader" Middle East – 28 states, including Israel. Following the Oslo Agreement of 1993, it became clear to many specialists that the Middle East conflict, or more specifically the feud between the Israelis and the Palestinians, could be best resolved by widening the circle of engagement to include most Arab-Muslim nations. Thus, North Africa became a player in the peace process.

With the September 11, 2001 attack on the World Trade Towers and the U.S. Pentagon, the territory of consideration expanded overnight to include Central Asia,

Pakistan and Afghanistan, seven countries with a primarily Muslim (though non-Arab) populace.

From that day forward, resolution to the conflict and recovery in the Middle East would be impacted by events in these 28 countries (plus perhaps Turkey.) The fight against terrorism adds to the lexicon of variables.

Specialists in the region have been arguing ever since the disintegration of the Soviet Union that Central Asia should be considered, in terms of foreign policy, part of the Middle East. Not only because of its geographic contiguity through Iran (formerly Persia) but also because of the similarities (diplomatic intrigues, religious foment, cultural frustrations, the existence of oil) that the region shares with the Arab-Middle East.

David Fromkin, author of *A Peace to End All Peace* declared, "The Middle East, as I conceive it, means not only Egypt, Israel, Iran, Turkey, and the Arab states of Asia, but also Soviet Central Asia and Afghanistan…"

The U.S. Department of State continues, for historical reasons, to refer to the Middle East as the Near East, which includes North Africa's coastal Western Sahara and Morocco, eastward to Iran, Persian Gulf nations, Oman and Yemen. To avoid confusion, I will refer to the "Middle East" as the traditional Middle East, and also the "broader Middle East" indicating a grand total of 28 nations forming a primarily horizontal linkage of nearly 500 million people..

The Bush administration now refers to the "broader" Middle East to include Afghanistan and Pakistan. It remains a huge territory of differing populations, cultures, languages, history, conflicts, expectations, and living standards.

Clearly, stabilization and nation-building in Afghanistan and Iraq will take precedence over other areas of the Middle East. Nevertheless, the creation of a post-Arafat Palestinian state and the securing of Israel's right to exist go hand in hand with the Afghans and Iraqi efforts to rebuild their countries after decades of brutal oppression.

In his insightful post September 11th 2001 article *Why Do They Hate Us?- The Politics of Rage*, Fareed Zakaria, *Newsweek* Magazine's International Editor argued that "To dismiss the terrorists as insane is to delude ourselves. Bin Laden and his fellow fanatics are products of failed societies that breed their anger. America needs a plan that will not only defeat terror but reform the Arab world."

Though coming at the issue from a completely different angle, hawkish theorists in the present Bush Administration support the democratic transformation of the broader Middle East.

Former US Deputy Secretary of Defense and current World Bank President, Paul D. Wolfowitz sees a "liberated Iraq" as a vanguard of democracy, "the first potential tile in a kind of reverse domino theory in which the United States could help foster the fall of authoritarian regimes in a reshaped Middle East..."

Another high ranking Defense Department official John Deutch, now retired, was less optimistic when in November 2006 he called for the U.S. to have a secondary track, "simultaneous with a military withdrawal, centered on new economic and diplomatic initiatives in the Middle East to re-establish America's credibility and purpose."

\*   \*   \*   \*   \*   \*   \*   \*   \*   \*

Have we learned our history lesson? Following World War II, victorious leaders realized that the punitive Versailles peace treaty after World War I had helped pave the way for Adolf Hitler. In 1948, the U.S. government established the generous, Marshall Plan and it succeeded beyond all expectations.

The following flowchart, in sequence, succinctly identifies events from 1945 to 1951 in the reawakening of Western Europe:

END OF WORLD WAR II
DESTRUCTION
POVERTY
NATION-BUILDING
COMMUNIST THREAT
U.S. CONGRESS
THE MARSHALL PLAN-16 NATIONS
EUROPEAN RECOVERY PROGRAM
EUROPEAN UNION-25 NATIONS
STABILITY AND PROSPERITY

Fifty-five years later, in 2003, President George W. Bush and other world decision-makers called for strategies to begin political reform and economic rebuilding in Afghanistan, in the Palestinian Authority, in Iraq, and throughout the region.

The following flowchart, in sequence, succinctly identifies events from 2000 – 20?? in the reawakening of the broader Middle East:

NO END TO KILLINGS
SUICIDE BOMBINGS
INSURGENCY
POVERTY
NATION-BUILDING
TERRORISM THREAT
U.S.CONGRESS/UNITED NATIONS
MIDDLE EAST RECOVERY PROGRAM
MIDDLE EAST COMMUNITY-28 NATIONS
STABILITY AND PROSPERITY

"A Palestinian state will require a vibrant economy where honest enterprise is encouraged by honest government," President Bush said. "The United States, the international donor community and the World Bank stand ready to work with Palestinians on a major project of economic reform and development." His orientation and focus appears to be on Palestine; now his words must turn into deeds. Much work remains to be carried out during the president's second term.

The President's strategy for a final peace arrangement between the Palestinians and Israelis will be different, by necessity, from those of past administrations, especially that of Bill Clinton. His close ally Ariel Sharon is no longer Israel's Prime Minister and Iraq continues to command most of his attention. However, the interconnection betweenthe Palestinian/Israeli conflict and the on-going war in Iraq is often missed by the White House.

The President has long avoided a direct push for peace in favor of the basics for a future deal, such as new aid monies and business opportunities. Bush wants to begin with the construction of democratic and peaceful Palestinian institutions, alongside the building of schools, hospitals, and the like. Increasing Palestinian employment will also certainly be an initial goal.

------------------------------------------------------

The United States, the European Union, and many of the Arab nations have spent hundreds of millions on dollars for reform in the broader Middle East. They have little to show for it. Major mistakes have been made in the past trying to assist the region.

A formal, structured approach, borrowing the best from the 1948 Marshall Plan, followed by proven institutional structures and means of governance will overcome most of the perils of "action and reaction." Impulsive and blind strategy making must be replaced by clearly defined concepts with the means of step-by-step procedures, some borrowed from history, others generated by careful study and analysis.

This volume examines the means of nation-building aid today and gradual economic integration as a viable tool for reinventing a glorious past, part and parcel of a great experiment to reconstruct a modern day crossroad of trade and peace. Rebirth comes via negotiation and sacrifice. All sides must be prepared for the inevitable reinventing of the neighborhood.

I will argue for inclusion by nation, from the circumference, working carefully inward towards a nucleus, focused on the Triangle of Israel, Jordan and Palestine. (Iraq could at this time in history replace Israel.)

A fitting long-term solution can only come about by resolving the Palestinian-Israeli dilemma, which is why I concentrate initially on that conflict before reaching out across the region to focus ultimately on models of treaties and free-trade agreements, to be signed by an expanded Middle East Economic Community which will include nations of the Middle East, North Africa, and Central Asia.

## THE MIDDLE EAST - ISRAEL AND THE PALESTINIAN AUTHORITY AND THEIR NEIGHBORS

The U.S. State Department recently collected political and economic information about the Middle East, North Africa and Central Asia that supports these beliefs:

. The United States, the European Union, and other nations, and institutions which are not part of the Middle East, such as the United Nations, have limited, but critical roles to play as facilitators, mediators, and/or as "honest brokers." However, any outcome and that any final outcome ensuring stability and security, must ultimately rest with the participants;

. The United States' greatest contribution today lies in being supportive of negotiations among all parties, becoming a benefactor to all, becoming the primary contributor of financial assistance to help erase poverty, and unemployment for the impoverished citizens of those nations willing to halt their aggressive ambitions against Israel;

. Timing is everything. The Oslo Accord generated excitement for nearly a decade, encouraging people to search for a just and fair solution to the conflict. If the ideologies and plans of Oslo have run their course, or if Oslo is dead, then an alternative must be found;

. The Spring 2002 Saudi peace initiative and President Bush's June 2002 declaration of a "road-map" for the Middle East conflict, must interface with and respond to the strongly worded, competently prepared United Nations *Arab Human Development Report 2002*. An updated 2003 and most recently 2004, appeared in April 2005.

The horrific violence in the region will someday end. Now that Arafat and Sharon are gone from the political scene, new leaders will seek their own legacies. Economic assistance will be required, and should immediately be placed on Bush's post re-election agenda to spur both dialogue and planning. A great worry will be the administration putting excessive conditions on the money

"Regime-Change" can be good and "Nation-Building" is crucial. But foreign policy will ultimately be judged by our ability to finish what we've started. The United States, the European Union, the United Nations, non-governmental agencies, and others must forge specific programs that may be risky, expensive or both.

*   *   *   *   *   *   *   *   *

After World War II, Jean Monnet, of France, put forth his grand scheme of "Containment" as a means to keep the Germans within a box, with defined limits of activity that would attempt to resolve antagonisms of the past. He advocated dealing with former and present "Conflicts" between neighboring countries, he identified identifying ongoing national issues, such as continuing hatreds and resentments. "Common problems" inevitably appear as borders become less relevant and unprotective with the spread of disease and pollution. Ultimately, a "Common management" of institutional structure and governance is required and ultimately, created. Thus, his four Cs.

So great was his influence that French Foreign Minister Robert Schumann was able to take Monnet's vision for a peaceful and prosperous Europe to the French National Assembly, where he skillfully convinced a cynical group of politicians that an open relationship with Germany, against a background of three wars in 100 years, was the best route to an acceptable future for Europe.

Monnet's model of harmony via regional economic integration (Winston Churchill had already called for a *United States of Europe*) and his 4 Cs envisioned loosely defined state borders and encouraged foreign direct investment and joint-projects. Free trade accords gradually lowered tariffs and overturned pre-World War II protectionist policies that stood in the way of prosperity.

France had to embrace Germany and Germany, France. But the United States government and its people had to provide the financial assistance that made recovery possible.

French writer Raymond Aron, indicated that the prosperity of Western Europe would never have attained its present levels were it not for the generous gift of the United States, envisioned in 1948 with Congress' European Recovery Program, popularly known as the Marshall Plan. "...But in point of fact direct investments in Europe by the American corporations did not go hand in hand with the Marshall Plan, but started to flourish only in 1955 and onward, that is to say several years later, attracted primarily by the acceleration of European growth and the prospect of the Common Market.... The objectives which the framers of the Marshall Plan set themselves were the rehabilitation of the ruined countries and the reconstruction of the European economies with a view to containing Communism and reducing the dangers of domestic subversion."

How can national economies best be integrated with former enemies? Can Israel accept an economic link with Iran, Iraq, Libya and others who continue to deny their right to exist? Were Israel's former Prime Minister Barak and his supporters right to think "Good fences make good neighbors?" Were they justified in pursuing "separation" rather than "integration" with the desperate people of the West Bank and Gaza? Was Prime Minister Sharon's withdrawal plans from Gaza in the summer 2005 a step forward? And will it ever be known what his strategy for the West Bank was to be?

\*    \*    \*    \*    \*    \*    \*    \*    \*

Peace and prosperity cannot exist in the long-term unless enemies embrace. The U.S. State Department Bulletin contained Secretary of State Dean Acheson's claim: "The German stalemate heightened the general European crisis. The European Recovery Program (Marshall Plan) could not succeed without the raw materials and finished products which only a revived German economy could contribute." Refusal to deal with past enemies creates isolation and exacerbates an already messy situation. Conversely, a humbled people currently on their knees, such as the Palestinians, will in time strike out for what they consider to be justice.

By the fall of 1947, the U.S. State Department realized that Europe needed immediate economic relief if there was to be any hope for recovery. President Harry Truman appointed three special committees to study the impact on America of the proposed aid to Europe. The most important group, the President's Committee on Foreign Aid (chaired by Averall Harriman), enthusiastically endorsed what would come to be called the Marshall Plan.

On December 19, 1947, President Truman, backed by bipartisan support and endorsements from special committees, asked Congress to approve the Marshall Plan: "The next few years can determine whether the free countries of Europe will be able to preserve their heritage of freedom. If Europe fails to recover, the peoples of these countries might be driven to the philosophy of despair - the philosophy which contends that their basic wants can be met only by the surrender of their basic rights to totalitarian control."

The Marshall Plan paved the way for the reinvention of the European continent and ensured a stable and prosperous future. Without the billions of US dollars in aid, Communism would have been far more attractive to the peoples and governments of Western Europe.

Without the Marshall Plan, one last hope of the new start in Europe would have been unlikely. This is, assuredly, a dramatic lesson for those studying the broader Middle East.

Without the Marshall Plan, the nations of Western Europe may have suffered the same fate as the Soviet satellite nations, sinking gradually into economic decay and enduring low standards of living.

Europe needed economic assistance, at least in the short-term, and the United States was willing and able to respond.

Certainly, the forces, dynamics and times are very different in both the United States and in the Middle East, North Africa and Central Asia. Some will question the need for any aid to the region; some will argue that Communism is no longer a threat.

Unfortunately, we are now faced with a more urgent challenge, one that has finally come to our shores. Since September 11, 2001, a new challenge faces the world; citizens in every nation are threatened by terrorists. They are our newest enemies, with unrelenting anger, resentment and determination. And time is on the terrorist's side. Remember that nearly eight years passed between the first bombing of the World Trade Center in 1993 and the devastation of 9/11/2001.

In 1947, Marshall invited Germany and the Soviet Union to participate in the European Recovery Program. We too, will be asked to negotiate and hopefully come to an accord with our enemies. It is possible, perhaps even likely, that Hamas will have to be a partner for peace.

Ideally, foreign aid and its organizational implementation will follow the cessation of all violence in the region. New peace treaties with Israel's neighboring states would assure rapid Washington and United Nations acceptance. But, realistically it cannot be expected that new peace overtures will come.

The Marshall Plan didn't make peace, for it followed the conclusion of war. But it may well have prevented future clashes. The lexicon of peace is more than just the end of killing. There is peace in stability, in economic growth, peace in a higher standard of living, in the recognition of another's right to exist, peace in trust and, cooperation.

The governments of the broader Middle East must move towards transparency and accountability, and critically, must build basic institutions of governance so that the flow of funds to legitimate entities can follow.

Israelis and Palestinians may need to reach a sense of exhaustion, of war-weariness, whatever, so that they might make compromises, accepting new definitions of peace, rather than continue fighting.

There will someday be a state of Palestine. This was evident even before Arafat's death. Ariel Sharon, in part to preserve the jewishness of Israel knew that a state of Palestine was inevitable. But so, too, will Israel continue to exist. Neither side is going to win a meaningful military victory, so the only way to end the conflict and killings is for both sides to agree to negotiate.

The alternative to waiting, is to commence preparation for a day that will arrive sooner, not later. Timed release of monies should be determined by donors and recipients. Long-term aid should be tied to non-aggression towards Israel (and vice versa). The promise of still more funding should stir participation.

Whether a Democrat or a Republican controls the White House, funds will be needed for nations of the broader Middle East. Democrats, were there for President Truman and helped push through the Marshall Plan.

Will today's Democrats take the plunge and enter onto its platform for the future a huge cost of more than $1 trillion to create a friendlier, prosperous and non-threatening broader Middle East alongside Israel? And how will a 2007 Democratically controlled Congress, with a Republican Administration, and the taxpayers cope with such expenditures?

2006 has reinforced the ideology of President Bush. His call for increased levels of freedom throughout the broader Middle East appeared to be on target. In 2007 we await the follow-up to the Iraq Study Group report.

The U.S. Department of State under Condoleezza Rice must maintain its vigilance in the Middle East and never permit its commitment to wane. Bush and his Administration, as a non-party to the conflict, especially remains the hope for peace and prosperity between the Israelis and the Palestinians and therefore the entire region. As such, they must maintain an announced willingness to rescue the neighborhood from violence and self-destruction with proper and fair funding.

There is the perception of many in the Middle East that the United States is no longer an "honest broker." Five years ago, the phrase "why do they hate us," was but an introduction to a worsening situation. Today, the U.S. is despised uniformly across the Middle East, and the Palestinian people don't trust us as far as they can throw us.

Our future behavior is therefore ever more critical to defining our stance.

Seven years ago, *The Economist* editorial called on the United States' new soldier-statesman, then-U.S. Secretary of State Colin Powell to mobilize American technology and finances, both public and private, on behalf of the economic development of the world's poor countries, suggesting that would be a fitting follow-up to the Marshall Plan. It is now in the hands of Condoleezza Rice and National Security Advisor Hadley.

Some nations will not qualify for funding at the outset of MERP; some will not wish to apply; some, with riches from natural resources will have too high a gross domestic product; others will be disqualified for longstanding, rampant corruption; still others will refuse or be unable to cope with the stringent transparency requirements that will be set in advance; and some, with continuing aggression towards Israel, will not be eligible.

Of paramount importance, the ideological split between Shiites and Sunnis remains unresolved throughout the region. Shiites, with the much smaller population of the two, historically considers worldly success as an indication of Allah's favor; political engagement and empire-building have been religious callings for them. This group would more likely accept the coming of MERP.

Sunnis, with the majority of people, emphasize moral victories finding meaning in physical restraint, material loss, and personal martyrdom. This group would more likely resist the coming of MERP. Shifts in attitudes will be needed.

Islamic nations could benefit from MERP, but would they accept financial assistance, assumed to have conditions, from western hands? No matter the answer, no Muslim nation should be kept away from a seat at the table.

No matter the decision, it is clear that a crisis is brewing. Leading Arab intellectuals warned in the third update, April 2005, of the UN-*Arab Human Development Report* against "premature" western euphoria over political progress in the Middle East, judging that reforms remain largely cosmetic and fragmented.

Making matters more complex, roughly half the Arab world is under 25 years of age, and these young people will need 100 million jobs over the coming decades. These opportunities is within the grasp of MERP.

Funds from this recovery plan can go a long way towards restoring a more civil and just society throughout this broader Middle East, with its population of half a billion. Those possessing both the wisdom and the authority will have to set conditions that some nations will find difficult to meet, and which may be challenged. The list of expenditures of many billions of dollars, probably exceeding one trillion, should go beyond the more traditional, appropriate, and obvious needs, such as humanitarian support, infrastructure, housing, employment creation, education, etc.

This aid package will demonstrate to the region and to the world that President Bush and the international community remain committed to a universal hope for cultural and economic harmony among the more than six billion people on the planet, of which as many as 500 million are within the reach of MERP.

The time for compassion, accompanied by an open wallet, is upon us. Which political party will subscribe to these huge expenditures? The pieces for the resolution of Israeli-Arab conflicts are nearly in place. A recent Saudi peace initiative calls for normal relations of the 22-nation Arab League with Israel; President Bush, in his remaining years of his second term, will seek significant Middle East changes; the Road-Map is tattered; the European Union is poised for greater involvement; new leadership has surfaced in Palestine, Israel, and Iraq; and the UN's *Arab Development Reports* plead for global assistance.

The Middle East needs the United States to lead the way, to show the worthiness of this investment for future peace. At the same time, the US needs support from Europe and other nations of the world. A *Middle East Recovery Program* could hold promise for a brighter future of stability and peace for citizens living throughout the Middle East region.

It is time to plan for this Middle East reawakening. In 1944, one year before the end of World War II, 44 nations were represented at a planning meeting in Bretton Woods, New Hampshire to initiate structures after the Nazi defeat. These included the International Monetary Fund and The World Bank, both to be run by the United Nations, and the General Agreement on Tariffs and Trade (GATT). These institutions have changed the course of history over the past 60 years. Now it is the Middle East's turn.

The new face of the twenty-first century indicates an economic invasion of exports from India and China. Future outsourcing activities in the search for talent and low cost wages move forward. Today, India and China, representing approximately 1/3 of the world's population, or slightly more than two billion people, have captured the manufacturing needs of richer nations. In short time, the 500 million citizens of the broader Middle East can likewise offer similar services, thereby restarting their economies and sustaining the growth of employment.

## CHAPTER II

## DECLINE AND THEN REAWAKENING

**"I think it is fair to say that I believe we've got a great chance to establish a Palestinian state, and I intend to use the next four years to spend the capital of the United States on such a state."**

**George W. Bush
(after the death of Yasir Arafat)**

For years the U.S. approached the situation in Israel and Palestine with due deliberation. But since the death of Yasir Arafat in November 2004, and then the election of Mahmoud Abbas, and especially since the passing of the mantle of Prime Minister Ariel Sharon in January 2006, a renewed sense of urgency has formed U.S. policy in the region. Time can no longer be wasted.

Hamas' January 25, 2006 victory in the Palestinian parliamentary elections was followed on March 28th with the selection of Ehud Olmert as prime minister of Israel, strongly suggest that dramatic shifts were underway. Throughout the campaign Olmert's cry was for disengagement from the majority of Palestinians within four years. It remains to be seen whether this is merely rhetoric. Does it call for the closing of doors, without economic or cross-border trade? Hopefully not.

In addition, without anyone realizing it, the West Bank and Gaza Strip may be transformed into two separate entities, where most of the ministers will be Gazans, and the Gaza Strip will become the Palestinian Authority's main headquarters.

Gaza may be transformed into *Hamastan*, and the West Bank will be transformed into *Fatahland*, according to Dr. Riad Malki, the head of the Panorama Research Institute in Ramallah. Instead of a two-state solution with a united Palestine and Israel as neighbors, the new map may have Gaza as one country and the West Bank as another, with Israel set between them. Three states for two peoples raises great concern for many.

\*   \*   \*   \*   \*   \*   \*   \*   \*   \*   \*

A senior Israeli intelligence officer was heard to say shortly after Sharon's "severe stroke": "We have an ailing prime minister and the Palestinians have an ailing Authority, and both are on life support."

When Sharon became prime minister on February 6, 2001, Israel's economy was flat on its back. Today, it is quite sound, though not great, and the ranks of its poor have grown. The rebound in Israel's high-tech industry however has recharged its economy.

On the other hand, the PA is in deep financial difficulty. All further complicated by the Hamas' successful election to gain control of the Palestinian Parliament. Assuredly, a blow to Prime Minister Abbass and to the United States government.

By 2006, the PA had spent almost its entire yearly revenue of some $1 billion on salaries, which were raised despite calls of alarm from donor nations and The World Bank. According to the Authority's former financial minister Salam Fayad, it is essentially out of money and unable to secure financing from international banks.

Not surprisingly, donor countries at an aid conference in London in December 2005 refused to release a semi-annual $60 million in aid because the Palestinians had broken their commitments to fiscal responsibility. The situation was described by the regional director of The World Bank, Nigel Roberts: "in any given month now, they might find themselves unable to pay their basic salaries and minimal operational costs."

The PA now faces a deficit of $900 million, with only a projected $300-350 million of promised new funding from the Arab world and donor nations within the year, resulting in a net deficit of about $600 million.

Investment and job creation is needed, especially as the young population rises. In 2006, overall Palestinian unemployment was about 23 percent, but some 75 percent of men from 16 to 25 years old in refugee camps are not working.

Checkpoints and other Israeli barriers are costing the Palestinian economy about 5 percent real growth each year. This is significant, given that 10 percent real growth is needed to solve the unemployment situation.

A temporary rescue was made by the European Union on February 26, 2006 after receiving a dire warning from James Wolfensohn, the special Middle East envoy of the Road-Map Quartet. He pleaded that the PA was so short of money that it might collapse in a matter of weeks, offered $144 million in aid to the Palestinians before a Hamas government took power.

## NATION-BUILDING

President George W. Bush met with British Prime Minister Tony Blair immediately following the death of Yasir Arafat. No longer would the U.S. sit by as historic changes were wrought in Palestine and Israel.   Bush promised the U.S. would "hold their feet to the fire to make sure democracy prevails (in Palestine), that there are free elections."

During the 2000 election campaign Bush made it clear he was opposed to nation-building. In a debate with Al Gore, he said of the U.S. mission in Somalia: "It started off as a humanitarian mission then changed into a nation-building mission and that's where the mission went wrong. The mission was changed.  And as a result, our nation paid a price, and so I don't think our troops ought to be used to fight and win wars. I think our troops ought to be used to help overthrow a dictator when it's in our best interests. But in this case, it was a nation-building exercise."

But 9/11 changed all that. A month after September 11, 2001, at his White House news conference to update efforts to respond to the attack he stated: "We've got to work for a stable Afghanistan so that her neighbors don't fear terrorists activity again coming out of that country....I believe that the United Nations could provide the framework necessary to help meet those conditions. It would be a useful function for the United Nations to take over the so-called nation-building."

## BEGINNING WITH THE TRADITIONAL MIDDLE EAST, THENI.

An eventual solution to the violence, terror, and conflict in the Middle East was within sight, especially the passing of Arafat. Years of suspicion and mistrust have exacerbated the problems in the Middle East, as at first one government and then another pursued violent policies in an effort to wear out the other side. Both the Israelis and Palestinians are exhausted from cyclical, and seemingly unending, violence. The time has never been more propitious for the pursuit of a lasting peace not just between Israel and Palestine but throughout the region. A solution that looks only at Israel and Palestine will be insufficient. What is needed is a regional master-plan, dedicated to fostering cooperation and prosperity throughout the Middle East.

The cycle of violence inevitably will be broken. And when it is, aid, including financial assistance for countries in the Middle East will be called for, perhaps sooner than later. When the Middle East cries out for assistance, will the United States government, supported by other rich nations of the world, respond quickly and commit enough resources to ensure success?

Peace followed quickly by assistance could restore the Middle East to its role as a central actor in the global economy, enabling countries in the region to reclaim their status as an economic conduit between Europe and Asia. With wisdom, decision-makers inside and out of the region can once again show that the Middle East has the potential to return to its past days of glory.

## GLOBALIZATION BYPASSES THE MIDDLE EAST

In 2005 and 2006, oil prices were at their highest level in two decades resulting in revenues of some $600 million a day gushing into Gulf state treasuries. The monarchies of the Gulf Co-operation Council earned $35 billion more from oil exports in 2004 than in 2003. Huge profits were evident throughout the Middle East.

Egypt and Algeria, two economic basket-cases in the 1990s, today are showing renewed signs of vigor and opportunity.

However, this recent good fortune has been poorly distributed. Regional economic growth is a mere 5 percent. This follows almost twenty years of sluggishness that has left 80 million-out of nearly 300 million-Arabs living below the poverty line. Five percent is simply not adequate enough to create the 2.5 million new jobs each year necessary to contain Arab unemployment, let alone lower it from its current level of about 18 percent.

Excessive trade barriers, investment restrictions, regional fragmentation, commodity dependence, and trade policy isolation have all contributed to the decline of Arab economies. A major United Nation's report (UNDP) written by fifty leading Arab intellectuals, shows that progress in the Arab world has been made with life expectancy increasing by 15 years over the past three decades, and infant mortality dropping by two-thirds. Arab income per head is higher than in most other developing regions and, combined the 22 nations have less abject poverty (income of less than $1 a day) than any other developing region in the world.

Nevertheless, they point to significant problems:

(1) The population in the 22 members of the Arab League continues to grow, rising from 175 million in 1980 to nearly 300 million people today, and with the largest proportion of young people in the world (38 percent of Arabs are under 14). It is calculated that the population will top 400 million in 20 years.

(2) During the 20 year period, from the early 1980s through 2000, the Middle East's share of world exports declined from 13.3 percent to about 2.9 percent. Its share of world imports also dropped from 6.4 percent to 2.9 percent.

(3) The region's share of world foreign investment has fallen by three-quarters since 1985, dropping from 4.8 percent to 1.6 percent. Arab GDP, at $531 billion, is less than Spain's.

(4) One in five Arabs still live on less than $2 a day.

(5) Over the past 20 years, growth in income per head, at an annual increase of 0.5 percent, was lower than anywhere else in the world except sub-Saharan Africa.

(6) Around 12 million citizens, or 15 percent of the labor force, are unemployed; this number could rise to 25 million by the year 2010.

Overcoming these significant problems ultimately rests with the leadership within Arab societies. Professor Fouad Ajami, a leading academic on the region boldly argues: "In the end, the battle for a secular, modernist order in the Arab world is an endeavor for the Arabs themselves."

## EXPORTING TO THE SILICON VALLEY, NOT THE NILE VALLEY

United Nation's statistics reveal the critical role of trade relations where Palestinians were almost entirely dependent on trade with the Israelis. According to the UN, in the early 1990s, over 96 percent of Palestinian Authority (PA) exports went to Israel. By decade's end that figure dropped to 80 percent. A report issued by the United Nations since violence began on September 29, 2000 shows a devastated economy for the people of the Palestinian territories.

Terje Roed-Larsen, then, the UN Middle East envoy, pointed out that over a million Palestinians had suffered economic difficulty as a result of the uprising, "The harsh situation could lead to a regional war."

"Separation," from the West Bank and Gaza, as demanded by several past Israeli prime ministers, claims Saeb Erekat, the veteran Palestinian peace negotiator, "is a declaration of economic war."

Border closures have prevented Palestinians from working in Israel and as a result the decline in gross national product reached $630 million for the year 2000, with income per capita down 11 percent. Palestinian Authority (PA) households were forced to reduce their savings, and the share of population living below the poverty line moved from 21 percent to 28.2 percent in just one year. The poverty rate reached 43.7 percent, while unemployment in Gaza hit nearly 50 percent. Seventy-eight percent of Palestinians in the Gaza Strip were unemployed by May 2002 according to a report by the Palestinian Labor Ministry. The report said the number of unemployed reached 597,000 including more than 100,000 who worked in Israel before the current conflict, blaming Israel's closure policy for the high unemployment figures.

Of the 1 million people in the Gaza strip, four-fifths fell below the poverty line, compared with one-third before Intifada II began the day following Ariel Sharon's pre-election visit to the Al-Aksa mosque in Jerusalem; more than half survived on emergency UN rations. As of August, 2001, two-thirds of the workforce were idle, compared with one-fifth before the Intifada, either because they could not go to jobs in Israel, or because local businesses had closed for lack of supplies and markets.

With no solution in sight and without swift foreign financial assistance, a situation by desperate people and their sympathizers could spill across neighboring borders, the region, and eventually the world.

There is no way to comprehend the Intifada-Palestinian uprising without examining the economic and social reality that the Israeli policy has created. With Oslo I and II, the nearly 3 million Palestinians living in the territories are expected to be self-governed (by the Palestinian Authority) and want the immense inequalities between themselves and the Israelis to be redressed. At the very least, Palestinians hoped to be rid of an occupying government – Israel. But the Palestinian's unequal conditions did not improve significantly after Oslo, and in the ensuing years, anger increased with hardship.

Even were Israel to lift the closures imposed on the Palestinian territories that prevent the free movement of goods and people across the border, Palestinian economists believe that the gains made in the Palestinian economy up to Intifada II have already been wiped away. Many experts worry that any long-term investment projects will be replaced by anti-Palestinian government groups, promising short-term programs aimed at preventing poverty and coping with unemployment. These stop-gap measures may prove insufficient.

Palestinians working in Israel helped bring unemployment down from over 20 percent to under 14 percent. But, with the Palestinian population of approximately 3 million in the territories (West Bank and Gaza Strip) and East Jerusalem growing at a world-high rate of 4 percent, robust job creation is an absolute necessity. (The United Nations foresees the population of the occupied territories rising from 3.3 million today to almost 12 million by 2050.)

In the first six years (1993-1999) of the Palestinian Authority (PA), when foreign donors provided more than $3 billion in aid, Saudi Arabia and most other Arab states kept a conspicuous distance. Support from all of the Arab states combined rarely reached even 10 percent of total donations, and by design, almost none of it went directly to the PA, which was continually dogged by reports of corruption and mismanagement. Reasons abound, including a dislike and mistrust of Yasir Arafat.

In November 2000, the Arab League agreed in principle to donate $1 billion (representing just 2 percent of the Arab countries' annual earnings from their investments abroad) to Palestinian aid projects. Nearly $700 million was quickly pledged to the fund. But by February 2001, only $10 million had been disbursed.

On March 19, 2001 the Persian Gulf oil nations announced a $300 million aid package to the PA, making Arab donors the Authority's chief source of budgetary support for the first time. Circulated via the Islamic Development Bank, up to $40 million a month, for six months was to support a new "intifada fund" and head off the bankruptcy of the PA. Most of the funding came from Saudi Arabia, the United Arab Emirates and Kuwait. This amount was in addition to the previously unpublicized transfer of $80 million in Arab grants and loans to the Authority since December 2000.

The United States, on the other hand, barred by Congress from giving aid directly to the PA, contributed $57 million in January 2001 to Palestinian social programs. (After Arafat's death, the U.S. Congress appropriated in December 2004, $20 million in aid as a symbol of the Bush administration's recommitment to the PA, and as a goodwill gesture prior to the Palestinian elections in January of 2004.)

The frantic and horrific fall-winter 2000-01 weeks were accompanied by suicide bombings within Israel. Israel's Prime Minister Ehud Barak reaffirmed his position as he campaigned for reelection in February of 2001. He wanted separation between the Israeli and the Palestinian economies, particularly in infrastructure, and believed that this could be achieved in three to five years, according to Yossi Kucik, Director-General of the Prime Minister's office. Barak was solidly defeated in that election by Ariel Sharon.

Terje Roed-Larsen, former UN Special Coordinator for the Middle East Peace Process, released another UNSCO report, covering the first year of the uprising to the end of September 2001, a period in which the West Bank was closed for two days out of every three. In the last quarter covered by the report, severe internal closures were in force every day.

The closures meant that the Palestinian territories were in effect split into some 200 separate entities. Unemployment had more than doubled from 11 to 25 percent, with an underlying jobless level of as high as 50 percent in the Gaza Strip.

The first year of the crisis, according to UNSCO, cost the Palestinian economy between $2.4 billion and $3.2 billion while Palestinian Authority revenues declined by 57 percent in the first nine months of the Intifada alone. With real incomes down by an average 37 percent, some 46 percent of the 3 million Palestinians were living below the poverty line, double the pre-Intifada figure.

The UN analysis now claimed that the economic situation was so severe that it was only donations from abroad, including from the European Union and Arab countries, that were keeping the Palestinian Authority going.

According to Palestinian Authority figures, "63 percent of households in 2004 saw their income cut at least in half during the Intifada, and 58 percent now live in poverty." This latter figure contrasts with the World Bank's 47 percent.

Israeli incursions into the West Bank and the Gaza Strip cost the Palestinians billions of dollars. Israeli soldiers had severely damaged the Palestinian economy and the infrastructure of the Palestinian Authority, according to the International Committee for the Red Cross, The World Bank and other international organizations. The World Bank, which is one of the largest donors to the Palestinian territories, estimated that the direct physical destruction of the public infrastructure was $600 to $800 million. World Bank officials concluded that most of the $5 billion of international donor aid to the Palestinians since the Oslo accords had been inappropriately used. The economic loss in gross domestic product alone was about $5 billion.

Terje Roed-Larsen noted that Israel's dismantling of the Palestinian Authority had left large swaths of the West Bank overrun by "lawlessness and anarchy." Ironically, at about this time, Prime Minister Sharon called for a Marshall Plan for the Palestinians.

UNRWA was distributing emergency rations to 90,000 Palestinians. Compounding the human disaster, the economy of the West Bank and Gaza was impoverished. The UN's economists estimated that three-quarters of all production in the West Bank had come to a halt, and that three-quarters of the workforce was either temporarily or permanently unemployed. The end of the Palestinian Authority was fast approaching.

"De-development" was the term used by the United Nations Conference on Trade and Development secretariat to describe the "complex humanitarian emergencies," in the occupied territories. The continuing crisis had forced the PA into a heavy dependence on donor support for basic activities, "while diverting attention from long-term development goals and activities."

In December 2002, UNRWA issued an appeal to international donors for an additional $94 million for emergency relief work A third of that total was earmarked for food to more than one million Palestinians. Peter Hansen, UNRWA's commissioner-general, told donor representatives, "So rapid has been the humanitarian collapse that it will take an emergency program of the scale we present today to prevent a complete breakdown in Palestinian society."

Christian Aid, a British charity, issued a report indicating that Palestinians were currently living in a state of extreme, worsening poverty and feared for their future. William Bell, the report's co-author said, "Almost three-quarters of Palestinians now live on less than $2 a day, below the United Nations poverty line." He said that doctors were reporting a sharp increase in child malnutrition, anemia in pregnant women, and underweight babies, as well as stress-related conditions, such as heart disease and hypertension. The organization also reported a 100 percent increase in new cases at mental health clinics since the start of the current Intifada, most of them children.

According to the United Nations Office for the Coordination of Humanitarian Affairs:

a.  Of the 2.2 million Palestinians on the West Bank, 50 percent now live below the poverty line, compared with 22 percent in 2001; the figure is 68 percent in teeming Gaza, wth its 1.3 million people.

b.  The number of Palestinians who worked daily in Israel was more than 150,000; today it is fewer than 35,000.

c.  Before the second Intifada-September 2000, about $500 million each year was provided in aid. Today, the average annual figure for the last four years is more than $1 billion, about $310 a person, the highest per capita rate in the world.

d.  Some ½ million of the 3.5 million Palestinians are in dire economic straits. Some 40 percent feel insecure about feeding their families; 29 percent feel severely insecure, and half of them feel severely insecure and are heavily dependent on foreign aid.

e.  30 percent of the population are watching their savings rapidly decrease.

Two decades after the United Nations Conference on Trade and Development program of assistance to the Palestinian people, a report was submitted in October 2004. Critically, the UN secretariat concluded that: ".....adequate resources are required in order to enable the secretariat to respond fully to its mandate. In order to capitalize on the secretariat's long experience, it is now necessary to secure more predictable resources (comprehensive extrabudgetary support) for its work in this area."

Always sensitive to the casualties of conflict, Natan Sharansky, Israel's Deputy Prime Minister in Sharon's first government stated "By building democratic societies on the ruins of tyranny, the Marshall Plan helped create a prosperous and peaceful Western Europe. Now is a historic opportunity to do something similar for the Palestinians."

Sharansky is the author of *The Case for Democracy*. He shared his thesis with President Bush in the winter of 2005 that the Palestinians should be helped with the hundreds of millions of dollars in taxes that have been withheld from the PA during the Intifada. These funds would be used as a kind of Marshall Plan to feed and care for the Palestinians so as to lessen their suffering.

Following the decades of control by Arafat, a new leadership has to point the way for returning to the people of Palestine the rights of both self-rule and economic opportunity. Assuredly, the outside world will come to their assistance.

## CONSEQUENCES FOR ISRAEL

The economic fallout from disturbances in the region was likewise negatively affecting Israel and her seven million people. There were plunging company valuations, rapidly disappearing cash reserves, and sorrowful venture capitalists. The share prices of most Israeli hi-tech firms have suffered considerably more than their U.S. counterparts over the same amount of time.

For the first time in more than two years, the amount of venture capital into Israel dropped, beginning in 2000, one year before Ariel Sharon defeated Ehud Barak for prime minister. Company valuations for start-ups plunged by as much as 70 percent, meaning that founders and entrepreneurs have had to surrender more equity to outside investors to receive comparable amounts of cash they would have otherwise accrued. Israeli venture-capital funds increased their share of total hi-tech funding to 50 percent from 37 percent; a bad sign.

Likewise, closures have paralyzed dozens of Israeli construction projects and other joint efforts, as well as scaring away greatly needed foreign investment. The Israel Manufacturers Association said that Israeli companies marketing in the Palestinian Authority lost $250 million, according to a survey of damage to industry from the current violence. The study showed that 14 percent of the enterprises suffered severe damage, while 20 percent had moderate damage.

The contrast is both defining and sobering. At the beginning of the new century, the Israeli economy grew by 5.1 percent; in the second quarter in 2000, by 7.8 percent; and in the third quarter, prior to the outbreak of the new Intifada violence, the Israeli economy grew by an impressive 9.1 percent. Exports were up 48 percent; per capita gross domestic product reached $18,643. For the year, Israel's GDP grew by 5.9 percent despite a fourth quarter drop to 8 percent, the sharpest single three-month decline in Israel's history.

For the year 2000, GDP per capita, at $17,700 set a record, up 3.4 percent from 1999; business GDP was up 7.7 percent, compared to a 2-percent rise in 1999. In 2000, Israel registered the lowest inflation rate in its history, and the lowest rate in the world outside of Japan (which had negative inflation of 0.7 percent.)

In addition, the year 2000 set a record for foreign investment in Israel. Total direct and financial foreign investment had been $8.6 billion since the start of the year, 1.5 times the $5.58 billion raised in 1999. However, there was a sharp ebbing of foreign investment beginning with October during the Intifada II disturbances. The total investment of foreign citizens in Israeli securities and real estate, for example, fell in November to an all-time low of $128 million. The outbreak of violence sent foreign investment down from $417 million to only $250 million. In August, the total was $1.2 billion, while the year's high was recorded in March at $2.3 billion.

In a further indication of the declining situation in Israel, a special Business Data Israel (BDI) study of investment trends in the Israeli market by foreign companies and concerns shows that the sum of these investments declined in one year from $60.2 billion to $53.8 billion, a 10.6 percent decrease.

Arguments were now showing that Israel's economy was only mildly impacted by events in the Territories.

The Federation of Israeli Chambers of Commerce reported that: "The Israeli economy is hardly dependent on trade relations with the Palestinian economy. Total exports to the Palestinian territories account for only 8 percent of total exports. Even today, most export-led activity to this region continues to be conducted, since the Palestinians are absolutely dependent on Israel for its supply of basic food products and other commodities.....In the first nine months of the year, private foreign investment activity in Israel has doubled, while foreign investments in Israeli securities have grown four-fold compared to the same period last year.

Even after the recent security-related events, no clear downtrend in the business activity between Israel and abroad has been noted, or the pulling out of investors from Israel for that matter."

However, the Federation claimed that the unrest had already cost Israel over $1 billion, amounting to a loss of 1 percent of Israeli GDP. The Israeli Tour Guide Association reported that some 2,000 of its 2,500 registered tour guides were without work.

Tourism continued to drop in January 2001, by 16 percent. The average hotel occupancy rate was less than 40 percent, with the greatest drop in Jerusalem and in the North of Israel, followed by Tel-Aviv (on the other hand, hotels bordering the Dead Sea were packed, not necessarily with tourists, but instead mostly with Israelis whose stay were subsidized, thus keeping staff employed, and guests happy.)

In September 2000, 350 hotels were operating in Israel, totaling 46,500 rooms. One year later, thirty hotels, with 2,500 rooms had closed. The number of foreign tourist bed nights was the lowest since 1967, with hotel occupancy for the year 2002 at 40 percent, the poorest yearly average ever recorded.

A total of 862,300 visitors from abroad entered Israel during 2002, making it the worst year for tourism in 20 years. The figures for 2002 were 29 percent lower than those for 2001 and two-thirds lower than those recorded in 2000. (Only since 2004 has the downslide reversed itself. Tourism, a major factor in Israel's economy, is today improving.)

Foreign shipping companies that used to make occasional calls at Israeli ports were refraining from doing so due to fear of the Arab boycott and/or out of concern that insurance firms would charge a war levy. It was simply economically unfeasible for ships to stop in Israel. These shipping companies do not have permanent offices in Israel, but their ships used to call at Israeli ports every few months to deliver various consignments while visiting regional ports.    Attempts to ship consignments through these companies were turned down by consignor executives, and it was understood that the refusal stemmed from the latest instability apprehensions.

Israeli exports to Arab countries plunged 39 percent in the spring 2002. Exports had reached $21.3 million with the largest drop of 47 percent ($12.1 million) to Jordan, Israel's largest trading partner in the Arab world.

Intifada II and the September 11th terrorist attacks caused at least $7.5 billion in overall damage to the Israeli economy. The fallout from the World Trade Towers and Pentagon attacks had a relatively small impact on the Israeli economy, compared with the U.S. and other Western countries, totaling $562 million, or 0.5 percent of GDP. A loss 0.2 percent of GDP was expected due to the drop in demand for Israeli exports, while each 10 percent decline in Nasdaq stocks represented a loss of 0.1 percent of Israeli GDP. Further damage, assessed at 0.1 percent of GDP, was caused by a decline in private consumption. The overall damage caused by the Intifada was a 2 percent loss of GDP, while the impact on the high-tech sector of the economy was estimated at 2 – 2.5 percent of GDP.

By the end of November 2002, it was announced in a government report that one in five Israelis was living in poverty, a major increase since the start of Intifada II began in 2000. Sharon was rightfully preoccupied with Israeli security and failed to react to the financial plights of his citizens.

* * * * * * * * * *

The year 2003 began with more bad news. The Central Bureau of Statistics reported that gross domestic product contracted for the second straight year. After record growth of 7.4 percent in 2000, GDP shrank by 0.9 percent in 2001, and an additional 1 percent in 2002, making it the worst on record since 1953. Other critical indicators, such as consumer spending and per capita GDP, also declined, while unemployment hit a depressing 10.4 percent, with an estimated 265,000 people out of work. That was a rise of 1 percentage point since the end of 2001.

In addition, inflation increased to 6.5 percent for the entire year 2002, the highest since 1998. The rise in inflation was more than double the government's 2 - 3 percent target following two years of very low inflation, 1.4 percent in 2001 and zero in 2000.

33 percent of Israeli children were living below the poverty line in 2004, while 1.5 million of the entire population of 6.2 million were living below the poverty line in 2004. That calculates to 19 percent of Israeli families living in poverty.

Israel's rising poverty rate was second only to the U.S. among western industrialized countries.

Further exacerbating the situation, the Israeli economy lost approximately $1 billion, as a result of the war in Iraq. This estimate assumed a 1 percent loss of GDP, similar to the loss in the 1991 Gulf War, which cost the Israeli economy $650 million.

And the 34 days summer 2006 intrusion into southern Lebanon was estimated to cost Israel about 1 percent of her GDP.

## ISRAEL'S COMEBACK

In 2004, Israel's GDP underwent a dramatic prosperity, growing by 4.2 percent, double Europe's growth rate. "After the worst recession in the country's history," *Business Week* (January 2005), "Israel is staging an economic comeback. A rise in global demand and dramatic improvement in the security situation helped real gross domestic product to grow..."   Sharon's cabinet was increasingly optimistic about Israel's financial future, as was the prime minister.

A 20 percent jump in exports led the 2004 recovery, especially strong in high-tech gear, such as software and semiconductors, which presently accounts for half of Israel's industrial exports. Israel's defense, aviation and aerospace exports could grow by an annual 7 percent over the next five years, reaching $6.5 billion in 2009.

Israel has more start-ups than anywhere , except for Silicon Valley. From only 50 start-ups in 1982, Israel now has over 2,500.

Israel has the highest proportion of engineers per capita: 135 per 10,000 residents. Workers are characteristically inquisitive, creative and risk-taking; critical features for entrepreneurship and development.

In addition, the condition of Israel's tourism industry has been gradually improving over the past two years. 1.75 million tourists entered Israel during January-November 2005. Tourism to Israel was up 48.2 percent in November 2005. New hotels jobs rose by 7 percent. Foreign tourist bookings dropped to only about 50,000 per month in 2003, but has now rebounded in 2006 to more than 425,000 per month.

The Bank of Israel increased its 2006 economic forecast for Israel to 4.8 percent from 4.6 percent, thereby supporting Ehud Olmert's assertion of growth, despite the war in Lebanon.

More good news. *The Economist Intelligence Unit* predicted that the Israeli economy would grow 4.1 percent in 2006, (it grew at 6.6 % in the first quarter, faster than the 5.2 % growth in 2005) and updated its forecast for 2007 to 4.2 percent.

By mid-2006 Israel's population of seven million, makes it roughly equivalent to medium-sized European countries such as Switzerland (7.5 million) and Austria (8.1 million.) Her annual growth rate jumped to 1.7 percent.

Since the end of the Intifada II in mid-2003, Israel's economy has grown by 15 % and GDP per capita has grown by over 9 %. This shows the importance of a "no intifada" to her economy. Unfortunately, these post-intifada positives are not reflected in the present Palestinian economy.

## AFTER GAZA DISENGAGEMENT

The Gaza Strip was evacuated by Israelis during the summer of 2005, along with several West Bank settlements. This heroic and costly act was based on a political decision of Sharon's government and supported by the United States and international community. Other withdrawals appeared inevitable. Israeli citizens held their breath awaiting the prime ministers next move; they never would come.

The cost of physically ending Israel's presence in Gaza and compensating the civilians its evacuated was estimated to be more than $1.6 billion. $1.1 billion in additional pullout costs are part of a compensation package to be paid. These significant monies are based on the removing of Jewish communities from Gaza:

. 3 high schools, 7 elementary schools, 36 kindergartens, and 42 day-care centers which were closed.

. 5,000 school children who need to find new schools.

. 38 synagogues that were dismantled.

. 166 Israeli farmers who lost their livelihoods and some 5,000 of their Palestinian workers who lost their jobs, and,

. 48 graves in the Gush Katif Cemetery that will be exhumed and moved to Israel.

In the relative calm of disengagement, Gaza settlers who moved to neighboring Ashkelon, a few miles north, built 80 housing units. These costs are significant and will ultimately become part of a reimbursement request.

Following the evacuation of Israeli settlers and soldiers from Gaza, James Wolfensohn, former head of the World Bank and President Bush's former representative to Gaza, expressed the hope that tens of thousands of jobs would be created for Gazans after the Israeli pullout. He identified about $3 billion in aid from the international community, a mini-Marshall Pan all its own.

Nevertheless, Wolfensohn realized the need for Israeli cooperation in securing employment opportunities for Palestinians in Gaza: "It is still Israel that can do most to improve the economic lot of Palestinians, not only in Gaza, where it will continue to control the flow of people and goods across the border, but also in the West Bank, which despite the ceasefire remains under a harsh regime of closures and roadblocks." Certainly, there is the suggestion that bilateral integration of economies will benefit both Israel and Palestine.

## ISRAEL'S CLOSEST NEIGHBORS

### Jordan

Across the Jordan River, workers were also suffering. Jordanian businessmen had bet heavily on the peace process, spending over $1 billion building hotels in Jordan after 1998. A 40 percent drop in western tourists means that most of the hotels were either half-finished or half-empty. Jordan expects the country's economic growth to barely match its annual population growth of 3.3 percent.

According to Omar Salah, a leading Jordanian entrepreneur, about half of all Jordanian businessmen carried on some type of cross-border trade with Israeli firms. That percentage had plummeted to only 5 percent.

Nevertheless, the s36 year old businessman remains optimistic "Listen, there has obviously been a breakdown between the two sides, but there is going to be a cessation of violence sooner or later…Compare the situation to the Marshall Plan in the aftermath of the Second World War. Instead of ostracizing Germany, the allies helped rebuild the economy of Germany and helped bring Germany back into the economy of Europe. In the long run, this approach was much more successful than the reaction of the victors following World War I….Similarly here--once the second Intifada dies down, we will have to try something different from what was done following the first one."

Opportunities for Jordan remain high. Her exports in the early part of this century to 115 non-Arab countries rose by 19.7 percent to $1.1 billion, selling goods worth $884.2 million. There was a significant jump in U.S.-bound exports from four Jordanian-Israeli industrial zones.

Jordan was the most eager of Israel's neighbors to engage in close cooperation. Unlike Egypt, where economic interaction with Israel was not encouraged by President Mubarak, "the economic fruits of peace" were for Jordan's King Hussein (especially since the post 1991 Gulf War) a major driving force behind the search for an accommodation with Israel. The King did not share Mubarak's fears about Israel's pursuit of regional economy hegemony. But, following Rabin's assassination days after the Amman Economic Summit in 1995 and the election of Bibi Netanyahu as the new prime minister, promise turned to disinterest and futility.

## Egypt

Egypt, along with Jordan, has a peace treaty with Israel. Nevertheless, unemployment in Egypt remains at 9 percent. Egypt requires a half million new jobs each year as the population increases by 3,655 per day. She also has more natural gas (about 1 percent of the world total) than she can use and wants to earn badly-needed hard currency by exporting gas. The natural market right next door is Israel, but Israel was put off limits while the Israelis and Palestinians remain in conflict.

An ideal way to improve Egypt's economy would be to build a natural gas pipeline that connects Egypt to Israel, a huge gas consumer, and then build north and east to other countries. With strong pro-Palestinian sentiment among Egyptians, the participation of Israel in any pipeline is doubtful; this severely impacts Egypt's plans to spend needed funds for pipelines that bypass Israel, the largest gas consumer in the region.

The developers who conceived of building Egypt's first private airport had visions of tourists by the thousands coming to a new $1.2 billion resort on Egypt's southern Red Sea coast. But when the Marsa Alam International

Airport opened in early November 2001, it attracted just one weekly fight, from Germany.

Tourism, the government's largest source of revenue, is crucial to Egypt's economy. The country drew 5.4 million visitors who spent $4.3 billion, accounting for 10 percent of Egypt's gross domestic product. About 2.2 million of Egypt's citizens have jobs related to tourism.

As soon as the violence began between the Israelis and Palestinians, Egyptian tourism started slipping. In the first half of 2000, (before Intifada began in September 2000), 430,000 people came from Israel, but fewer than 37,000 came in the first half of 2001. In addition, one month after the September 11th attacks on the U.S., tourist activity dropped nearly 45 percent. Some improvement has been noticed in 2004, mostly from European nations.

The 1990s were not good years for Egypt. Israel's ascendancy as a regional economic powerhouse and Israel's new diplomatic links with Arab nations eroded Egypt's perceived weight as a "regional power and her relevance as a peace broker."

## Lebanon

The summer 2006 conflict between Hezbollah, Lebanon, and Israel lasted for 34 days a humiliating time span for the perceived superiority of the Israeli military power. By its end, border communities were devastated.

Lebanon had before the war achieved significant progress in advancing its position as a modern, thriving Middle East nation. The brief battle would be a huge economic setback. The cost of direct structural damage from the war was estimated at $3.6 billion.

Adding to this following the destruction of personal properties, plus indirect losses incurred by such things as factory closures, higher insurance premiums and lower tourist revenue, amounted to losses of as much as three times the original estimates. This cost is about equal to half of Lebanon's gross domestic product.

## Iraq

James Traub in his informative *New York Times* article "Making Sense of the Mission," concluded that the current Bush administration failed to learn the lessons of the 1990s as it turned toward post-conflict efforts in both Iraq and Afghanistan.

On the other side, the U.S. Department of State, when it comes to Iraq in 2006 points to "A Path To Democracy and Prosperity." By February 2006, they argued critical successes:

a.  Free elections transformed Iraq in 2005, with two parliamentary elections and a constitutional referendum. 76 percent of the nation's registered voters participated in the December 2005 elections.

b.  Economic recovery was on the rise. The International Monetary Fund estimated GDP growth by 2.6 percent in 2005, and a projected growth by 10.4 percent by 2006, adjusted for inflation.

c.  A stable currency, introduced in October 2003, allowed the Central Bank of Iraq to manage inflation. The IMF estimated inflation was 32 percent in 2004, remaining stable at this level in 2005.

d.  Iraq was on the road to membership in the World Trade Organization, and its first World Bank loan was made in 30 years.

e.  Debt relief agreements are helping Iraq with its
    economic outlook; Iraq secured an agreement to
    forgive at least 80 percent of its Saddam-era debt.
f.  Iraq's stock market was established in April 2004
    currently listing nearly 90 firms.
g.  Iraq had virtually no cell phone subscribers in 2003.
    Today, there are more than 5 million cell phone
    subscribers, and an estimated 2,000 Internet cafes.
h.  77 percent of Iraqi businessmen anticipate growth
    in the national economy over the next two years,
    and 69 percent are "optimistic about Iraq's future."

Much of the above is attributed to the monies given
to Iraq by the United States. A mini-Marshall Plan
approach – the *Iraq Relief and Reconstruction Fund*
(IRRF), although only for one country and not for regional
cooperation among nations, illustrates the potential for
reconstruction.

The U.S. Congress authorized $20.9 billion in
civilian funds to help rebuild Iraq in the three and one half
years immediately following *Operation Iraqi Freedom* in
April 2003. Paralleling the aspirations of the 1947 Marshall
Plan, the IRRF assistance is to help the Iraqi government
develop "a democratic, stable, and prosperous country, at
peace with itself and its neighbors, enjoying the benefits of
a free society and a market economy.

Following the attack into Iraq in 2003, the U.S. was
aware of the existing hardships of the people, and the huge
task ahead. It was determined that Iraq's per person income
had dropped from $3,836 in 1980 (higher than Spain at the
time) to $715 in 2002 (lower than Angola.)

The White House was well aware that the *Fourth
Geneva Convention* demanded that going to war in Iraq
required U.S. soldiers to protect the local people, restore

law and order, maintain local hospitals and health services, facilitate the education of children, and ensure that food supplies are available. In short, to rebuild the country. Unfortunately, the past four decades of the Cold War had taught U.S. presidents to prepare combat soldiers for battle, not to be peacekeepers and rebuilders.

Iraqi public services infrastructure were on the verge of collapse after 20 years of neglect, with little or no investment in many key areas. The few investments made were highly politicized, and the south in particular was under-funded, affecting health, education, and standard of living.

A team of U.S. officers on the Central Command stafsdf began the initial reconstruction planning in the summer 2002. At the same time at the State Department, a group called the *Future of Iraq* project was anticipating what would be needed should Iraq collapse or Saddam Hussein be overthrown.

The Central Command, according to Colonel Oliver,

"realized that they did not have the expertise to prepare a full plan for the recovery of Iraq after the war. Additionally, they were told that postwar reconstruction would be the responsibility of other U.S. departments, but it was not clear who these were to be."

By late October 2002, the Joint Chiefs of Staff developed a new approach for the management of postwar Iraq. The Pentagon would form a team led by a retired three-star general and draw on other agencies and departments to prepare and carry out the postwar reconstruction.

On January 22, 2003, President Bush created the Office of Reconstruction and Humanitarian Assistance

(ORHA), headed by retired General Jay Garner. ORHA, with 500 people, went into Iraq in April 2003, with objectives to deal with organization, humanitarian assistance and reconstruction in Iraq after the collapse of the Ba'athist regime.

Then, in March, a final plan for post-conflict Iraq was prepared by key coalition members, the UK, the US and Australia. It envisioned the following end state: "A stable Iraq, with its territorial integrity intact, and a broad-based government that renounces WMD development and use and no longer supports terrorism or threatens its neighbors." Organization, humanitarian assistance, reconstruction and civil administration were designed to address every aspect of rebuilding Iraq.

Numerous questions arose. Prominent members of the team knew that there had not been sufficient information to complete their goals. There were too many gaps about the status of facilities and infrastructure in Iraq prior to the conflict. Added to this was a limited degree of data regarding what was destroyed as the war moved forward.

Jay Garner formed three teams to manage three regions (the Danish army would take the lead in a fourth region.)

The Reconstruction and Humanitarian Assistance Office, on April 22$^{nd}$ moved into one of Saddam's palaces and commenced the management of reconstruction.

Throughout Iraq, the record indicated that there was no humanitarian crisis. Arguably, there were a host of major humanitarian issues, but "surgical precision of the American weapons resulted in few Iraqis being forced from their homes....The Iraqi people had access to food and water. Hospitals were functioning and electrical power was restored, albeit in limited amounts. The government of Iraq distributed sixty days of food rations from the *Oil for Food* Program, so for the most part people did not go hungry.

Then, in mid-May 2003, Ambassador Paul Bremer assumed the reigns of managing the overall efforts for the coalition. Garner, a military official was replaced by Bremer, a civilian administrator and an experienced State Department official who would now report to the Secretary of Defense, Donald Rumsfeld.

Unfortunately, the U.S. was not ready to take on the responsibility of reconstruction in Iraq. The planning and management was late in coming accompanied by many gaps in information.

The post-midterm U.S. election of November 7, 2006 held numerous surprises. Equally important, and long anticipated was the release of the *Iraq Study Group* report co-chaired by former Secretary of State James Baker III and Congressman Lee Hamilton.

This bipartisan team and its committee are looking at alternatives on behalf of Congress. One recommendation is to withdraw "over the horizon" and control Iraq from a neighboring country. Another is for the U.S. to be less fastidious about establishing democracy, and to concentrate on the smaller aim of establishing a government that works.

At the same time, Senator Joseph R. Biden, Jr., along with Leslie H. Gelb, the former president of the Council on Foreign Relations called for the establishment of three regional governments-one Kurdish, one Sunni, one Shiite-responsible for administering their own regions.

## Syria

When it comes to Syrian relations, Prime Minister of Israel, Ehud Barak made some dramatic and costly miscalculations. For example, he insisted on a "Syria First" strategy, with the Palestinian question removed to the back burner. His plan was to neutralize Assad's northern front before shifting to dealing with Arafat.

The President of Syria showed little interest in economic matters, especially in relation to Israel. He chose not to discuss economic possibilities with Barak.

Barak on the other hand put the carrot out for trade and economic development, even suggesting before the signing of a peace agreement to the creation of a Free-Trade Zone on the disputed Golan Heights. "This was utterly unacceptable to the Syrian President. Peace to him was about the end of the war, not about cooperation. In addition, Barak expected the Americans, as well as making available to Israel an astronomic financial package and agreeing to a strategic upgrading of their relations with her, to convince one or more Arab countries to start full diplomatic ties with the Jewish state." Former foreign minister of Israel Ben-Ami believes: "Such was the extravagant package of confidence – building measures and down payments on the fruits of peace that Barak felt he needed in order to convince his skeptical countrymen of his Syrian undertaking." Matters have deteriorated since.

**Afghanistan**

After the September 11, 2001 attacks, the U.S. response to the failed state of Afghanistan was to overthrow the Taliban, then track down and eliminate al Qaeda. Nation building was initiated by a United Nations team, but they recognized that in such a volatile region, nation building was not possible without a secure environment.

Before the U.S.coalition bombing in October 2001, Afghanistan was one of the poorest nations in the world.

(Little changed during the first Bush administration.) Few schools or hospitals existed, one in four children died before reaching the age of 5, three-quarters of her 26 million citizens could not read and the country lacked basic facilities, such as water distillation, and sewage systems. Average life expectancy was 40 years. (United Nations' estimates for rebuilding Afghanistan included a cost of up to $6.5 billion for the thirty months following the October bombings.)

Towards the end of 2002, at the time the U.S. was preparing to invade Iraq, the U.S. military decided that Afghanistan would never become a functioning country unless other parts of its state underwent nation building. The concept of Provisional Reconstruction Teams was suggested to bring rebuilding outside of the capital, Kabul.

Three years after the U.S. drove the Taliban out of Afghanistan, the war-shattered economy ranked 173rd of 178 countries in the United Nations 2004 Development Index. The February 2005 survey "National Human Development Report: Security With a Human Face" warned that Afghanistan could revert to anarchy if its economy, health facilities, and security were not improved.

Afghanistan has made considerable progress since 2001, but it remains far behind its level of achievement of 20 years ago. Average life expectancy for its 28.5 million citizens is 44.5 years, at least 20 years lower than that of neighboring countries. One of every two Afghans are classified as poor, and 20.4 percent of the rural population do not have enough to eat.

One quarter of the people have at some time sought refuge outside of the country, and 3.6 million remain refugees or displaced citizens.

Most glaring are the inequalities that affect women and children. One woman dies from pregnancy-related causes about every 30 minutes, and maternal mortality rates are 60 times higher than in industrialized nations.

One fifth of her children die before the age of five, 80 percent of them from preventable diseases. Only 25 percent of the population has access to clean drinking water, and one in eight children die from lack of clean water.

Afghanistan now has the worst education system in the world, and one of the lowest adult literacy rates, 28.7 percent. Annual per capita income was $190 and the unemployment rate 25 percent.

Despite four years and $10 billion of foreign aid, Kabul remains a depressed city. And the most buoyant sector of her economy remains the drug trade, which is equivalent to around a third of Afghanistan's GDP.

On the positive side her economy grew by 14 percent in 2005 and exports climbed 40 percent to $500 million. (Coca-Cola opened a factory in Kabul, complete with its own water-purification plant.)

Described by a Rand Corporation study "Successful nation building needs time and money." Rand concluded that twenty-five times more money and fifty times more troops were provided to Kosovo than to postconflict Afghanistan.

During the October 2001 bombing campaign, President Bush promised that  following the military victory the U.S. could not just walk away from the country. He approved an initial $320 million in aid for Afghanistan, with more to come. These monies would be used to feed the more than three million refugees who had left the country prior to the coalition bombing, and another 1.5

million starving people crossing the borders in Pakistan and Iran.

Once disbursed, funds would be used to build up infrastructure -- roads, bridges, electric plants, water treatment facilities; then schools and hospitals. Ultimately, the proposed MERP (Middle East Recovery Program) would help finance institutions, the government and legal system, the formation of political entities, elections, a banking system, federal means for tax and customs collecting, internal and external trade, and the list continues.

## Pakistan

Pakistan is awash in drugs, guns, and refugees, and the country's mounting anarchy and poverty makes it anxious to receive military and economic support from the United States, especially since it cooperated with the coalition against the Taliban. The lack of stability during and following the coalition bombing in Afghanistan frightened Pakistan's foreign customers, raised freight-insurance charges, and contributed to an uncertainty that hurt her economy. Short-term losses in trade, manufacturing, foreign investment, and government revenue amounted to nearly $2 billion, with economic growth for the fiscal year down a full point to 2.5-3.1 percent.

Pakistan, with $38 billion of foreign debt, even with new loans and easier terms on old ones, suffered significantly during the months leading up to and following the September 11th attack on the U.S.

## Central Asian countries

These are the newest post - September 11, 2001 strategic partners. The Muslim nations "stans", which are not Arab, came from the five former Soviet republics of Central Asia. Financial assistance is needed to overcome their poverty, corruption and lack of infrastructure. Tajikistan, the region's poorest country, is a central corridor for heroin smuggling; Uzbekistan has one of the worst records of human rights in the region; Kazakstan, has emerged as one of the world's biggest new sources of oil.

Indeed, The World Bank, has loaned $3.5 billion to Central Asian nations in the 10 year period with an additional $1.5 billion expected in the coming decade. The European Bank for Reconstruction and Development likewise plans to invest $300 million over several years to these nations. The United States plans to provide hundreds of millions of dollars in new assistance-probably a most inadequate funding effort.

## North African countries

The African nations on the southern rim of the Mediterranean Sea include Morocco, Algeria, Tunisia, Libya, and Egypt. Egypt has a dual geographic identity, also being a nation of the Middle East.

North African nations, most Muslim and Arab, long subdued by their former colonists, France and England, are today determined to reach out and find new export opportunities throughout the world. In particular, Morocco, Algeria, Tunisia, Libya, and Egypt are finding a greater reception not only in Europe but also in the United States, countries throughout Asia, other nations of the African continent, and South America.

## ISRAEL'S FAILED APPROACH

Former Israeli Prime Minister Ehud Barak often quoted America's distinguished poet Robert Frost "Good fences make good neighbors" as he called for a trial separation that he said might also become permanent. His staff busily prepared contingency proposals in which Israel would separate unilaterally from the West Bank and Gaza should a peace accord not be realized. The plan called for Israel to withdraw its soldiers from some areas of the West Bank, stake out new borders, and ultimately erect barriers along these boundaries, with carefully controlled crossing points. For Barak, political and geographic border separation promotes a "healthier relationship" between the two peoples.

"If it becomes clear that there is no partner for peace on the other side, we will go for unilateral separation," Barak informed a parliamentary committee. His planners had already recommended a permanent militarized border between the two entities, a strategy for replacing Palestinian workers with mostly unemployed or underemployed Israelis, and for disentangling Israel from the network of utilities (primarily electricity and water), and other services it shared with the Palestinians. (In Gaza, the electricity networks to Jewish and Arab customers are separate, so it would be possible to effect an economic separation there. But the West Bank grid is shared - the lines that supply electricity to the settlements also carry it to the Palestinian villages. Thus there is no way to execute a separation, except by establishing two parallel grids, which could never be done.)

Following his ascension to Prime Minister in February 2001, Sharon revised definitions of separation and the approaches to closures. By the summer of 2002, Sharon had created buffer zones and was installing cement and electronic walls - barriers that were electrified to catch penetrators - along the Green Line with the West Bank. The economy continued to tumble.

## THE EUROPEAN UNION'S ROLE

During the optimistic years following Oslo, the European Union committed monies to their neighbors across the Mediterranean Sea. On November 28, 1995, in Barcelona, the EU and its 12 southern Mediterranean partners created a new policy framework - the *Euro-Mediterranean Partnership*. The European Union promised $4.1 billion over five years to help nations on the southern rim of the sea. This equaled 70 percent of the aid offered to Central Europe's countries (most now members of the 27 nation European Union.). By the end of 1999, only 26 percent of that commitment had been paid out. Yet, to the remaining 74 percent, the EU decided to add another $4 - plus billion for a program lasting through 2006.

(In 2004 following President Bush's second-term election, the EU leadership has already committed new energies - perhaps as a counterbalance to a distant U.S. track record - in being involved in the Middle East conflict.)

The EU's initiatives in the Arab world are based on the Euro-Med Partnership or Barcelona process, which, since 1995, was to bring southern rim nations of the Mediterranean into free trade relations. In addition, the EU has continued to work to bring the Gulf Cooperation Council nations into closer trade relationships.

The cornerstone of the Euro-Mediterranean Partnership is the establishment of a large free trade zone around the Mediterranean basin by the year 2010 that will, it is hoped, ensure the prosperity of the region. In essence, the partnership intends to dismantle the tariffs that the Mediterranean countries impose on imports from the European Union, since they already enjoy comprehensive duty-free access to the EU for their manufactured goods. If this agenda is to be fulfilled, the EU must express strong sentiments and action to fulfill the promise of the road-map.

Nearly $6 billion (far greater than US funding) was invested by 15 nations of the EU in the 12 Mediterranean countries in 1998. Almost one third of that total went to Israel, and another 25-30 percent to oil and gas exploration and distribution in countries such as Algeria, Egypt, Tunisia, and Syria.

Intra-regional trade remains significantly low, and high customs barriers protect small markets.

## ISRAEL'S STRATEGY UNDER BARAK

At the outset of 2000, the Israeli government prepared a plan for a regional cooperation association, whose nations were to shape a framework for improved relationships between countries. Modeled after the *Association of Southeast Asian Nations (ASEAN),* the plan called for international disputes to be solved through talks and without violence, as well as the pursuit of regional economic cooperation and security. By January 2001, though, everything was put on hold, and throughout the first term of the Bush Administration remained inactive.

Israel's major free trade agreements include the European Union Free Trade Agreement (EU FTA); the United States of American Free Trade Agreement (USA

FTA); the European Free Trade Association Free Trade Agreement (EFTA FTA): and many more. These accords provide unparalleled access to the world's most important markets. Most importantly, Israel has tariff-free entry to both the U.S. and the European Union.

As late as September 2000, Israel and the Palestinian Authority appeared close to establishing a Free Trade Area (FTA) as part of their final economic accord. "But first," spoke Oded Eran, Barak's one-time peace negotiator, an "effective economic border" needs to be established. Eran explained that an interim period would be required to enable the two sides to prepare the administrative infrastructure and work out the details for the new economic border arrangement. The final agreement was to provide for the free, although monitored movement of workers between the Palestinian and Israeli economies. This FTA was based on economic separation, with each side enjoying economic independence. By January 2001, the FTA was also shelved.

The brake was pulled by Mohammed Isktayyeh, the Palestinian official negotiating on economic affairs who said it was premature to say that there had been an agreement in principle since "everyone knows the economic scenario comes after the political."

Gamemanship had won. By the beginning of November 2000, the hope of creating a free trade agreement, of integrating the economies of the region, and of pursuing the impressive goals of Oslo had been all but shattered. Oslo was bleeding, with little optimism for its future. It appeared near death.

## STRATEGIES UNDER SHARON

Sharon, formed a unity government in March of 2001. *(The month before at a meeting in Jerusalem he spent a few minutes with me to discuss his supportive position on an eventual integration of nations in the region. And then, just one year later, he called for a Marshall Plan for Palestine.)* He quickly set his own agenda, which included a close examination of policies of his predecessor. The crisis in the region, and the downfall of Barak, after only 21 months in office, intimated a period of upheaval.

Sharon was aware that the Palestinians, and the Israelis were here to stay, neighbors to the end, whether friendly or antagonistic. Any unilateral separation would be problematic for a host of reasons. By design, Israel had, over the years, made the Palestinians dependent on them, as seen by the grid patterns for electricity, telephone connections, etc. Condemnation would be heard around the world were Israel to deny the Palestinians their critical sources of supply. If separation was the ultimate solution, then the question for Sharon became, what form of separation would be best?

Israeli and Palestinian independence will, in all probability, follow an agreement that provides for Israel's security and a Palestinian state, and their own economies. The result will, by necessity, require the creation of a free trade zone – free of customs, tariffs, quotas and other trade barriers. Both Israel and Palestine would be free under such an agreement to determine their own tariffs and, independently, to sign trade accords with the Arab world.

A free-trade agreement between the Israelis and the Palestinians would in all probability require the inspection of goods at the various crossings. Inevitably, border stations would cause delays and increase the costs of trade, but the tradeoff would be security and the ability of both parties to control the quality of goods entering their states.

And what of Gaza and the West Bank, separated by the land mass of Israel proper? A route must be constructed to enable Palestinians to move and to trade freely between the two regions and bypass any interaction with Israelis. In all likelihood, the solution will be found with a super-highway, lengthy bridge someday connecting the  nascent state of Palestine.

In addition, there is a need to promote bi-national industrial parks in order to encourage and enable cooperation between Israelis and Palestinians. There is also a need to create foreign enterprises that include work for Palestinians within designated zones. A typical park would have entrances on each side of the border, where certified laborers would enter freely. With this approach, any closure for security reasons would be unnecessary.

Over time this may lead to a gradual reduction in the number of Palestinians working in Israel. This would have the benefit of protecting Palestinian workers, who in the past could lose their jobs at a moment notice. I believe it would require the PA to anticipate a solution to the problem created by designing jobs in the West Bank and Gaza with its own industry. To fulfill this goal, foreign investment would be required, investment that could serve as another incentive to maintain the peace. The objective is for Palestinians and Israelis to accept that they must learn to live together. This security and stability would be based on a strategy of cooperation through separation.

Is it possible to cut the links between the Israeli and Palestinian economies, forged over three decades? Yes, but the links were designed to be ties that bound the two peoples together. After more than thirty years of occupation, their economies are closely interlinked. Some links could be readily severed, but attempts to severe them would only create larger problems for both sides.

Colin Powell, on his first Middle East trip as U.S. Secretary of State in mid-February 2001, raised the possibility of an administrative collapse in the Palestinian Authority. Powell said this would only contribute to the escalation of the conflict with Israel. He also added that economic pressure by Israel did "nothing to improve the security situation." The trade blockade on Palestinian areas remained a blunt instrument that did more to incite Palestinian outrage. If, as many claimed, the Oslo process was dead, then Powell's statements suggested he was willing to look at the Israeli-Palestinian conflict through fresh eyes. Sharon was pleased.

Complicating matters at the time, were concerns that Arafat was interested in the deterioration of the situation between Israelis and Palestinians in the hopes of international intervention. No matter the mistrust between the two sides, sustaining a certain minimum standard of living for the Palestinians was and remains a clear-cut national priority in the PA.

Based on the economic situation, it was conceivable that a Palestinian welfare state was likely (with little reason for comfort in 2005 and 2006.) Additional aid of $1 billion, or more, from the United States, the European Union, and other nations would be needed to keep the West Bank and Gaza afloat and functioning. More monies would be required later.

(At a meeting in Jerusalem late in February 2002, Ariel Sharon and other senior government, military, corporate officials, and advisors discussed the severe economic plight in the territories, which had already caused the complete paralysis of many of the Palestinian Authority's institutions. Without the money, goods, and raw materials that flow from Israel into the West Bank and Gaza Strip, the condition was likely to degenerate into mass starvation, collapse of institutional units, and a concomitant escalation of violence.)

Shimon Peres, while foreign minister in Sharon's first government had no illusions. He did have plans – a partial invention of his existing vision for a *New Middle East*. He would begin pushing to:

a.  make significant changes in the economic condition of the Palestinians, since the present crisis was encouraging PA citizens to join the terrorists. Peres believed that, without economic revival in the West Bank and Gaza Strip, the conflict would continue and expand;

b.  re-open selective closures permitting Palestinian workers back into Israel;

c.  transfer funds owed by Israel to the PA;

d.  increase international contributions to the PA; and

e.  create a long-term joint common market for Israel, the Palestinians, and Jordan.

Unlike the Prime Minister, Peres was willing to entertain these strategies, even before the violence subsided, an approach that was believed would also comfort governments around the world.

Now, Ariel Sharon is no longer leading the government in Jerusalem. The "warrior" has made his mark and along with the passing of Arafat, a new generation steers the course of events in the Palestinian/Israeli conflict.

## ENTER CONDOLEEZZA RICE

With a second-presidential term for George Bush, a new Secretary of State – Condoleezza Rice, a new National Security Advisor, a new prime minister in Israel, and a stunning Hamas election victory, dramatic shifts were expected after 2004.

During the first term of George W. Bush neoconservative strategies pushed for taking a hawkish line in the Middle East. Since taking command of the State Department in January 2005, Condoleezza Rice has been labeled by some as a reborn neo-realist. While she shares the neoconservative's belief in the importance of spreading democracy, she does not favor going it alone. She wants to work closely with U.S. allies, and the United Nations is central to her style of engaging support around the world.

Whether Dr. Rice orchestrated the shift, the President now allows her to pursue a more multilateral foreign policy than he permitted Colin Powell. Her actions to date have been disappointing to many.

During his first term in office, the President shunned Chairman Arafat and refused to engage the Palestinians. Secretary of State Rice went in a different direction. She encouraged the opening of a border crossing between Israel and Gaza, became a player in increased travel and commerce within Gaza and the West Bank, and has worked hard to support Sharon in disengaging from Gaza.

An embarrassed administration following the January 2006 electoral parliamentary victory of Hamas caught the Secretary of State off guard, as it did most followers of Palestinian/Israeli events. As part of the faultering Quartet's road-map, the U.S. ruled out any threat of an immediate rolling back of aid, which is crucial to the survival of the basically bankrupt Palestinian government, where $100 million per month is required in order to remain afloat. By now, the PA's total expenditures reached about $1.6 billion, and revenue totaled about $1.1 billion, leaving the PA with a $500 million deficit.

The Secretary of State knew that Arab League countries had only given the Palestinians in 2005 about $200 million, down from the $388 million contributed in 2001. A State Department strategy of limiting contributions is a way of countering Hamas' continuing call for the destruction of Israel and further support for terrorist activities.

## APPROACHING CHAOS

Each day, $2.4 million has been lost because of the closures along the borders between Israel and the PA. Palestinian unemployment, which even in ordinary times was high, tripled to 38 percent since the beginning of the al-Aksa Intifada on September 29, 2000. Construction ceased, alternative sources of employment inside Israel dried up, and the salaries of Palestinian civil servants were only partially paid, if at all.

With nearly every second Palestinian worker jobless, the gross national product of the PA dropped by 20 percent in one year, whereas a 2 percent increase had been projected. Per capita income in the PA in 2000 was as low as $1,650; it has continued its decline.

The 125,000 Palestinians that were denied access to work in Israel after the al-Aksa Intifada began had earned enough money to support 7 others Palestinians, or about 1 million people. The same could be said for the 115,000 police officers and government employees of the West

Bank and Gaza Strip - while working and being paid, they were able to sustain nearly two thirds of the population.

Under the Oslo Agreement of 1993, Israel remained responsible for collecting income taxes from Palestinians working in Israel and for transferring those funds to the Palestinian Authority. But with the Intifada, the Israeli government began holding back these monies. By January 2005, more than $75 million was owed by Israel to the Palestinians. Likewise, the PA owed money to the government of Israel for water, energy, and infrastructure. This reduced Israel's debt to the PA by millions of dollars.

The European Union meanwhile, delivered $25 million to the Palestinian Authority in December 2000. (The EU gave nearly $2.7 billion to the Palestinians between 1993 and 2005.) By February 2001, they had planned to convert loans worth $57 million into direct grants to the PA budget, but only as part of a broader international effort. EU foreign ministers called upon Israel to lift the border closures and resume paying the PA for tax revenues and customs on behalf of the Palestinian Authority.

The PA needed about $50 million a month to stay afloat. They borrowed $60 million from the international community to pay for February 2001 salaries. They were forced to transfer Arab pledges of $1 billion to tide them over for the rest of the year.

Even with rapid reversals in the economy of the Palestinians, which seems unlikely, the three and a half million citizens of the bifurcated West Bank and Gaza Strip could be locked into dependency from outside government funding to sustain daily life.

By the spring of 2002, chaos was fast approaching. The combined West Bank and Gaza economy, roughly one-

20$^{th}$ the size of Israel's, was dependent on exporting goods and sending day workers to Israel. The border closings and severe restrictions on movement inside the territories imposed by Israel during April and May of 2002 doubled Palestinian poverty and unemployment. Relief officials revised their figures -- 50 percent of Palestinians were living below the poverty line and up to 60 percent were unemployed. A massive bailout was necessary. Both fragile and destitute, the Palestinian Authority was well on its way towards becoming a welfare state.

And, what will the White House do to prevent this catastrophe? The nation's debt continues to grow, finances are very tight and increasingly limited, and unilateralism is not succeeding. Failure to reach out to the international community will become the counter-voice of the contenders for the U.S. presidential election in 2008.

## A MIDDLE EAST "MARSHALL PLAN"

President Bill Clinton cannot be charged with insouciance on issues of peace in the Middle East. His administration committed more than seven years to resolving this torturous conflict, indeed, down to the very last days of his tenure in the White House.

President George W. Bush responded differently to the conflict from that of his predecessor. His June 24, 2002 Presidential speech from the Rose Garden of the White House spoke of hope for the Middle East. Ensuing action did not support this optimism. Throughout his first term, Bush never once invited Arafat to Washington. Instead, the president chose a path of disengagement from the growing conflict. He never presented any long-term strategy, including the use of financial incentives that could help resolve the entire Middle East conflict.

The President had announced his "road-map" for the region. Sharon was never impressed with Bush's new strategy. The President repeatedly refers to its loosely defined, but necessary steps, emphasizing U.S. commitment to finding a solution to the conflict between Israel and the Palestinians.

## RESETTLING AND COMPENSATING THE DISLOCATED

*The relocation of people is now considered a vital part of the concept of a soft partition, to prevent chaos and civil war. Shepherding people who want to flee toward areas where they feel safe will require both humanitarian assistance so they can get back on their feet.*

Refugees are people displaced during war. Palestinian refugees resulted from the War of Independence of 1948. They included Palestinians who lived within Israel's Green Line. Jewish refugees were those ejected from Arab countries. Displaced Palestinians are people who have been displaced from the West Bank and Gaza Strip as a result of the 1967 war. Expired "Permit Palestinians" are former Palestinian residents who went abroad and overstayed their permits. As a result, they have not been allowed to reenter the territories. There are approximately 50,000 cases of expired permits, although Jordan claims 90,000.

### A. Palestinian refugees

Many Palestinian refugees have demanded the right to return to their ancestral homes in Israel, buttressed by

UN Resolution 194 (December 1948) (adopted at the 186th
Plenary meeting) recommended under Section 11:
"Resolves that the refugees wishing to return to their homes
and live at peace with their neighbors should be permitted
to do so at the earliest practicable date, and the
compensation should be paid of the property of those
choosing not to return and for loss of or damage to property
which, under principles of international law or inequity,
should be made by the governments or authorities
responsible."

696,000 Arabs lived within the 1948 Armistice
Lines. 157,000 remained in their homes after the Israeli
War of Independence, leaving 539,000 Arabs who left
Israel in 1948. Today, Palestinian refugees live in camps in
some 60 locations in Gaza, the West Bank, Jordan, Syria,
and Lebanon. Some 3,737,534 refugees were registered
with the UN Relief and Work Agency in Lebanon, Syria
and Jordan, with an additional 90,000 registered in Iraq.
Most are the children and grandchildren of the original
refugees, living lives without a country for two generations.

Well over half of Jordan's population of 4.8 million
is of Palestinian origin. The country hosts 1.57 million
registered refugees, or slightly more than 40 percent of all
Palestinians listed by the United Nations. Some 300,000
people live in 13 refugees camps throughout the Hashemite
Kingdom of Jordan.

The Jordanian government in Amman not only
seeks the right of return to the PA and compensation for all
refugees but also tens of billions of dollars in compensation
for having hosted the refugees all these years, claiming to
have spent $350 million annually in response to their needs.
Israel, meanwhile, does not recognize a "right," nor does it
recognize "responsibility," and it will not allow the return

of refugees into what is now its territory. According to Israel, UN General Assembly resolutions have no binding standing; they are merely recommendations. Sharon's first government had attempted to dispel all Palestinian hopes of return or compensation.

Rather, Israel urged resettling refugees in neighboring and "third" world countries, which would not constitute a "return" to Israel lands. However resolved, the reinvented Marshall Plan will cover all or most of these costs.

## B. Israelis in the West Bank and Gaza

Similarly, the Palestinian Authority continues to insist that Israeli citizens leave their settlements in the Occupied Territories, beginning with disengagement in Gaza of 9,000 Israelis in the summer 2005. For those who leave settlements in the Gaza Strip, (and the West Bank) enormous sums of money are required to enable a quick and comfortable exodus of settlers. In this case, settler's homes, and other buildings should be maintained for future use by Palestinian occupants. The reinvented Marshall Plan will pay for some or all of these expenses.

## C. Jews from Arab countries

In 1948, there were 740,000 to 856,000 Jews in Arab countries; by 1976, 97 percent had fled or been evicted. 400,000 of these refugees entered Israel between 1948 and 1951; a total of 586,268 had entered by 1972, becoming citizens of Israel.

In practically all of the Muslim countries in the Middle East and North Africa, Jews were forcibly evicted from their homes. As a result, most of the Jews who left Arab nations for Israel were unable to profit from the sale of their properties, lands, homes, etc. Financial records are scarce or non-existent. Jewish claims for restitution will be difficult, if not impossible, to prove.

Between January 1950 and December 1951, Israel airlifted more than 119,000 Jewish citizens from Iraq, almost their total Jewish population. (Today, about eleven Jews remain in Iraq.)

Israel's Foreign Minister Moshe Sharett had earlier responded to Iraq's extortion and state-sponsored theft as "robbery by force of law." He was reacting to the decade old anti-semitism toward the Iraqi Jewish community of 2,600 years in the making. "We have a reckoning to conduct with the Arab world...the value of the Jewish property frozen in Iraq will be taken into account by us in calculating the sum of the compensation we have agreed to pay to Arabs who abandoned property in Israel." In the end, Iraqi Jewry were airlifted to Israel at the rate of 15,000 per month.

Now, the total of over 800,000 Jewish refugees from Arab countries (in 1948 there were 856,000 Jews in Arab countries, today there are 25,870 remaining) is almost identical to the 789,000 Arab-Palestinian refugees (539,000 in 1948 and 250,000 in 1967.) Jewish and Arab refugees were both settled in refugee camps.

Thus, the pressure of abandonment and the right of return to Israel remains a testy issue and unlikely to disappear from the front burner. How this will play out is difficult to determine. Canceling Jewish emigration with Arab emigration is a strange and improbable solution and will only increase tensions.

In the end, Israel had no alternative but to accelerate the rescue of Iraqi Jewry by as many as 15,000 per month. Between January 1950 and December 1951, Israel airlifted, bussed, or otherwise smuggled out nearly 200,000 Jews, all but a few thousand who were mostly elderly to leave.

Israel intends to pursue compensation, to the tune of tens of billions of U.S. dollars on behalf of Jews who fled to Israel from Muslim lands in the aftermath of the establishment of the Israeli state, officials in the Israeli Justice Ministry say. The move is widely perceived as an Israeli countermove, invoked in response to Palestinian claims for compensation under any formula that would resolve the Palestinian refugees issue.

Monies from the reinvented Marshall Plan will cover some or all of these costs.

## D. Israeli-Arabs living in Israel

As funds might be used for assisting those people who remained behind in the new State of Israel following the outbreak of war in 1948, MERP funds could also be used to vastly improve the living conditions of all Israeli-Arabs.

There are about 1 million Arabs living in Israel. These Arabs, comprising about 18 percent of the country's population, have been deprived of their full rights and benefits as citizens of Israel. Following the war of independence in 1948, approximately 150,000 Palestinians remained within the boundaries of Israel. Their population has grown to about 1.2 million. On the whole, they are poorly educated and receive less than their share of government funds; they have an unemployment rate that averages at about 15 percent, twice that of the Jewish Israelis; and only 5 percent of government jobs are allowed to be given to them. Indeed, 95 percent are in the lowest socio-economic level within the State of Israel.

## LAST CHANCE?

The Middle East crisis does not allow for delay; we no longer have the luxury of time. For Israel, Palestine and the broader region, the advice given to Macbeth is sound: "If it were done when 'tis done, then 'twere well/It were done quickly" (a message straight down the Ages from Shakespeare to President George W. Bush.)

The conflict in the Middle East is more than an Israeli-Palestinian issue. Bandaid treatment is counterproductive. A full scale international effort though costly and requiring the creation of institutions is necessary. In this corner of the world, 28, mostly troubled nations can determine, individually or collectively, whether the future will remain centered around their struggles-right or wrong- or whether calm can return and lead the way to prosperity.

The data is not reassuring:

(a) Population is exploding in the region while a decline in the economy is predicted. According to World Bank estimates, the total population of MENA (the Arab nations, Israel, Iran, and Turkey), will grow from 279.3 million in 1997 to reach 393.9 million in 2015, and to 481 million in 2030. Eight countries have population growth rates of well over 3 percent per annum. Syria, which had a population of 8.7 million in 1980, was recently estimated to have a population of 17 million, a figure that is expected to balloon to 28 million in 2030.

And populations are getting younger. Contemporary Iran is a case in point: two-thirds of its 69 million inhabitants are currently under 25.

In Central Asia, as the "leaders age, the population gets younger: more than 60 percent of the region's 50 million people are under the age of 25. This new generation is unemployed, poorly educated, and hungry – how long will they tolerate the decline in living standards and the lack of rudimentary freedoms? A social and political explosion seems inescapable unless the demands of the young are addressed."

(a) Egypt and Jordan now have peace treaties with Israel, while Syria and several others remain staunch enemies of Israel. Hesitating until additional peace treaties are sealed is shortsighted.

(b) Critical water shortages are predicted within 15 years unless regional and long-range planning soon begins. Middle East leaders must agree on ways to conserve and share water, while forging ahead with nascent plans to build desalination plants. Residents of Amman are permitted to turn on their water faucets just one day a week, even as Jordan's population continues to increase. Syrians already ration water, and its population is expected to double in 22 years. Palestinians are in an even worse situation. Israel, whose population is expected to increase by 20 percent over the next decade has declining aquifers and shrinking rivers.

(c) Reconstruction is not going well in Iraq.

President Bush declared in October 2003 that "the more jobs are available, the more kids that are going to school, the more desperate these killers become."

The electricity and jobs that were supposed to make make the killers desperate never arrived. Iraq produced less electricity by the end of 2006 than in October 2000. The Iraqi government estimated that the unemployment rate at 27 percent, but the real number is probably much higher.

The desperate facts of life in the West Bank and Gaza have crushed optimism for those living there. Since Oslo in

1993, unemployment is higher, wages are lower, and, worse, the promise of a better life does not appear to be within reach. Despair has replaced hope. And Sharon's absence, not only concerns Israeli citizens, but also the people of a proposed future state of Palestine.

## A BINDING ECONOMIC COMMITMENT TO THE PALESTINIANS

Lost in the swirl of events is the historic April 29, 1994 *Paris Economic Agreement* which was enacted over six months of arduous Israeli-Palestinian negotiations. This accord, which should be binding, granted Palestinian economic independence and cemented the two economies. The final agreement ensured the free movement of goods into Israel except for five items on which quotas were imposed for five years. In addition, Palestinian restrictions were lifted on exports to other markets.

More importantly for the Palestinian Authority, this agreement was supposed to substantially lower their longstanding trade deficit with Israel by providing them with virtually free access to Israel's markets, and by allowing them to purchase goods from other cheaper suppliers outside of Israel.

This economic accord provided for free trade and the establishment of a limited form of customs union, initially between Israel and the autonomous areas of Gaza and Jericho, that was to be extended eventually to the rest of the West Bank.

## TO THE FUTURE

The *Middle East Recovery Program* would encourage cross-border regional economic integration over time, through the creation of JIPTA - the Jordanian-Israeli-Palestinian (Free) Trade Agreement.

I envision JIPTA - the initial phase of my idea for a Middle East Economic Community - as the seed for future opportunity. JIPTA argues against fences and closures, and would work to reduce and ultimately eliminate tariffs and quotas to forge an open trading community of capital, goods, and services between the three entities. In essence, JIPTA would someday bear witness to the fruits of the Middle East Recovery Program with tariff-lowering and the increase of tariff-free imports and exports, all in pursuit of employment, higher living standards, and stability for people of the region.

The *Middle East Recovery Program* – a reinvented Marshall Plan – will promote interaction and expansion to other nations of the region, such as Egypt, Lebanon and those of North Africa to incorporate other Arab countries into a Middle East/North Africa Economic Community of 300 million people. Such a model could someday be expanded to include non-Arab-Muslim nations from Central Asia, plus Afghanistan, Pakistan, and perhaps Turkey, thereby evolving into a 28-nation economic powerhouse - a Middle East/North Africa/Central Asia Community (MENACA).

The near 500 million citizens living in the 27 nation European Union, (Bulgaria and Romania ascended in January 1$^{st}$, 2007) free of the burden of war and the disaster of trade barriers and restrictions, consume one quarter of the world's goods. Just as the Marshall Plan paved the way

for the EU's economic prosperity, the Middle East
Recovery Program would likewise be a historical program
to bring stability and prosperity to a region of the world that
has suffered for far too long. But MERP can only succeed if
doner nations commit to an aid package of many billions of
dollars, and if those nations look at solutions that
encapsulate the broader Middle East.

This greater region could conceivably cover
territories from North Africa, the traditional Middle East,
and the 8 nations from Central Asia, as well as Pakistan,
Afghanistan, and possibly Turkey. One half a billion
people currently live in this broader Middle Eastern
neighborhood. This newly extended boundary might
include as many as 28 nations, all an outgrowth of the
original Triangle of Israel, Palestine, and Jordan. (A new
Triangle can be created substituting one nation for another.)

"The Middle East is a cemetery of missed
opportunities," argues Shlomo Ben-Ami. Imagine the
possibilities that lie ahead; imagine once stability sets in
how this region of nearly ½ billion people could supplant
the growing influence of both India and China as the
manufacturers of the world. The end of the killings in the
region would encourage government and private financial
investments across the broader Middle East of 28 nations.
Those unemployed, underemployed will then share in
attracting work and factories to their nations, all purporting
to create the glue for sustaining the peace process. All
attempted past directions appeared to have failed. "Oslo"
via a reinvented Marshall Plan and a future regional
economic community remains plausible. Alternatives are

grim. Abraham Lincoln, reflecting on the Civil War said: "All dreaded it, all sought to avert it, and the war came."

# CHAPTER III

## THE MARSHALL PLAN

**"A working economy has to be revived to permit the emergence of political and social conditions in which free institutions can exist."**

**George C. Marshall**

President Bush has described Afghanistan, the first front of the war on terrorism; as a success. Compared with Iraq, perhaps it is.

In 2002, Bush promised a Marshall Plan for the country, which would turn the nation into a stable, democratic state. Neither security, stability, prosperity, nor the rule of law could be found in Afghanistan at the start of 2006.

We continue to shift from country to country, with interest waxing and waning based on changes in policy, economics, and the politics of the moment. The "Road-Map for peace" is but another failure awaiting renewed attention. (Prime Minister Sharon, shortly before his massive stroke had renounced any possibilities for this Bush plan.)

In order to halt this decline and begin towards rebirth in the Middle East, a new means to move the process along is needed. Let's turn our attention now to that plan, which certainly had its ups and downs before passage and implementation.

There is much we can learn by reviewing the events of the late 1940s. Though there are, admittedly, significant differences between Europe in the 1940s and the Middle East today, the similarities will prove instructive. With a thorough understanding of the Marshall Plan we can apply familiar concepts to the present day Middle East conflict, passing the torch down half a century to reinvent one of the most successful attempts at post-war reconstruction and stimulating prosperity and increased living standards to the Middle East.

Before the world became fixated on the phrase "nation building" the more prosaic way to describe this endeavor was "reconstruction accompanied by financial assistance." Certainly the Marshall Plan is the model for this reconstruction and assistance, one of the noblest gestures of humanitarian aid. In 2000, the Brookings Institution poll of 450 historians and political scientists ranked the Marshall Plan as the U.S. government's greatest achievement of the past century. Or more succinctly put,

*The Economist* referred to the Marshall Plan as "an act without peer in history."

As described by Dr. Barry Machado, "Nemesis, the goddess of retributive justice, visited Europe when mass killings stopped in 1945." The malfunctioning of market mechanisms made the peace almost as bad as the war that had cursed the continent since 1939. "Given its hazardous economic, political, and psychological conditions, 1947 had replaced 1931 as the twentieth century's real 'annus terribilis.'"

The desultory conditions of the post-World War II period has been well documented; devastation of the infrastructure, economic disarray, and distrust between friendly nations was offset by the Soviet threat from beyond the borders of Western Europe. The steady growth and mounting influence of indigenous Communist parties, especially in France, Italy and Greece, reflected popular disaffection with capitalism and talk of a better Europe. That the European economy might, as a consequence of enormous pressures, suffer a wholesale collapse seemed likely at the time to concerned Americans.

David McCullough, author of *Truman,* notes that one of the ironies of history is that President Truman became the first world leader to recognize Israeli statehood six months after passage of the Marshall Plan, on May 14, 1948.

Truman did this despite the urging of Secretary of State George Marshall, who warned that support for a Jewish nation would incite the Arabs, risk compromising America's oil supply, and possibly give the Soviets an opportunity to expand their sphere of influence in the region.

Between the end of World War II and the beginning of 1947, the United States had already loaned or given nearly $6 billion to save the starving and unemployed in Europe, money appropriated for both friend and former foe. President Truman repeatedly argued that any country that had avoided physical damage to its land during the war was obligated to come to the assistance of needy countries. Relief was attractive, moreover the answer was that outright funding was required for reconstruction. Europe was to be remade by American power at its most intelligent and benevolent best.

As Undersecretary of State for Economic Affairs, Will Clayton was a key figure in Marshall's State Department. He was convinced that the balance of payments - the relationship of a nation's imports and exports - between countries was a pretty reliable guide to the depth of financial trouble of each country after the war. He calculated that $5 billion annually, over a five-year period would get Europe's economy jumpstarted and eventually lead to a self-supporting level. Returning from a fact-finding European mission in 1946, Clayton reported to both Truman and Marshall that he had found life there far worse than he had anticipated.

In 1948, Congress approved funds for the European Recovery Program. Claiming it would not pass Congress were it to be named for himself, President Truman insisted it be called the Marshall Plan after his Secretary of State, the "greatest living American." Following the cold winter of 1946 and the crop failure of 1947, Marshall knew that Germany, as before the war, was destined to be the future economic engine of Europe. Germany had to be revitalized, or there might well be no European recovery.

The situation in West Germany was dire. Unemployment was rampant and many Germans went to bed each night on the verge of starvation. Marshall knew that large-scale aid was needed to avert disaster. Not everyone agreed with Marshall.

Some European leaders were reluctant to offer assistance to their former enemy, but Marshall insisted that without Germany's resurgence, European recovery would only be a dream.

Marshall worried that the disintegrating European situation might "quickly permit the development of a police state regime."

The terrible winter of 1946-47 took its toll. For example, following the December-January blizzard, most production in Great Britain was shut down for three weeks and rehabilitation consumed one-third of a U.S. loan that was intended to carry the country into 1949.

"At the bedrock of George Marshall's thinking about aid to Europe were two articles of faith: a devout belief in 'economic health' as a prerequisite to 'political stability' and a conviction," according to Machado, "that Western Europe could achieve neither without both initiative and cooperation.....Marshall rejected as unworkable a unilateral American solution to the perceived crisis in Europe." Marshall foresaw no lasting improvements through a strictly bilateral approach either. Only within a regional, multinational framework – and in close partnership rather than through charity – could permanent recovery emerge.

Industrialist and chairman of the John Mansville Corporation, Lewis Brown offered in the October 1947 issue of the *Wall Street Journal* a stark choice: either back

the Marshall Plan, or go to war with the Soviet Union now
or later.

As the winter gave way to the transient stability of
1948, and the Americans prepared to unload the supplies
from the Marshall Plan in Europe, the atmosphere turned
from gloom to joy.

Eventually 16 nations participated in the plan. "In
all the history of the world," President Truman wrote soon
after passage of the Marshall Plan, "we are the first great
nation to feed and support the conquered."

Without Truman's determination to share American
bounty with war-stricken citizens of Europe, the European
Recovery Program would not have gone forward to
Congress.  The President was committed to spread "the
faith" of freedom and democracy, and was convinced that
the stricken nations of Europe needed everything and could
afford to purchase nothing: "We are the giant of the
economic world. Whether we like it or not, the future
pattern of economic relations depends upon us."

Truman wrote to his sister: "I've got to face the
situation from a national and international standpoint and
not from a partisan-political one. It is more important to
save the world from totalitarianism than to be president for
another four years."

The U.S. Administration received ammunition from
international sources to support its position for Marshall's
package. England's Winston Churchill emphasized the
plight of Europe, "It is a rubble-heap, a charnel house, a
breeding ground of pestilence and hate." Later, Churchill
spoke in London, calling upon the British and other
governments to seek a European solution for European
problems.

At the time, Marshall's aid package was the largest U.S. grant in American history, approved at nearly $17 billion. This donation by the American people contributed significantly to European stability and economic rehabilitation, and led ultimately to the creation of the European Economic Community, later renamed the European Union. In the end, only $13.3 billion, (less than $150 billion in today's dollars) was actually spent.

"Presented with what seemed to be almost overwhelming challenges of nature, war damage, ideological challenge, and political opposition at home and abroad," argues John Bonds, "a remarkable group of policymakers changed the course of history by working beyond partisanship for the recovery of Western Civilization in Europe."

Marshall introduced the world to his historic plan on June 5, 1947 during a 10-minute, low profile, commencement speech at Harvard University: "Our policy is directed not against any country or doctrine, but against hunger, poverty, desperation, and chaos. Its purpose should be the revival of a working economy in the world so as to permit the emergence of political and social conditions in which free institutions can exist."

His address was deliberately short on specifics, such as dollar amounts, so as not to galvanize opposition in the U.S. before the Europeans could react. His goal was to revive agriculture and trade in Europe so that stricken nations might become self-supporting.

He spoke of the need for the U.S. to do something about Europe's economic plight. He wanted the Europeans to assume the responsibility for initiating the program; insisted that all European nations were eligible for funding; and that Germany's economy needed to be rehabilitated.

Not for Western Europe alone did Marshall design his plan. He also reached out to the Soviet Union: "It would be neither fitting nor efficacious for this Government to undertake to draw up unilaterally a program designed to place Europe on its feet economically. That is the business of the Europeans. The initiative, I think, must come from Europe. The role should consist of friendly aid in the drafting of a European plan, and of later support for such a program so far as it is practical for us to do so. The arrangement should be a joint one, agreed to by a number, if not all, European nations."

Throughout 1947, the U.S. State Department became increasingly aware of and concerned about Europe's economic collapse. A once-hoped- for rapid recovery after the war had not materialized. Undersecretary of State Dean Acheson, who later replaced Marshall as Secretary of State, warned that "America might have to support the reconstruction of Europe." The Policy Planning Staff, created by Marshall to be the new think-tank of the Department was quick to respond.

The State Department and the State-War-Navy group had filed reports on the conditions in Europe--the latter report was ninety-three pages long. The news was dismal.  "Disintegrating forces are becoming evident," reported Marshall on national radio.

In late May, Clayton wrote a gloomy message to Marshall, "It is now obvious that we have grossly underestimated the destruction to the European economy by the war." He urged a grant of "six to seven billion dollars worth of goods a year for three years." As the former head of the world's largest cotton brokerage firm, far from being altruistic, Clayton envisioned huge markets for the U.S. that would sell products across the Atlantic. (He also recommended a European economic federation nearly ten years before the European common market was created.)

It was time to commence the process of confidence-building and outreach. Marshall determined that Europe must lead the way with information, recommendations, and calls for assistance, each having to be supported with accurate evidence. On June 12, 1947, U.S. diplomatic mission representatives commenced surveys in countries to which they were assigned to determine: the current economic situation and the immediate help needed; the seriousness of the economic situation for the coming year; whether matters would improve with the exchange of goods with other countries of Western and Central Europe; the obstacles to overcome; the extent of contribution each country could make to general European rehabilitation; and the degree of Soviet or Communist pressure likely to inhibit the country's initiative and cooperation in a recovery program.

At times on the defensive, always tuned to the political swings of the day, the U.S. State Department demanded to know (1) why was European recovery proceeding so slowly; (2) what could Europe do to help itself; and (3) with minimum aid from the United States, how long would it take Europe to get back on its feet?

Both Truman and Marshall were concerned that some European governments might resist U.S. involvement and outreach with this aid package (there was considerable wrangling and positioning, especially among the leaders of France, the U.K., and the Soviet Union.)

Ernest Bevin, Foreign Minister of the United Kingdom, "warmly welcomed" the Marshall Plan proposal. His encomium for Marshall's approach was visionary. He considered the Secretary of State's Harvard address to be of the greatest historic importance and upheld the General's belief that Europe should be responsible for the next move.

Upon learning of Marshall's speech, Bevin stated "I assure you, gentlemen, it was like a lifeline to sinking men. It seemed to bring hope where there was none. The generosity of it was beyond my belief."

Bevin compared the position of the U.S. with that of Britain following the Napoleonic wars. He found a precedent for America's aid, in both money and goods. At that time, Britain possessed 30 percent of the world's wealth, while in 1947 the United States held half. After the Napoleonic conflicts, the British practically gave away their exports for nearly eighteen years, resulting in one hundred years of stability on the Continent.

Emotions ran deep when it came to assisting a former enemy. The issue of supporting Germany remained in the forefront of the debate. The French wanted a weak Germany. England worried that a weak Germany would mean the perpetual support of her shattered economy, which would prohibit the U.S. and other countries from assisting England.

The United States argued that the economic calamity faced by the Germans was far worse than that of France. With its population of 66 million, Germany must be involved if the Marshall Plan was to have a major impact on the future of Europe. Following analysis of overseas data, a summary report was approved on September 12, 1947 by representatives of Austria, Belgium, Denmark, Ireland, France, Greece, Iceland, Italy, Luxembourg, the Netherlands, Norway, Portugal, Sweden, Switzerland (Switzerland ultimately participated in various recovery programs, but did not get any funds), Turkey, and the United Kingdom. It was rushed by Marshall to the

President for consideration: "It is easy to propose a great plan, but exceedingly difficult to manage the form and procedure so that it has a fair chance of political survival."

Realizing that Congress was in no mood to approve large, self-perpetuating projects, Marshall presented a restricted four-year program. The objective was the promotion of economic recovery in the sixteen participating nations and West Germany by: making strong efforts to restore agricultural production levels to prewar standards, and industrial production to somewhat higher totals than those established immediately before the outbreak of the war by creating and maintaining stable internal economic conditions; establishing and continuing an organization to promote and increase economic cooperation among the countries involved; and undertaking to solve the dollar deficit in each country through expansion of exports.

Initially, it was assumed that the sum required would amount to $22 billion, (at one time estimated by the Europeans to approach $29 billion or approximately half the remaining funds in the US Treasury at the end of World War II) but under pressure, especially from Congress, the amount was scaled down to $17 billion before it was formally presented to Congress.

Marshall and Truman devoted considerable energies to convince Congress that the recovery plan was not just affordable but a necessity. It wasn't easy. The Republicans in 1947 were determined to reduce taxes and expenditures following the great costs of the war. Under attack for what some considered to be wasteful spending was the $3.25 billion in foreign relief that had already been loaned to the United Kingdom. That was before Marshall came forward for further funding.

Naturally, Europe praised the plan. The consensus

among European nations was that the initiative taken by Marshall was the most important single step that any government had taken since the end of the war to improve conditions in the region. Members of a European mission to the U.S. feared Congress would only approve half-steps and argued vociferously that if they achieved only partial relief, "Europe had gone so far downhill that full recovery would not be possible...The forging of the recovery of Western Europe can only be done once and it has to be done now."

There was considerable muscle-flexing and arm-twisting required to secure approval. Increasingly, Marshall warned that the choice was between good and evil, and that the U.S. had to lead the forces of good.

The debate raged seven months after Marshall's Harvard address and concern began to grow that the drawn-out process might temper interest in the plan. In testimony before the House Foreign Affairs Committee, Marshall knew he had to intone the same warnings again and again: "....so long as hunger, poverty, desperation, and resulting chaos threaten the great concentrations of people in Western Europe-some 270 million-there will surely develop social unease and political consequences on every side."

Congress reviewed reports from sixteen countries that, for the first time in history, had collectively outlined their economic contributions and facilities and described measures that would be needed by all to assure recovery.

To institutionalize the plan over a four-and-a-half year period was of great and proper concern to the House Foreign Affairs Committee. Marshall believed that there should be an executive agency run by one person "fitted into the existing machinery of government." He wanted the organization to be named the Economic Cooperation

Administration (ECA) to relate to the nation's foreign policy without being controlled by the Secretary of State.

Congress had different ideas which were ultimately accepted. It wanted a man with an industrial background to head the Administration, a person with impressive business credentials who operated outside diplomatic circles. Truman initially wanted to have Dean Acheson, by now back in private law practice, to become the ECA's first administrator. Acheson convinced the President to look elsewhere, certain the Republicans would reject his name during an election year. Truman did finally nominate Acheson, but the Senate would not confirm him.

The Czechoslovakia coup in February 1948 elevated growing fears of Communism, disarming lingering opponents for the Marshall Plan, and clinching its passage in Congress.

On April 3, 1948, the President signed into law the *Foreign Assistance Act* that launched the Marshall Plan by creating the Economic Cooperation Administration.

With his signature, Truman broke fundamentally and irreversibly with the U.S.'s isolationist past. The sense of national emergency had redefined traditional foreign policy. As John Bonds, a scholar of the Marshall Plan, in addition to numerous other scholars, has hailed this event as "the high watermark of bipartisanship in foreign policy."

Two days later, on April 5th, the name of Paul Hoffman, a Republican, President of the Studebaker Corporation, and Chairman of the Committee on Economic Development was submitted and approved by the Senate. Once Hoffman was appointed, he was responsible only to the President himself. Marshall left its operation to this talented executive. "He never made a suggestion on appointing anyone, never made a suggestion on how to run the show," Hoffman said of Marshall: "I kept him informed because he was Secretary of State, but I think his feeling was that as long as it was going all right, that was it...we never had any differences ourselves." Hoffman's end goal became a fixture of determination: "nothing less than the creation of a 'new' Europe." He always believed that "the way to combat Communism is with prosperity."

Often referred to in the sweep of economic diplomacy, where the expansion of trade was a U.S. strategy, the following sentiment was aired. "Dollars," according to Frenchman, Raymond Aron, "were indubitably used as a weapon against Communism and as an instrument in the policy of containment." Marshall had come back from the Foreign Ministers' Conference at Moscow in the spring of 1947 convinced that the Russians meant to have all of Western Europe.

The journalist Theodore H. White summarized that tension: "The Russians, he (Marshall) felt, would never cease pushing Western European democracies on the downspiral of 1946-47 unless we, the Americans, did something to reverse that downspiral. In this sense, the Marshall Plan was the most successful anti-Communist concept in the past fifty years."

Though invited to participate in the Marshall Plan, the Soviet Union soon withdrew from negotiations with other major European powers and also prevented its satellites from joining the program. Czechoslovakia, which had indicated a strong interest in participation, yielded to Russian pressure and retreated. To this day there remains a mystery as to why Generalissimo Stalin rejected the U.S. offer of financial help. Was it suspicion of American motives in view of the earlier requests for loans, or a resistance by the U.S. for a list of requirements for multilateral relations?   The Marshall Plan, designed to transcend the Cold War, became an extension of containment following the Soviet Union's rejection, thus virtually assuring that Congress would approve the Administration's request.

*Pravda*, the official daily newspaper of the Soviet Union saw in Marshall's proposals: "evidence of even wider plans of American reaction, of a new state in Washington's campaign against the forces of world democracy and progress.......Marshall proposed or rather demands quick formation of a notorious western bloc but under the unconditional and absolute leadership of American imperialism......From retails purchase of several European nations, Washington had conceived this design of wholesale purchase of the entire European continent." By now, most members of Congress chose not to argue this claim with the Soviets.

The Truman administration, as a matter of policy, chose not to use the anticommunist logic to secure support for the Marshall Plan and thus deepen the widening gulf that was developing between east and west. Bonds reveals: "The Soviets were not only willing for Europe to disintegrate into chaos; they were actively promoting that end in the expectation of ultimate communist success in the democracies of western Europe."

Marshall was now puzzled: "What do we do if the Russians accept?" Kennan suggested that it was necessary to "play it straight" and treat them as full partners in the task. The assumption was that the US would supply the capital, and that the Soviets would provide raw materials, and between the two, Europe would be rebuilt.

Stalin's version of communism included massive strikes, large demonstrations and vigorous campaigns against the Marshall Plan. He and Molotov were suspicious of U.S. motives. The terms Marshall proposed were found by them to be incompatible with the USSR closed economy.

On July 2, 1947, Soviet Foreign Minister Molotov explained some of his nation's objections to the Marshall Plan: "It would lead to interference in the internal affairs of European countries, particularly those which have the greatest need for outside aid, this can only complicate relations between the countries of Europe and hamper their cooperation...."

An October 5, 1947, formal Communist communique to Washington, condemned the program as only: "a farce, a European branch of the general world plan of political expansion being realized by the United States of America in all parts of the world .... The aggressors of yesterday--the capitalist tycoons of Germany and Japan -- are being prepared by the United States of America for a new role, as tools of the imperialistic policy in Europe and Asia of the United States of America ....... In these conditions, the anti-imperialist democratic camp has to close its ranks....and work out its tactics against the chief forces of the imperialist camp." (Most experts, then and now, believe that had the Soviet Union accepted the invitation, Congress certainly would have defeated the European Recovery Program initiative.)

Communist aggression was never spoken of in Marshall's Harvard speech, but he knew that its mention would overcome resistance to funding a program for reconstruction, and he warned once again that the nation had to accept the consequences that a collapse could end in the formation of dictatorships and police states.

A last surge to win approval was needed. Marshall's campaign to win approval became more forceful as weeks passed. Speaking at the University of California in Berkeley in the Spring of 1947, he talked of "a world-wide struggle between freedom and tyranny, between the self-rule of the many as opposed to the dictatorship of the ruthless few."

US Department of State experts spread across the country, delivering speeches on the need for European recovery monies. During the fiscal year 1947, ending in June 1948, the department offered speakers for the 878 audiences, totaling some half a million people, and distributed some three million leaflets of printed material.

The Chairman of the Committee asked whether the ideology in the U.S. offer of aid would not be seen as a form of American imperialism, an attempt to overpower the sovereignty of nations. Marshall responded that were the U.S. engaged in such a conspiracy of economic imperialism, we would need to "have a basis of a more Machiavellian approach than is exhibited here with public hearings and public discussions on every side with regard to every issue."

President Truman acted quickly. On October 23, 1947, he called Congress into a session to commence debate on November 17th. Marshall would be present at the joint meeting of the Senate Foreign Relations Committee and the House Foreign Affairs Committee to outline reasons for interim aid as a part of a larger, long-range program. His peroration was decisive.

Writing to his wife Bess, Truman told how preoccupied he was with the immense projected cost of the Marshall Plan... "If it works out as planned it will cost us

about $16 billion over a four-year period ...... just the
amount of the national debt when Franklin (Roosevelt) took
over. He ran it up to 40 odd and then the war came along
and it is 257...." Several days later, he told her "Our war
cost that year (1945) was set at $105 billion. The $16.5 is
for a four-year period and is for *peace*. A Russian war
would cost us $400 billion and untold lives, most civilian.
So I must do what I can."

The President pressed forward and addressed the
joint session of Congress on November 17th, proposing
short-term aid of $597 million to cover needs until the end
of March 1948.Truman would ask Congress for the
Marshall Plan on December 19[th:] "The next few years can
determine whether the free countries of Europe will be able
to preserve their heritage of freedom. If Europe fails to
recover, the peoples of these countries might be driven to
the philosophy of despair -- the philosophy which contends
that their basic wants can be met only by the surrender of
their basic rights to totalitarian control." Congress, in turn,
passed an interim aid bill to carry Western Europe through
the winter.

The President was so convinced of Marshall's
influence with the public and his outstanding leadership
that he began to refer to the ERP measures as the "Marshall
Plan." (The January 5, 1948 cover of *Time* Magazine had
the caption "Hope for those that need it" as Marshall was
declared "Man of the Year" for a second time. The first
time was in 1944 when he was General of the U.S. Army.)

Increasingly, Congressional opposition to the
Marshall Plan was rooted in the fear that the U.S. economy
could not bear the financial burden and that American
funds were being poured into the rat holes of Europe. At
another moment of suspicion, Congressman Hubert Ellis of

West Virginia, addressing the House, insisted that now was the time to resist Marshall's program by yelling, "Stop, thief; police… A bankrupt and demoralized America can make no contribution to the suffering of the world."

In September 1947, the President made public the three economic studies he had ordered, each of which concluded that the United States was not only, but indeed obligated by self-interest to make a massive effort for Europe's reconstruction.

There was opposition to the Marshall Plan even from the most unexpected quarters. Loy W. Henderson, head of the Office of Near Eastern Affairs at the State Department worried about the consequences of the Marshall Plan should Arab oil be severed. Europe was dependent on Arab states for 80 percent of its oil and the formation of a Jewish State, he stressed to the Secretary of State, could be disastrous to the long-range interests of the United States. (For similar reasons, both Secretaries of State Marshall and his successor Dean Acheson opposed Truman's desire to quickly support the creation of the State of Israel.)

Marshall, though sensitive to Washington pressures, remained firm. Taking the stand in 1947 before the Senate Foreign Relations Committee on the proposed European Recovery Program, assured the panel and the nation in his usual calm fashion, "This program will cost our country billions of dollars. It will impose a burden on the American taxpayer. It will require sacrifices today in order that we may enjoy security and peace tomorrow."

Until May 1948 Marshall was virtually a one-man talkathon. His whirlwind swing around the nation took him to "a chamber of commerce here and a church group there, as well as to business councils, university bodies, farmers' association and women's clubs."

Early into 1948, the Department of State presented the bill to Congress. The big battle was fought in the Senate where some thought the amount requested was too great. Opponents wanted to slash the amount and reduce the time from fifteen months to twelve.

Moderates in Congress, to preclude creating a permanent financial mandate, limited the plan to four years' duration.   They also insisted on a new and autonomous operating agency distant from existing bureaucracies, i.e., the State Department; and critically, that the Administrator report to Congress, not to the President of the United States.

$$* \quad * \quad * \quad * \quad * \quad * \quad * \quad * \quad * \quad *$$

Known officially as the *U.S. Foreign Assistance Act of 1948,* Congress had approved of "a plan of European recovery, open to all such nations which cooperate in such plan, based upon a strong production effort, the expansion of foreign trade, the creation and maintenance of internal financial stability, and the development of economic cooperation, including all possible steps to establish and maintain equitable rates of exchange and to bring about the progressive elimination of trade barriers."

Entered as *Chapter 169-Public Law 472,* the plan begins with a statement of principle "An Act to promote world peace and the general welfare, national interest, and foreign policy of the United States, through economic, financial, and other measures necessary to the maintenance of conditions abroad in which free institutions may survive and consistent with the maintenance of the strength and stability of the United States."

The Act's *Declaration of Policy* concluded:

*"Provided,* That no assistance to the participating countries herein contemplated shall seriously impair the economic stability of the United States. It is further declared to be the policy of the United States that continuity of assistance provided by the United States should, at all times, be dependent upon continuity of cooperation among countries participating in the program. In brief, President Truman called for (1) authorization for the expenditure of $17 billion in support of European recovery from April 1, 1948 to June 30, 1952; (2) an immediate appropriation of $6.8 billion to carry the program for its first fifteen months, from April 1, 1948 to June 30, 1949; and (3) authorization to create an Economic Cooperation Administration, an independent agency answerable to the President, to administer the program. I know that the Congress will, as it should, consider with great care the legislation necessary to put the program into effect. This consideration should proceed as rapidly as possible in order that the program may become effective by April 1, 1948. It is for this reason that I am presenting my recommendations to the Congress now, rather than awaiting its reconvening in January...I recommend this program, in full confidence of its wisdom and necessity as a major step in our nation's quest for a just and lasting peace."

\* \* \* \* \* \* \* \* \* \* \* \* \* \* \* \* \* \* \*

At the end of February 1948, on the eve of opening debate on the European Recovery program legislation, informed observers for the first time were optimistic about swift passage in the U.S. Senate.

Senator Vandenberg's support was essential when he opened debate on Monday, March 1st. He deprecated Soviet charges of economic warfare, repeating Marshall's early explanation that the aid program was intended solely to combat chaos, disorder, and confusion. As the close of debate approached, he urged that the U.S. accept greater responsibilities of leadership. He employed the Soviet threat effectively. He concluded powerfully: "It is a plan for peace, stability, and freedom. As such, it involves the clear self-interest of the United States. It can be the turning point in history for 100 years to come. If it fails, we shall have done our final best. If it succeeds, our children and children's children will call us blessed. May God grant his benediction upon the ultimate event."

During the week, *Newsweek* Magazine reported on March 8th that the administration had released a statement by Secretary of Commerce Harriman in a closed session of the House Appropriations Committee: "There are oppressive forces in the world coming from the Soviet Union which are just as destructive in their effect on the world and on our own way of life as Hitler was, and I think are a greater menace than Hitler was."

The administration's strategy would work. Stalin merged with Hitler in the popular mind, and the Soviet Union's unitary government was seen increasingly to resemble the Nazi state....There was an undercurrent of foreboding and a growing sense of vulnerability that had been totally lacking in the early postwar period," according to John Bonds. Truman was now ready for the critical Congressional vote; he had done his homework and prepared the history books for passage of the Marshall Plan.

Following two weeks of argument, thirty-eight Democrats were joined by thirty-one Republicans to pass the *Economic Cooperation Act* by a vote of 69-17 at five minutes past midnight on March 14, 1948. Then the fight turned to the House of Representatives.

While in Los Angeles on March 19th, Secretary Marshall echoed the President's speech to Congress: "Never before in history has the world situation been more threatening to our ideals and interests than at the present time. A depressing aspect of the situation is the duplication in Europe of the highhanded and calculated procedure of the Nazi regime....A special appeal is now being made to carry through the European Recovery Program promptly to final approval.......This is fundamental of all our future decisions in dealing with a situation as grave as any that has ever confronted this nation. The President has presented to the Congress the further measures which should be taken.

The President had to do a lot of armtwisting to secure the Marshall Plan. He broke the logjam. A Republican resurgence had taken place, outstripping almost anyone's expectations. The GOP controlled both houses, 51 to 45 in the Senate and 245 to 188 in the House. Far worse, the mood of the new Congress seemed decidedly anti-New Deal, a sign of problems ahead for programs of humanitarian assistance.

On March 31st, most of the Senate's version was accepted. A loud shout of the bill was heard in a voice vote of 32 to 74 and authorizing economic aid of $5.3 billion ($4.3 billion in appropriations and $1 billion in flexible credit) for Europe.

After intense Congressional debate, the Marshall Plan bill (the European Cooperation Act of 1948) passed both houses and was signed by President Truman on April 3, 1948. On June 28, 1948, Congress passed the *Foreign Aid Appropriation Act of 1949* funding the Marshall Plan's first year of operations.

On April 16th, representatives of the sixteen participating countries and the occupying powers of western Germany met in Paris and signed a multilateral agreement for economic cooperation. Two weeks later implementation of the Marshall Plan commenced.

The Marshall Plan was about 12 percent of the entire federal budget, and 1.2 percent of U.S. GNP. Between 1948 and 1951, some $13.3 billion was distributed, more than $100 billion in today's currency value. (Over the life of the program, the costs to each American taxpayer was roughly $80, now equal to about $650.)

(It is critical to note that in 1945, at the end of World War II the United States possessed a gross domestic product (GDP) that was 50 percent of the world's total; today it is less than half that amount, assuring that the debate about future financial aid to the Middle East will be contested, not only in Washington, but by the public.)

For three years, Western Europe required U.S. help. Clark Clifford recalled, "I think it is one of the proudest moments in American history. What happened during that period was that Harry Truman and the United States saved the free world." The next Secretary of State, Dean Acheson described it more biblically, as being "present at the creation."

To help administer the plan, the Organization for European Economic Cooperation (OEEC) was set up, eventually consisting of eighteen European nations including West Germany, together with the United States and Canada. In the early years, the Marshall Plan dollars crossed the ocean to provide European participants with the foreign exchange they needed to buy more goods abroad than they could have traded for with their exports.

The Marshall Plan underwent frequent course corrections. The aid was conditional, containing an emphasis on accountability.

Before the Act terminated, U.S. support for war-torn Europe (pre- and post-Marshall Plan) ultimately totaled $19,541,000 billion in economic assistance (82 percent in grants). In 1951, when U.S. funding ended, the Plan's implementation was transferred to the Mutual Security Program, which continued to operate until 1956. In 1961, the OEEC was superseded by the Paris-based Organization for Economic Cooperation and Development.

Within two weeks of Congress' approving the appropriation for European Recovery, the freighter *John H. Quick* sailed out of Galveston, Texas for Bordeaux, France, with 9,000 tons of wheat, the Marshall Plan's first cargo. Truman wrote privately after approval "In all the history of the world, we are the first great nation to feed and support the conquered...." The United States had never appeared so great or so generous.

Secretary Marshall and his advisors recognized that assistance, security, restoring infrastructure, and restarting the mechanisms of government were insufficient to bring long term peace. They were convinced that an economically viable Europe was essential to American prosperity and security.

Greece and Turkey were ultimately incorporated into the European Recovery Program. The Marshall Plan cost the U.S. taxpayer less than originally expected. More importantly, it did save the free and independent governments in Western Europe; it did put Europe on the road to a booming industrial prosperity; and it did pave the way for European economic integration.

Some considered the Plan to be a capitalist plot against European workers; other a finance plot against European industry itself; still others a plot against Russia; yet others a plot against European culture, what the Communists of Europe called the *Coca-Colanization.*

As pointed out by the journalist Theodore H. White: "The story of the Marshall Plan, it turned out, began with the meaning of money. It was also about money and Europe, and money and the peace – but above all, money and power and America ...... Marshall Plan money was a field of force, as invisible yet as energizing as electricity ..... What was novel about the Marshall Plan was that the command quality of money, used on such a scale between nations, was being used for the first time not to kill but to heal; money provided the energy ......."

At its peak, the Paris headquarters of the Marshall Plan occupying the Talleyrand mansion on Rue de Rivoli, held only 587 people on its payroll, and another 839 all across Western Europe. A resident mission was established in the capital of each participating nation. These people dispensed $13,350,000,000.

The Atlantic was an ocean of American humanitarian aid. For example, in one day in 1950, an estimated 150 ships, all bearing goods for Europe showed in their manifest a feast of cargo. There was one shipment heading for France with five cotton-carrying vessels to supply the mills and lofts where 170,000 French textile and clothing workers awaited American cotton. The *S.S.Godrun Maersk,* out of Baltimore on the same day contained tractors, resin, and cellulose acetate; the *S.S.Gibbes Lykes* pulled into Marseilles with American Gulf sulfur; the *S.S. Rhondda* was arriving with more farm machines, chemicals, oils, and so on.

By the end of 1950, industrial production in Western Europe was not only 45 percent higher than in 1947, the year the Marshall Plan was proposed to Congress. It was also, despite all war devastation, 25 percent higher than in 1938, the last prewar year.

And to the pleasure of American businesses, 83 percent of all dollar purchases were spent in the United States, an often forgotten payback.

The GNP of the participating nations grew 32.5 percent between 1947 and 1951, mainly due to high rates of investment by those countries. Economist Imanuel Wexler points out: "Such high rates of investment probably could not have been sustained, especially during the early years, without the financial resources provided through Marshall Plan aid. This is probably the key contribution of the Marshall Plan to Europe's industrial recovery."

Local administrators closely monitored the use of funds. With transparency and accountability screening they usually had veto power over proposed projects. Every U.S. dollar granted to a government had to be matched by local currency held in a special account to be used for infrastructure projects.

*The Overseas Technical Assistance and Productivity Program* (TA&P) was supported by the Economic Cooperation Administration. It outlived the Marshall Plan and between 1949 and 1958, it extended approximately $1 billion to European governments. The TA&P funded over 19,000 foreign-business managers and labor leaders in spending six to eight weeks studying U.S. industrial techniques. In addition, between 1950 and 1952, over one thousand Western European companies received special funding for managers to attend training courses at U.S. universities on new management practices.

In December 1951, the Economic Cooperation Administration closed its doors. The Marshall Plan was for all intents and purposes finished. The closure was urged by conservative critics in Congress and made possible by a shift in Presidential strategy from economic assistance to military aid and rearmament. As the Cold War geared up, economic diplomacy, as practiced by Secretary Marshall, quickly became a thing of the past.

The war on the Korean peninsula gradually redefined the Marshall Plan midway. The focus shifted more to a military-oriented and less-economic minded enterprise. Thereafter, concerns for international security and Europe's western defense became paramount. The Marshall Plan would end on December 31, 1951;new priorities had been set.

But what a spectacular legacy the Marshall Plan left in its wake. Celebrating the fiftieth anniversary of the European Recovery Program in 1997, Germany's Helmut Schmidt said: "The United States ought not to forget that the emerging European Union is one of its own great achievements; it would never have happened without the Marshall Plan."

In total, 270 million Europeans benefited from this amazing humanitarian aid package. The Marshall Plan "must be judged as one of the most successful peacetime foreign policies launched by the United States in the century," wrote Michael J. Hogan in his 1987 prize-winning book.

Differing events bring new dreams and opportunities. Let's hope that future world leaders say the same thing about a Middle East Recovery Program some fifty years hence.

## THE McCARTHY ATTACKS

When the American public protests government policy and policy makers, most citizens find it worthy -- an act reflecting cherished democratic principles. On the other hand, they are often unnerved when one of their few elected officials dedicates his or her career to vindictive attacks on national heroes, past and present.

Several books written about Senator McCarthy detail his harsh and belligerent treatment of Marshall. My intent here is to    suggest the possibility of a similar performance from the floor of the U.S. Congress, from other halls of power, and from the streets of America when it is time to take a position on the MERP. (Years after implementation of the Marshall Plan, it was concluded that it kept the Soviet Union at bay and her soldiers away from the most eastern of Europe's borders.)

Many praised Marshall for his role in proposing, supporting, and gaining legislative approval for the European Recovery Program, which was instrumental in rebuilding war-torn Europe.   "There are few men whose qualities of mind and character have impressed me so greatly as those of General Marshall," wrote England's Prime Minister Winston S. Churchill. "He is a great American, but he is far more than that ... He has always fought vigorously against defeatism, discouragement and disillusion. Succeeding generations must not be allowed to forget his achievements and his example."

During the period of anti-Communist hysteria in the United States, however, attacks on President Truman, General Marshall and the Marshall Plan persisted. None were more aggressive than the prolonged assault by U.S. Senator Joseph McCarthy. Judging General Douglas

MacArthur "the greatest American that was ever born," McCarthy undertook the destruction of MacArthur's most formidable adversary -- Marshall.

McCarthy, the elfin-like, junior Senator from Wisconsin, was certain the Soviet Union was planning world conquest and in light of that decided that anyone, even war heroes, were fair targets. In his short Congressional career, McCarthy brought down some of the country's most celebrated people, many from Hollywood. His swung treason charges like sledgehammers but only brought himself down in the end.

McCarthy audaciously accused Marshall of conspiring with those who wished to see the Communists inherit the earth. On June 15, 1951, he went to the Senate with a briefcase full of manuscripts that would, he stated, be useful to the Senate Armed Services and Foreign Relations Committee. It was, according to historian Richard Rovere, "the most daring and seditious of McCarthy's actions. It stands today as the most famous of his speeches, and yet it is ….. a speech to which no one ever listened and which very few have ever read."

McCarthy stood on the Senate floor and delivered a small portion of his scathing 60,000 word speech against Marshall and his plan. He stopped speaking after reading about one-third of the text (by then most of the Senators had walked out of the Chamber) and stated that the portion he had just completed and the rest of the speech, all 48 pages of it, would be entered into the U.S. Congressional Record. Later the speech was published as a book - "America's Retreat from Victory." (At another time, McCarthy would accuse General Dwight D. Eisenhower of joining, part and parcel, in Marshall's "traitorous" scheme.)

"I think it is clear that, in these great matters of life and death," bellowed the Senator, "President Truman is in the custody of Marshall." Continuing, McCarthy said that Marshall was a man "whose every important act for years has contributed to the prosperity of the enemy."

Biographer J. Anderson claimed that McCarthy would blame both Truman and Marshall, for the loss in the free world of 100 million people a year to international Communism.

Although McCarthy stopped short of uttering the word "treason," he declared that Marshall's career was "steeped in falsehood and that when his story is fully told it would be of a conspiracy so black that its principals shall be forever deserving of the malediction of all honest men."

*Time* Magazine reported: "In familiar fashion, McCarthy twisted quotes, drew unwarranted conclusions from the facts he did get right, (and) accused Marshall of having made common cause with Stalin since 1943."

    \*   \*   \*   \*   \*   \*   \*   \*   \*   \*

In 1953, the Nobel Peace Prize was awarded to Marshall, not as soldier, but as statesman and humanitarian for his sponsorship of the European Recovery Program.

The five-day ocean voyage to receive his prize, aboard the *Andrea Doria* was a bumpy one. He had intended to use the crossing to draft his acceptance speech but his illness prevented him from doing so.

Tired and weak, he called upon General Andrew J. Goodpaster, who worked from Marshall's note cards and had a sit-down session with him. Goodpaster worked passionately to help complete the talk, and ultimately penned a statement in Marshall's terse, no-nonsense style.

Marshall's speech before a glittering audience at Oslo University's Festival Hall included his insightful vision of the Western world's future challenges. Straightforward, even blunt, Marshall was both eloquent and precise as he stated his case: "We must present democracy as a force holding within itself the seeds of unlimited progress by the human race. By our actions we should make it clear that such a democracy is a means to a better way of life, together with a better understanding of nations. Tyranny, inevitably must retire before the tremendous moral strength of the gospel of freedom and self-respect for the individual, but we have to recognize that these democratic principles do not flourish on empty stomachs and that people turn to false promises of dictators because they are hopeless and anything promises something better than the miserable existence that they endure."

The Secretary of State was aware that decisive military strength was needed to win World War II. Equally, he was aware that to keep order afterwards, battle alone would not bring peace: "The maintenance of peace in the present hazardous world situation does depend in very large measure on military power, together with allied cohesion ...... but, the maintenance of large armies for an indefinite period is not a practical or a promising basis for policy. We must stand together strongly for these present years ...... but we must, I repeat, must find another solution."

For Marshall, peace and security, economic prosperity and a stable democracy were interdependent. Though his plan couldn't have succeeded without the massive aid contributed by the U.S., still Marshall received the Nobel Prize much more for his vision of collective action in the pursuit of a common goal. He was now a member of a unique club winning for both leadership and for his inspiring, determined effort to rebuild Europe.

As Goodpaster later wrote: "The true heart and genius of the Marshall Plan was that it gave the people of Europe hope, restored their pride and delivered on the promise of something better. It proposed that the countries of Europe, acting in concert, should tell the United States what they deemed best to meet their needs – not the other way around."

At the end of his speech, with his characteristic humility, Marshall revealed his fear that his words had failed him: "Due to my inability to express myself with the power and penetration of the great Churchill, I have not made clear the points that assume such prominence and importance in my mind." He needn't have feared. His ideas helped shape the world we now live in and, more than 57 years later, can still impact the future.

---

Marshall's words augured well for the plight of post-World War II's Europeans. His words can be uttered decades later and still, the same phrases reach out to the people of the Middle East Recovery Program (MERP), suggesting that hope indeed burns eternal.

It is likely that the MERP supporters will have to survive attacks on their concepts and approach. The Soviet Union, the   perceived threat that helped get the Marshall Plan approved in Congress, began to dissolve and the fear of communism has all but disappeared.  Yet, new and serious threats have crested the horizon. The United States needs a plan that will not only prevent future terrorist attacks, but will assist nations in reforming their current, dysfunctioning forms of governance.

MERP funds can be used to encourage the movement in the Middle East towards moderation and reform, and help governments to become more transparent, democratic and, consequently, legitimate. Some of the monies will be used for regional education, to demonstrate that moderate Islam is compatible with western society, open to men and women, open to all faiths, open to differing ideas, cultures, and ideologies.

Marshall's portrait was an imposing fixture in Colin Powell's Washington office. The example of McCarthy's attacks on Marshall is a sharp message for the former Secretary of State and other officials that such a scenario might be replayed.

There will assuredly be a struggle for the hearts and minds of the American people when the debate over funding the Middle East Recovery Program commences. Congressional leaders in the not too distant future will take positions on the pros and cons of the revisited Marshall Plan; will juggle the trade-offs between the costs and benefits to our nation; will appease some constituents at the same time that they antagonize others. They will determine MERP's destiny.

Likely attempts to sabotage the proposed MERP by zealots within the United States and beyond her borders will be launched concurrently with the proposal of such a plan. Ultimately, the advantages of MERP, when listened to calmly and closely, should become apparent: the plan is not only an affordable one but essential if lasting stability and prosperity is to be achieved throughout the broader Middle East.

Americans won't ever forget that the most powerful nation in the history of mankind, was shaken and momentarily brought to its knees on September 11, 2001 by a highly motivated, 18-man operation wielding low-tech devices with nihilistic resolve to turn American power on itself.

Yet in the years since 9/11, since the French newspaper *Le Monde* declared, "Today, We Are All American," a dismaying portion of the world's population is furious with the United States. The U.S. government must develop long term plans to strengthen relationships with many of the world's citizens who remain both hungry and disenfranchised, and who feel the sting and injustice of violence and corruption. Hopelessness breeds despair and we have all seen the lengths people who feel they have nothing for which to live will go to find a purpose.

The Marshall Plan helped rebuild a devastated Europe; it also ensured U.S. security throughout the second half of the 20$^{th}$ century. Costs aside, a Middle East Recovery Program can defuse a world in peril and replace uncertainty with global order.

## THE MARSHALL PLAN (MP) and THE MIDDLE EAST RECOVERY PROGRAM (MERP) - A COMPARISON

**MP:** On April 29, 1947, then U.S. Secretary of State George C. Marshall summoned to his office George F. Kennan, a key participant on the Policy Planning Staff on European aid. He stated that "Europe is in a mess ... Something will have to be done." Marshall had complete faith in his staff and urged swift action, asking them to "avoid trivia."

**MERP:** Today, the Middle East, North Africa, and Central Asia region is a "mess." Iraq's march towards democracy remains stalled as does the Quartet's (U.S., U.N., Russia,

EU) Road-Map for the Israelis and Palestinians
.....Something will have to be done. A next step, an Arab-
Road Map, lies dormant. The U.S.'s past policies must be
re-examined and replaced with new ones. Trivia must be
avoided. Basic decisions are essential; details to follow.

**MP**: President Truman split once and for all from those
who argued for U.S. isolationism. He was determined to
project a new and inspiring image. He argued that this
(Marshall Plan) program of humanitarian and financial aid
fulfilled his perception of a national emergency and in its
passage redefined the foreign policy of the U.S.

**MERP**: For decades the U.S. has been closely involved in
conflicts around the globe. No greater national urgency
exists for the U.S. than working to create a Palestinian state
while at the same time ensuring the continued existence of
Israel, and bringing about an end to the conflict.

**MP:** Speaking in a nationwide radio address, Marshall
warned: "The patient is sinking while the doctors
deliberate."

**MERP:** Intifada II commenced on September 28th, 2000.
Its causes and aftershocks remain, providing further
evidence of the  inadequate movement towards resolution
in the Middle East conflict in this most promising post-
Arafat era.

Global and regional meetings without progress
leaves the Iraq, Lebanon, and Israeli-Palestinian struggle in
shambles. A decisive thrust forward is needed before time
runs out. Revised or new strategies are called for as the
situations are vastly different.

**MP:** The Marshall Plan not only encouraged, but even forced Western European countries to think together, not separately, about recovery programs.

**MERP:** Nationalism throughout the broader Middle East region is changing. Today, home- grown organizations are essential to stand above the nation-state for the sake of stability. Outspoken, but often contained, domestic institutions have become the vehicle for more open communication, transparency, and placement of common problems before participants. Inclusion by the United Nations and other international agencies is essential.

**MP:** Marshall said: "It was my feeling that the Soviets were doing everything possible to achieve a complete breakdown in Europe...." "That is, they were doing anything they could to create greater turbulence. The major problem was how to counter this negative Soviet policy and restore the European economy."

**MERP:** Historical enemies, such as Iran and Syria, of Israel and western society continue to call for the elimination of the State of Israel, perhaps even the subjugation of Europe and the United States. How to deal with global terrorism and biological/chemical attacks, while rejuvenating collapsing nations is a complex and difficult, but necessary, task.

**MP:** Kennan believed that the Communists would portray U.S. aid as a "sinister effort to further American hegemony onto the people of Western Europe."

**MERP:** Anti-Israeli governments will continue their attack against Israel, as will other potent groups who talk of yet another U.S. plot to control their destiny, and oil supplies, and those of other Arab/Muslim and non-Arab/Muslim cultures and nations. U.S. economic clout, though a force of significance, will be no match for political wisdom. Nevertheless, economic power remains available as the glue to sustain a positive movement towards stability and prosperity.

**MP:** The Planning Staff on European aid recommended to Marshall: "To avoid Communist interference it is suggested that U.S. assistance depend on guarantees from those European countries seeking aid that any assistance would not be misused or sabotaged by Communists."
**MERP:** The same approach must be employed to make certain that extremist groups/nations that seek aid would guarantee that they will not utilize the monies for subversive efforts, such as the destruction of the State of Israel.

**MP:** Anticipating the future European Economic Community, the Planning Staff on European aid urged encouragement of some form of "regional political association of Western European states."
**MERP:** Nations that receive funding should be obligated to enter into discussion with other funded countries in order to set an agenda of participative and shared decision-making across national boundaries. Realistically, economic integration would prove easier to create than political unification.

**MP:** Kennan wrote in 1946: "The formal initiative must come from Europeans, the program must be evolved in

Europe, and without questions that the Europeans should bear the basic responsibility for it."

**MERP:** Similarly, progressive steps from the United States should only follow dialogue and planning from eligible nations. The U.S. should not initiate the Middle East, North Africa, Central Asia (MENACA) policy, but should merely provide the opportunity for serious searching and dialogue. Engagement and participation must be decided freely by invited and qualified nations. Sooner or later, Middle East nations must bear the basic responsibility for MERP.

**MP:** Under Secretary of State Will Clayton, one of Marshall's writers and advisors said: "If there was no aid, economic, social, and political disintegration would follow."

**MERP:** Without funding and distribution, the same pattern may readily follow throughout the Middle East region. Once military intervention is curtailed, monies set aside for reconstruction goals must not be transferred to extend military objectives.

**MP:** Discussing the growing disintegration in Europe, Marshall argued that "it would be folly to sit back and do nothing."

**MERP:** The security of the Middle East and, perhaps, beyond, rests with those too complacent to see the results of their pettifogging and stalling. One could argue that at least six months were lost as the 2004 US-presidential campaign worked its way around the States. Hiding from action is foolhardy and irresponsible.

**MP:** During the economic collapse in Europe between 1929 and 1931, U.S. aid to floundering Europe was insufficient and came too late. The results in Europe included bank failures, bankruptcies, increased tariffs, blocked currencies, disrupted markets, and ruthless efforts at economic autocracy. These events are viewed as germinal for the rise of Hitler and the Nazis.

**MERP:** Timing is critical; peace is within reach. Funds could be made available; Congress can be convinced of the positive results that could emanate from a well-orchestrated and executed MERP. Inadequate funding for rebuilding is a crime itself.

**MP:** When President Truman launched the Marshall Plan, only 14 percent of the American people supported the idea of foreign aid.

**MERP:** Foreign assistance is now an established form of U.S. national security policy. Certainly, the nation can be expected to question, to debate, and eventually to conclude that the United States can afford to supply the needed revenues for MERP, were other countries to withdraw financial support.

Truman and Marshall demonstrated enormous fortitude, and leadership. Eighty-six percent of the U.S. polled population was not sufficient to discourage the Administration. Let's hope, should like numbers appear from the public, Washington will have the courage to stand up for its beliefs on the broader Middle East.

**MP:** The Planning Staff, according to Kennan, contributed three major elements of Marshall's speech at Harvard University: a) Europeans should assume responsibility for initiating the program; b) the offer should be made to all Europe; and c) a decisive element should be the rehabilitation of the German economy.

**MERP:** Likewise, a) MERP policy makers should initiate the aid program; b) the offer should be made to all Arab/Muslim and regional non-Arab/Muslim nations (including Iran) as well as to Israel; and c) primary focus should be on rehabilitating the destitute. This includes aid to Palestinians in the West Bank and Gaza, in other countries where they live in the Middle East, as well as in Afghanistan, Pakistan and other hotbeds of anti-US extremism, including Iraq, Lebanon, and Iran.

**MP:** Marshall warned at Harvard that: "governments, political parties or groups which seek to perpetuate human misery in order to profit therefrom politically or otherwise would encounter the opposition of the United States."

**MERP:** The same warning should apply in the Middle East, North Africa and Central Asia. The United States should remain firm in its human rights commitment, by returning to the ideals of America.

**MP:** "The truth of the matter is that Europe's requirements for the next three or four years of foreign food and other essential products - principally from America - were so much greater than her present ability to pay that she must have substantial additional help or face economic, social and political deterioration of a very grave character," Marshall said in 1947.

**MERP:** People of the West Bank and Gaza Strip, Palestinian refugees throughout the region, Iraqis, and other Arab and non-Arab/Muslims living on the edge remain a potential time bomb. Abject poverty begets terrorism. Welfare is only a negative construct when monies are wasted or misused and when the lives the welfare is intended to help remain desperate. Financial assistance can sustain people during periods of hardship; it can provide a new generation with hope and opportunity.

**MP:** The Marshall Plan helped Europeans to be feel better about their condition and themselves. It helped to severe the legacy of hopelessness, depression and authoritarian rule. It made co-ordinated economic policy-making appear normal rather than unusual.

**MERP:** These principles of self-awareness carry the means for feeling good about oneself and the future. The same can apply to nations throughout the Middle East.

**MP:** In his Harvard address Marshall said: "Our policy is directed not only against any country or doctrine but against hunger, poverty, desperation, and chaos. Its purpose should be the revival of a working economy in the world so as to permit the emergence of political and social conditions in which free institutions can exist. The Soviet Union and its dependencies could participate, if they chose to."

**MERP:** This is a doctrine worth reproducing. All former enemies of Israel, (and certainly funding nations of Western Europe and the U.S.) should be invited to participate – so long as they declare themselves no longer enemies.

**MP:** The Soviet Union's decision not to participate in the Marshall Plan almost certainly saved it from defeat in Congress. However, all nations involved in the European field of battle had been invited to share in the aid program.

Marshall's biographer F. Pogue notes that Soviet Commissar of Foreign Affairs, Molotov, claimed that the Marshall Plan "would lead to nothing good ….. and would split Europe into two groups of states." Furthermore, satellite countries of the Soviet Union also chose to reject the plan.

**MERP:** Existing enemies of Israel, and those not friendly to the United States, including nations in the Middle East, North Africa, Central Asia, and also Pakistan, and Afghanistan, should be approached as potential members. It is their decision whether to participate. Governments in power will have to weigh the reaction of their people very carefully when forging policy.

**MP:** Moscow said: "The United States has embarked with the Marshall Plan on the enslavement of Europe …. all an extension of American imperialism."

**MERP:** The same sort of response can be anticipated from numerous governments directly involved in the Palestinian/Israeli conflict. Other potential MERP member governments might   argue that the United States will be "buying" its way as a means for controlling the region.

**MP:** Speaking before the Senate Committee in 1947, Marshall said: "This program will cost our country billions of dollars. It will impose a burden on the American taxpayer. It will require sacrifices today in order that we may enjoy security and peace tomorrow."

**MERP:** This is an investment for the future; tradeoffs will be rewarded. The real GNP of the United States is significantly larger than it was when the Marshall Plan was offered to Europe. In the short run, the Plan and other post-

World War II packages cost Americans about 3 percent of
their GNP for ten years. With its $12 trillion annual
economy, the United States is well able to afford MERP
today.

**MP:** At hearings before the House Committee on Foreign
Affairs on January 12, 1948, prominent members of the
panel feared passage of the Bill would result in an
immediate tax hike, and worse, would be "throwing good
money after bad."
**MERP:** With its present economy and treasury, the United
States should readily be able to support MERP. More than
any other economic enterprise, MERP will stimulate the
speedy recovery of its member nations and in turn help
prevent the dislocations of violence, terrorism,
biological/chemical attacks, and general instability. The
U.S. devoted a small portion of its gross national product to
rebuild war-torn economies in the late 1940s, but about 10
times the percentage expended on foreign aid now.

**MP:** Testifying before the House Committee on Foreign
Affairs, Marshall said: "Durable peace requires the
restoration of Western European vitality."
**MERP:** Durable peace requires the restoration of the
MERP and MENACA nation's vitality. President Bush has
already called for a "Marshall Plan for Afghanistan" and for
economic reform with aid for the Palestinians. Former
Prime Minister Sharon, along with other leaders of the
world, have also called for a Marshall Plan for the
Palestinians. The same message will be forthcoming,
directed at all the other nations of the region.

**MP:** Congress wanted to know how soon they could expect Europe to get on its feet, and were interested in proposals for a more closely-integrated European economy. Strong hints for a common market of Europe were established, paving the way for today's 27-nation European Union.

**MERP:** Congress, will seek answers to similar questions for MERP, with the expectation that a common market of MENACA would, in the near future, be considered. Plans for a process of institution-building and governance would be part of it. Twenty-two Arab nations, plus Israel and another five from Central Asia could someday join together in reinventing the glories of the region.

**MP:** Clayton said: "The program should provide for the greatest possible European self-help, should provide for action on the part of the participating countries which they will, in fact, be able to carry out, and should be such as to assure the maintenance of the European economy without continued support from the U.S."

**MERP:** The same must apply in the MERP region. With time and hard work, self-sufficiency will likely emerge, especially following efforts at economic integration. Self-sufficiency will be written into the script. A fixed time span and cut-off date will be sound policy, even if they have to be adjusted to suit the unfolding circumstances on the ground.

**MP**: Marshall argued that "economic health" was a prerequisite to "political stability" and that Europe could not accomplish either without both initiative and cooperation.

**MERP**: The January 2006 electoral success of Hamas in winning control over the Palestinian Parliament will hopefully lead to compromising and peaceful initiatives and cooperation, first with Fatah and other internal forces, and then with the Israeli government and other nations throughout the region.

**MP:** At the end of the Second World War most Western European countries were predictably antagonistic towards Germany. Threats of isolation for the former enemy, wishes for division or annihilation, and economic boycotts were inevitable. The Marshall Plan dealt with most of these concerns, especially in its determination to promote future European cooperation and integration. It required an end to all talk of boycotting imports/exports to and from Germany.

**MERP:** After 1950, the Arab states, in order to increase the isolation of Israel, banded together to blacklist shippers carrying cargo or passengers to Israel. In 1955, this list was extended to all corporations doing business with Israel. Though the boycott was cancelled, the potential threat of a future boycott against Israel remains. MERP would both serve to counter such attempts, and should include a statement in its program outlawing all forms of economic boycott against Israel and the U.S. as a condition for receiving U.S. assistance.

**MP:** The Administrator of the European Recovery Program found corruption and misuse of funds was greater than originally expected. New controls were put in place, further accountability was demanded, auditing of spendings was tightened, and fraudulent practices were dealt with harshly.

**MERP:** Transparency and other detailed procedures must be the highest priority for the MERP. A tightly monitored unit must generate confidence and respect, and demand and receive open disclosure, with appropriate plans for penalties and cancellations of memberships.

**MP:** In 1999, the Brookings Institution surveyed 1,000 U.S. college professors asking them to identify America's most important accomplishments in the past 100 years. The Marshall Plan was ranked #1, as the greatest public policy of the past century.

**MERP:** Might not MERP, or its equivalent, rank high as a major public policy for the 21$^{st}$ century?

**MP:** In the post-World War II years, the Soviet Union was pressing westward in its spread of communism. At that time we referred to "satellite nations" occupied by the Russians. Today many of those counties have newly ascended into the EU.

Marshall and Truman were both determined to create a better and safer western European world out of the ashes of the war. The plan succeeded within a few short years, with unspent monies returned, creating a prosperous region that anticipated the European Economic Community.

**MERP:** Nearly fifty-seven years later, the threat of communism has been replaced by the threat of terrorism and religious extremism. Bush has promised during his remaining years in office to establish a Palestinian state and to guarantee Israel's sovereign rights. The tightrope of the "Israeli – Palestinian Road-Map" will demand both staying the course and spending the required funds, to provide humanitarian aid and to assist in reconstruction.

In addition, an evolving "Arab Road-Map" is on the horizon as change continues to sweep the broader Middle East.

The original Marshall Plan ended with a refund of unspent funds.  Hopefully, this good fortune can be repeated, but in any case, the MERP funds will be a welcome and needed light in this moment of darkness.

**MP:** The George C. Marshall Foundation states: "One intended consequence of the Marshall Plan was furthering American's national interest in a peaceful Europe. By forcing the West European nations into supranational cooperation The Marshall Plan indirectly influenced the precursors of the present European Union."

**MERP:** With proper funding, training, and communication, a path will emerge leading to the establishment of free-trade accords and an eventual Middle East Economic Community.

**MP:** The predecessor to the existing Organization for Economic Cooperation and Development was the Organization for European Economic Cooperation which helped coordinate post-war reconstruction under the Marshall Plan. As the first European institution dedicated to economic cooperation, the OEEC was a catalyst for economic recovery and integration on the western half of its continent.

**MERP:** Disassociation and disengagement between Israel and Palestine are inappropriate policies. These quixotic concepts will never fulfill the desired hope for stability or prosperity in the region. All neighboring nations having a common bond, will find a meaningful future only by sharing their very best with one another.

**MP**: Secretary of State Marshall did not attempt reconstruction as a U.S. unilateral action. He pursued cooperation and participation with regional multilateral inputs and close contacts with others. His leadership, accompanied by dedicated practitioners, were critical for passage in Congress.

**MERP**: Unilateral decision-making will not succeed, as proven by other efforts at nation-building. Working with many countries in the region can invite heightened morale and command greater effort and acceptance of any program. This certainly will hold true in the Middle East.

And of course, inspired and talented leadership will always be needed.

**MP**: As time moved forward, the benefits of the Marshall Plan and nation building enterprises were downplayed, and the U.S. engaged in the Cold War with the Soviet Union for four decades.

The national security strategy from the late 1950s was now focused on preventing a major war with the Soviets. Aid was primarily given to a range of countries to win influence and stem the spread of communism and promote democracy. Direct support to nation-building by the U.S. was limited as it was deemed too provocative. "The chess game lasted for more than forty years; a new generation of diplomats and soldiers grew up on Cold War national security strategies."

**MERP:** With the end of the Cold War, President Clinton gradually began to dismantle this tired and rather obsolete policy. It took 9/11 to bring many Washington politicians to their senses (perhaps not President George W. Bush) to realize that reconstruction and financial assistance to terrorist and/or failed states, in particular those in the Middle East, is a strategy that must be honed and implemented.

**MP:** T.H.White wrote in 1978: "The Marshall Plan had won because it had linked gain with freedom, had assumed that the movement of minds and the movement of peoples must go with the movement of goods and out of merchants. In the noblest terms, it had enlisted the good will of free peoples against the discipline of orderly peoples. In the crudest terms, it had enlisted greed against terror."
**MERP:** In today's struggle to secure a road-map to peace in the Israeli-Palestinian arena, along with the evolution of a broader Arab-Road-Map, the lessons of the Marshall Plan remain critical. Success in the Middle East demands U.S. and international support, encouragement, and financing. A regional, economic integrated community may one day follow.

---

Gordon Brown, the British Chancellor of the Exchequer, argued in December 2001 that there are strong parallels between the world today and the world when the Marshall Plan was launched. He proposed that the United States, the world's wealthiest country, should double aid to developing countries for health, education, and anti-poverty programs. This would mean a commitment of $50 billion annually for the next 15 years. The conditions that breed terrorism, Brown said, are similar to those that fed totalitarianism over a half-century ago. "How do you win the peace? That was the question in 1945 and it's what we face today after Afghanistan."

Chancellor Brown's challenge is no different from the post-World War II period. President Truman and Secretary Marshall's initial goal was to rescue Turkey and Greece from Communism, but their thinking evolved into a comprehensive plan to rebuild war-torn economies. As a result, the U.S. devoted one percent of its gross domestic product to the initiative, or about ten times the percentage expended on foreign aid in 2000.

It would be naïve to believe that a crisis of more than fifty-seven years could be eliminated with a mere duplication of the Marshall Plan. Certainly, times are quite different; new forces and personalities in the world have taken the stage; attitudes and perceptions have changed; former enemies are gone, only to be replaced by others. The broader Middle East, for a number of factors including its willingness and ability to export terrorism, become the most crucial region in the world for U.S. policy in the twenty-first century..

President Clinton's second Secretary of State, Madeleine Albright is clearly a George Marshall fan. Whether in working out U.S. strategy for the states of former Yugoslavia, or for the newly liberated Soviet countries of Central Europe, she cited the Marshall Plan as a great model for nation-building: "If the latter (integration and democracy) were to prevail, we needed to stop drifting from crisis to crisis and engineer a decisive shift. As models, we cited the Marshall Plan that helped Western Europe recover from World War II......."

---------------------------------------------

A study of the Marshall Plan is a reward in and of itself. Borrowing from its lessons and results both validates the genius of its founders and administrators and provides a basis for adding to a proven vehicle of cooperation, rather than having to invent one from scratch.

The European Recovery Program and the establishment of the State of Israel were both decided in 1948. The two events are linked in history books - both were dedicated to preserving freedom, and both were attempting to redress the evil of World War II.

Today, Israel remains center stage, as does the Palestinian Authority, Iraq, Iran, Lebanon, Syria and other nations of the Middle East, many locked in a struggle for a rightful place in the modern world.

Jeffrey E. Garten, former Dean of the Yale University School of Management has recently pressed for a worldwide economic stimulus plan, "In the immediate aftermath of World War II, the United States pushed for the establishment of the International Monetary Fund and the World Bank, and coordinated the Marshall Plan with European nations. Washington realized then that economic stability and prosperity were essential to a country's security. It's true today, too."

It is worth repeating that the Marshall Plan's hallmark was the requirement that European countries work together to devise a plan for postwar construction: "It would be neither fitting nor efficacious for this government to undertake to draw up unilaterally a program designed to place Europe on its feet economically. This is the business of the Europeans.  The initiative, I think, must come from Europe," said Kennan.

The U.S. Department of State, without trying to force Europe to a common market, nonetheless "pressed an idea on European which became the Common Market, for America would yield dollars only to the common consensus of all claimants ..... The U.S. was handing out tickets of admission to the circling globe of world trade which Europe itself had once dominated."

This should be a severe admonition for our current President. As Susan E. Rice, a former Assistant Secretary of State warned: "The goal was not only to rebuild Europe but also to encourage former adversaries to form partnerships that could endure after United States assistance ended. The plan succeeded so well that Europe has followed the road of cooperation all the way to the European Union." The mounting arguments for an Arab-Road Map are compelling.

There will be those who will gleefully remind us that the Marshall Plan led the way towards the creation of the European Union. Today, the EU appears to be in crisis, evidenced by resistance to the creation of a constitution and the June 18, 2005 heated collapse of its future budget negotiations. Some will argue that the Marshall Plan led to the establishment of European integration only to see it suddenly coming to a halt, leaving the institution in paralysis and self-doubt. There are lessons here that must be studied over and over again to avoid similar pitfalls.

In addition, having funds drift in without citizen participation would be a futile exercise. Leaders cannot unilaterally make decisions. Whether Palestinian, Iraqi, or other recipients of funding, they must not sit back nor just await the flow of monies, which must be finite in amount and duration.

Former Secretary of State Colin Powell worked in his office under a portrait of Marshall, and at the same desk once used by Marshall. Powell's noble legacy remains to be written, but judging his style of diplomacy, and the advice and support provided to President Bush, Powell would have argued for a strong and adequately funded program for reconstruction and nation-building. Unfortunately, he never was given the chance, although in retirement he feels free to speak out against President Bush's military strategies. Nevertheless, for the most part, these responsibilities are now passed on to the newest chair holder in the State Department, Condoleezza Rice.

President Bush, during the election campaign of 2000 spoke disdainfully of "nation-building": "I think what we need to do is convince people who live in the lands they live in to build the nations. Maybe I'm missing something here, I mean, we're going to have kind of a nation-building corps from America? Absolutely not."

"Americans, even today in this globally connected world, feel the pull to retreat into our isolationist comfort zone," wrote George Oliver. "The nation is blessed with a strong economy, a large supply of natural resources, and a skilled labor force. Any plan that offers a sizeable sum of taxpayer money to rebuild another country will face the same resistance that the Marshall Plan did. The lesson from those who believed in the Marshall Plan is to make the American people understand the purpose of such a project, and why it is important for America."

In the next chapter, we'll examine the models for a re-invented Marshall Plan (a new name needs to be claimed), from its founding concepts to its institutional structure and form of governance. It will be necessary to examine the many alternatives and options, consider inputs from the multitude of concerned parties, and exam the costly funding – one trillion dollars and more, over an extended time frame.

The debates will be many and intense and the political tug between Democrats and Republicans will be play central to the outcome. Motives will be suspect and the passions of past and present conflicts will continue to fog perceptions as we reach for peace and stability.

Following the release of the *Iraq Study Group* report, President Bush in January 2007 shifted course in Iraq and in the Middle East. His January 23rd State of the Union address revealed his determination to move forward.

Assuredly, as far as the Middle East is concerned, the parallel to Communism is not terrorism, but religious extremism because terrorism is not a form of government, religious extremism essentially is. And terrorism flourishes within religious extremism throughout the world.

Advances in economic and political concerns will be addressed. They await the restoration of stability and calm.

In the end, a master plan should find its supporters, distracters, and eventually triumphs. The United States, working closely with its international partners, will sort out the challenges and set the path for a reinvention of the entire region.

# CHAPTER IV

## REBIRTH BEGINS -
## THE MIDDLE EAST RECOVERY PROGRAM ACT

"As a soldier who knows the horrors of war, I seek a peace with every Arab country. We are ready to share our know-how with Palestinians, to help you and be helped by you. I see a Marshall Plan for Palestine – call it the Bush-Sharon plan – to solve your problem of unemployment. Together we can make tremendous achievements."

**Ariel Sharon**
**(Prime Minister of Israel, 2002)**

The 2004 *New York Film Festival* emphasized wartime and the implacable enemy that sought to sully the United States' image, alter its form of life, and undermine its coalition allies.

No, it was not the 21$^{st}$ century of Al Qaeda, Taliban, nor Iraq, but the post World War II Cold War of Communism and the Soviet Union. Films depicting western ideology, to charm and seduce European sentiments were produced for public consumption, today referred to as "public diplomacy." *Selling Democracy: Films of the Marshall Plan, 1948-53* long hidden from US citizens because of bureaucracy which only recently became available for viewing.

The 25 films were released 57 years ago after being shot in part to help answer the question, "Why, with this experience....has the U.S. failed so conspicuously since September 11$^{th}$ to bolster its image in another region it seeks to transform, the broader Middle East?

According to Roger Cohen of the *New York Times*, the 1949 film "Me and Mr. Marshall" was made to "humanize the economic vision of Europe first set out by Marshall at Harvard on June 5, 1947, in the hope of reinforcing a nascent West German democracy and binding it to America."

These brief films repeatedly discuss principles of empowerment, of returning control back to the Europeans, and of shortening the length of U.S. occupation. The order in which events must unfold to ensure a liberal democracy, as depicted, emphasizes "a job, money, security and then freedom."

More than 300 documentary films were made, mostly on specific European Cooperation Administration topics, with a niche marketing mind. Eleven to fifteen minutes in length, almost all played as shorts alongside features in movies houses. *The Shoemaker and the Hatter,* a prize winning animated cartoon pitched free trade and mass production, and was distributed in 1951, in 11 languages to cinemas throughout Western Europe. *The Island of Faith,* about the reconstruction of the dike system in The Netherlands, played to audiences in 9 nations and was dubbed in 8 languages. It was "stipulated that the Marshall Plan....will not be mentioned more than twice in a one-reeler and three times in a two-reeler."

These half a century old films concentrate on how employment bringing in the money that would create prosperity available only in a free world. They offer the viewer the possibility of consideration in the projected world of a reinvented Marshall Plan, or MERP. The films provide a splendid template from the past for a propaganda campaign today. Some themes may apply, while others seek clarification in a different time and place.

------------------------------------------------------------

The Republican candidate for President, George W. Bush, criticized the Clinton administration for its expansive agenda of nation-building. During the 2000 presidential campaign, Governor Bush derided the use of American soldiers for this purpose. Repeatedly, the candidate argued against this form of reconstruction. He spoke disdainfully, "I think what we need to do is convince people who live in the lands they live in to build the nations." Bush said: "Maybe I'm missing something here. I mean, we're going to have the kind of a nation-building corps from America? Absolutely not."

Prior to the Iraq war, Bush had been told that "the road to Jerusalem passed through Baghdad." With Iraq the present magnet for anti-Western fervor, it is believed throughout the region that the formula is the other way around.

Then, an apparent shift occurred when nation-building became the inescapable responsibility of the world's only superpower. Following 9/11, rebuilding other countries strictly with aid was considered appropriate by the Bush administration. In fact, once the counterattack against the Taliban was deemed a success, Bush called for a Marshall Plan for Afghanistan.

Bush reversed his position on nation-building during a speech on June 24, 2002 in the White House Rose Garden. With his address, Bush opened a new period of American diplomacy in the Middle East: "The United States, the European Union, the World Bank, and International Monetary Fund are willing to oversee reform in Palestinian finances, encouraging transparency and independent auditing. And the United States, along with our partners in the developed world, will increase our humanitarian assistance to relieve Palestinian suffering."

President Bush's *Millennium Challenge Account* called for the largest U.S. increase in foreign assistance in two decades. $1.3 billion would be earmarked for 2004 (Congress cut it back to $1 billion), $2.6 billion for 2005, and $5 billion annually after that. The Account attempted to deal with foreign aid abuses by corrupt regimes, to avoid having funds squandered on ineffective projects and inadequate monitoring. (Were the *Millennium Challenge Account* carried out successfully, it could become a major template in the creation of MERP.)

In November 2002, Congress passed the *Afghanistan Freedom Support Act*, providing $3.3 billion for reconstruction in Afghanistan over a four-year period. The legislation authorized $425 million a year for recovery projects and set up an enterprise fund that would provide a total of $300 million in seed money to start and sustain new businesses, a mini, but failed Marshall Plan, based on the recent anti-American protests.

The President's humanitarian gift to the world's poor was an optimistic response to join with 187 other countries to support the UN's *Millennium Declaration*, a manifest to eradicate extreme poverty, hunger and disease for more than one billion disadvantaged people. The project set a deadline of 2015 to achieve its goals. The objective is to have countries such as the U.S., France, and Britain offer 0.7 percent of their national incomes for development aid for poor nations.

The Bush administration has failed, however, to match its promises with action. The $5 billion promised for the future would have totaled just 0.04 percent of our national income. But even that amount has been withheld. By the end of 2004, the U.S. had not dispersed a single dollar towards fulfilling its obligation. Tragedy marches on across the globe including in Africa, where one in 16 pregnant women die in childbirth, 2.2 million die of AIDS, and 2 million children die from malaria every year.

Today, as the world's lone superpower, we are obligated to share our resources with the poorest parts of the world not only to alleviate poverty, but to promote employment and opportunity. As the leading contributor of funding to the Middle East, the U.S. will remain a major voice in the creation of MERP.

Funding of a *Middle East Recovery Program Act* would go a long way towards creating more civil and just societies in the Middle East, but also throughout the North African and Central Asian regions. Working closely with pre-existing regional institutions, MERP expenditures would go well beyond the more traditional and obvious needs to include humanitarian support, infrastructure development, housing construction, job creation, and financial support for education.

By the end of 2002, then Secretary of State Colin Powell had introduced what he called a *Middle East Partnership Initiative* (a potential precursor to a Middle East Recovery Program) asking for a new effort to spread democracy and political reforms in the Middle East. This phase added only $29 million, approved by Congress in July 2002, to the $1 billion that goes for foreign aid to Arab countries. Many experts believed that the United States would spend far more than $10 billion to reconstruct the region should there be an agreement between Israel and the Palestinians. (Following Arafat's death, the U.S. Congress quickly approved an emergency Palestinian aid package of $23.5 million.)

Though accepting the task of securing and rebuilding Afghanistan, the Bush administration still had reservations about nation-building. The attack on Iraq permitted the administration to continue its attack against such concepts. A considerable part of the chaos on the ground in Iraq was assuredly attributable to the aversion shared at the top levels of Bush's war-planning team.

By March 2003, the Bush administration prepared to award a contract valued at as much as $900 million (a one nation mini-Marshall Plan) to begin rebuilding a post-war Iraq, in what would be the largest government reconstruction effort since Americans helped to rebuild Germany and Japan after World War II.

One obstacle to winning the peace before reconstruction of a country is the long-standing issue of how best to handle any prewar debt owed to others by the defeated state. There is no better example of this dilemma than the desire of the Bush administration for obtaining "forgiveness" for the debt Iraq owed Western countries.

Forgiving the debt is considered almost as critical to Iraq's future as quelling the insurgency. Even if considerable aid was offered to Iraq, such as a reinvented Marshall Plan, the impoverished country would never attract enough foreign investment to revive its oil industry and its economy so long as it carries unsustainable debt of $120 billion.

In October 2004, the Group of 7 (the United States, Britain, Canada, France, Germany, Italy and Japan) working with the International Monetary Fund and the World Bank, gathered at its annual meeting to resolve the issue of debt. Exacerbating the situation was the claim by some African nations that the group of 7 governments showed favoritism for debt relief for Iraq with little concern for the well-being of African countries.

In fact, Iraq's debt, run-up by Saddam Hussein during sanctions, is nearly four times larger than the $32 billion needed to pay off the entire debt of several dozen nations. A partial debt relief remained another alternative, although Iraq owed $80 billion of its $120 billion to other Middle Eastern and Persian Gulf countries.

By November 2004, Germany and the United States had agreed on a proposal to cancel 80 percent, or about $33 billion, of the debt owed by Iraq to a group of creditor nations known as the *Paris Club*. The U.S. argued for a generous debt write-off for Iraq, trying to win support for wiping out as much as 95 percent of the country's debt.

## MADRID, THEN TOKYO AND MERP

More than twenty-five years ago, Iraq's per capita income was $3,600, similar to that of Spain at the time. Today, that income barely reaches $600. Based on the

United Nations Human Development Index, Iraq tumbled 50 places.

In October 2003, a mini-Marshall Plan was created at the International Donor Conference for the Reconstruction of Iraq which took place in Madrid, Spain.

Seventy-three nations (half of which sent delegations headed by ministers), 20 international organizations, and 13 non-governmental agencies (NGOs) together committed $33 billion for the period 2004-2007. At least $5.5 billion of this amount was to come as loans from the World Bank and the International Monetary Fund.

The host in Spain, Prime Minister Jose-Maria Aznar declared: "The economic reconstruction of Iraq is evidently the reason why we have called the conference. However, we should also stress the underlying motive: We want Iraq to return to the fold of the international community and return to normality as a state."

Secretary of State Colin L. Powell flew back to Washington with pledges of $13 billion to be delivered over four years. By the fall of 2004, only $1.3 billion of the pledged money had been provided, with more than half from Britain and Japan. The monies were to be used for reconstruction of water, power, health care and other systems devastated by the American invasion of Iraq six months earlier. By November 2004, the U.S. Congress had appropriated $18.4 billion, though little more than $1.8 billion had been disbursed.

On October 13-14, in Tokyo, the U.S. held a meeting with rich nations to raise additional monies in Europe and the Arab world to rebuild Iraq.

By the summer of 2005, Iraqi officials argued at a Brussels meeting, that their government was now sufficiently stable, secure and legitimate enough. Their discussion focused on the $13 billion pledged for rebuilding Iraq at the 2003 Madrid conference. Two years later, a mere 10 percent of the funds had been delivered.

## MERP AND THE UNITED NATIONS

In today's climate, unilateral action, whether it be military or humanitarian should be determined primarily by members of the international community. The United Nations with all its warts, remains the strategic organization for doing this. Though often criticized by conservatives, the United Nations remains the last best hope for world diplomacy.

Thirty years ago, the United Nations failed to implement the its General Assembly approved "Charter of Economic Rights and Duties of States." Passage was blocked by a handful of economically powerful nations sitting in the Untied Nations Security Council.

The fundamental purpose of this Charter was to promote "the establishment of the new international economic order, based on equity, sovereign equality, interdependence, common interest, and cooperation among all States, irrespective of their economic and social systems."

Had the Charter been implemented, I believe it would now serve as a partial model for MERP. Renewed consider of the Charter today is needed.

Probably perceived as a threat to the most powerful nations of the UN Security Council the proposed Charter was rejected. In today's climate of terrorism and debate, a renewed consideration of the Charter would advance the cause of stability and reconstruction. Five of the 10 primary articles of the Charter's "Economic rights and

Duties of States" as presented more than three decades ago are:

- Every State has the sovereign and inalienable right to choose its economic system as well as its political, social and cultural systems in accordance with the will of its people, without outside interference, coercion or threat in any form whatsoever.

- Every State has and shall freely exercise full permanent sovereignty, including possession, use and disposal, over all its wealth, natural resources and economic activities.

- States should cooperate in facilitating more equitable international economic relations and in encouraging structural changes in the context of a balanced world economy in harmony with the needs and interests of all countries, especially developing countries, and should take appropriate measures to this end.

- All States have the responsibility to cooperate in the economic, social, cultural, scientific and technological fields for the promotion of economic and social progress throughout the world, especially that of the developing countries.

- All States are juridical equal and, as equal members of the international community, have the right to participate fully and effectively in the international decision-making process in the solution of world economic, financial and monetary problems, *inter alia,* through the appropriate international organizations in accordance with their existing and evolving rules, and to share equitably in the benefits resulting there from.

The 1974, nearly forgotten "Charter of Economic

Rights" deserves renewed attention. Resolution of the Middle East conflict, whether it be Iraq alone, or the Israeli-Palestinian debacle, or in unison with the Arab-world demands an international strategic approval and plan before MERP is released.

Exacerbating and complicating the situation, the World Bank and the United Nations pointed to the inadequacy of donations to revitalize the economy of Iraq. Together, they announced in 2003 that $36 billion was needed over four years. This would be in addition to the $19 billion recommended initially by the United States. 14 different sectors were included, such as health, education, water and electricity for a total of $9.3 billion for the year 2004, and another $26.3 billion over the next three years, for a total of the stated $36 billion through 2007.

A MERP proposal must therefore take into account their calculations, where $55 billion in total will be needed for Iraq to rebuild everything from health care to infrastructure to agriculture and security infrastructure.

## MERP AND THE EUROPEAN UNION

As indicated by the the international outcry over the U.S.administration's invasion of Iraq and claims to be a neutral partner in the Israeli-Palestinian dispute, any effective arrangement to settle the dispute between the western world and the countries of the Middle East will require international cooperation.

To minimize potential strains between the European Union and the United States what will be necessary to conduct MERP negotiations. For example, in October 2004, the European Union and Syria initialed an association agreement that commits both sides to work towards free trade – as well as against weapons of mass destruction and terrorism.

Syria was the only Arab country in the EU's "Barcelona process" launched in 1995 not to have concluded an association agreement. The new accord provides for the creation of a free-trade area between the EU and Syria as part of the larger goal of a Euro-Mediterranean free-trade zone by 2010. Israel's government called this accord "a pity," claiming it keeps Syria from being a player in the Palestinian/Israeli Road-Map.

On the day of Arafat's burial in Ramallah on November 12, 2004, Tony Blair met with George W. Bush in Washington, pushing hard for a renewed effort by the U.S. president to reopen negotiations towards a fair and significant resolution of the Palestinian-Israeli conflict. Progress in this direction, Blair pointed out, must include the European Union into the process. Re-engaged, the U.S. and the EU should provide greater resources, energies, creativity, funding and a more positive relationship between great nations long separated by an ocean and differing ideologies.

## MERP AND THE MIDDLE EAST PARTNERSHIP INITIATIVE

Since President Bush's inaugural address in January 2005, calling for the sweeping adoption of democratic rule in autocratic countries, the administration has pressed more and more for aid to the Middle East (to date the nearest effort approaching a mini-MERP) to go, at least in part, to groups supporting change in their societies, with training and subsidies.

The administration first set up its own *Middle East Partnership Initiative,* which committed $300 million in aid over the last few years. MEPI is a presidential initiative to promote democracy and reform in the Middle East and North Africa through diplomatic efforts and through aid to individual nations. A key element of MEPI is creating links and partnerships with Arab, U.S., and global civil society governments and private sector businesses to jointly achieve genuine and lasting reforms at the local level.

In part, to remove American fingerprints in a region where anti-American sentiments run high, about $85 million was taken out of this initiative and used for the new *Foundation for the Future,* for support of democratic groups, and the *Fund for the Future*, for entrepreneurial efforts. Both became part of the Bush administration's so-called *Broader Middle East and North Africa Initiative,* set up by major industrial democracies at Sea Island, Georgia in mid-2004.

## MERP AND STOCKHOLM

Once Israel and Hezbollah agreed to end their cross-border killings at the end of the summer 2006, Hezbollah, with funding from Iran, would rebuild devastated Lebanon. In response, the United States, Europe, and nearly 60 foreign governments and aid organizations came forward with mini-Marshall aid plan in Stockholm on September 1st.

They had hoped to raise $500 million, and instead promised a total of $940 million as an early rebuilding multilateral effort.

The following day $500 million was also pledged for the Palestinian territories. (Unfortunately, history in the region indicates that pledges often fail to be fulfilled.)

## THE WORLD BANK AND THE INTERNATIONAL MONETARY FUND – MINI-MARSHALL PLANS IN DISGUISE

They were created following the Bretton Woods conference in New Hampshire in 1944, where the World War II allies, minus Russia, met to chart the economic order of the post-war world. The World Bank and the International Monetary Fund (IMF) are today the biggest nation-building pillars in the struggle to reduce poverty and to sustain economic growth in developing nations.

### Funding in Iraq

A recent World Bank Group study estimated that Iraq could handle only $5.2 billion in foreign reconstruction. The study's majority opinion was prepared by the World Bank, assisted by the United Nations and the IMF. The Bank estimates Iraq needs $55 billion in economic aid overall, partly to finance its rehabilitation of its oil fields.

The $55 billion estimate coincides roughly with the Bush administration's conclusion that Iraq would need $50 billion to $75 billion to recover from the rule of ousted Saddam Hussein and war damage.    However, only American firms are eligible for contracts financed by U.S. contributions.  Foreign companies, on the other hand, may obtain contracts under non-US international assistance. For instance, a British firm was able to print new currency for Iraq.

In January 2004, the World Bank released its *Interim Strategy Note* for Iraq.  It describes all of the Bank's planned support, most importantly, lending, studies, and other technical assistance.  The report, which builds on the Bank's earlier work in 2003, details the Bank Group's work program for Iraq over the coming years.

It draws on the Bank's experience with post-conflict nations and those in transition from a centrally planned economy to a market-based economy. As of March 2004, the World Bank has financed six active projects in Iraq amounting to over $ 170 million.

The International Monetary Fund is also a partner in the reconstruction of Iraq. It will provide Iraq with $2.5 billion to $4.3 billion in loans.

**Funding in Afghanistan**

After 23 years of civil conflict, Afghanistan's government is receiving over $750 million in grants and interest-free loans from the World Bank.  The Bank pledged $570 million for Afghanistan at the Tokyo conference, and delivered as much as $600 million between January 2002 and June 2004. The funds were focused on addressing urgent financial management and public administration needs as well as investment priorities, including education, infrastructure rehabilitation, job creation, health, and private sector development.

On May 19, 2005, the World Bank approved a $85 million grant to Afghanistan, of which $40 million will fund higher education, with the remainder to support the country's economic and social recovery through improved road access to goods, markets, and social services.

In the United Nations Development Program, the Asian Development Bank and the Islamic Development Bank created the Afghanistan Reconstruction Trust Fund, a coordinated way for donors to help the Afghanistan Government. Programs include rebuilding the country and facilitating the return of skilled expatriate Afghans to their country. It also provides short-term emergency funding for salaries of civil servants.

## Funding in Palestine

As dictated by the regulations of the World Bank and the IMF, since the West Bank and Gaza are not a sovereign nation, they cannot apply for membership. Therefore they are not eligible for normal funding sources, available only to member nations.

To overcome these barriers, the Trust Fund for Gaza and West Bank (TFGWB) was created in 1993. The TFGWB has periodically been replenished through allocations from the Bank's surplus. By 2005, a total of six allocations, worth $460 million in U.S. currency have been made. Over the past decade, the World Bank has had 17 projects in the Palestinian territories, ranging from housing to healthcare.

On March 1st, 2005, the Bank reaffirmed its commitment to support the reform efforts of the PA and it continues to raise short-term emergency budgetary support as well as medium-term development aid. The Bank also attempts to help investors provide funding to the private sector. By lending fiscal support to Palestine, the Bank assists in delivering basic services to citizens in the West Bank and Gaza. At least 100,000 people have benefited from this aid and not fallen into poverty.

The World Bank is focused on giving Gaza and the West Bank a working economy. The Bank recommends to:
.    speed up checks at crossings by improving technology,
.    abolish unloading and reloading of goods at Israeli-Palestinian borders,
.    re-open Gaza airport,
.    building a Gaza seaport,

. build a Gaza-Ashdod rail link,
. build a Gaza-West Bank rail link,
. restore 38,000 permits for Gazans in Israel,
. dismantle West Bank internal checkpoints,
. let Israeli firms stay in border industrial zones
. maintain a quasi-customs union for now,
. transfer Jewish settlement infrastructure and houses to PA.

The World Bank's president, Paul Wolfowitz has a full plate as he determines how best to lend the world's neediest nations $20 billion a year. To be sure, he is fully aware that he will face the wrath of many poor nations of the world if he bypasses their growing concerns.

At the same time, the former President of the World Bank, James Wolfensohn was engaged in critical work for the U.S. Department of State as their Middle East negotiator.

Likewise, the IMF is active. Managing Director Rodrigo de Rato said: "The IMF would continue to support the PA in strengthening its economic performance and building sound economic and financial institutions."

The United Nations Conference on Trade and Development (UNCTAD) urges Palestinian policymakers to press for immediate priorities in the economic area, including halting the public wage bill and workforce inflation; avoiding overdependence on donor aid to provide social protection and budget support; managing a transparent balanced budget without incurring unsustainable external debt, while divesting the PA of its remaining commercial and market assets; establishing accountable public sector institutions according to global best practices, promoting absorption within a distorted labor market of some 80,000 workers formerly employed in

Israel, and more than twice the number again of chronically unemployed; designing and managing a coherent economic policy and development program for a fragmented, landlocked territory surrounded by land and sea barriers with Israel and intersected by the built-up areas, access routes and buffer zones of Israeli settlements; and reinforce and develop the rule of law after years of deterioration and centralization of powers.

Following promises from the Arab League, on August 1, 2006 the European Union began to release donor funds to cash-starved Palestinian hospitals, as part of a broader relief package that will provide the Palestinian Authority with about $130 million over three months. The money is to be used to pay a half-month's salary to all of the government's 167,000 employees, with the remainder used for government operating expenses.

Arab League countries had already pledged $55 million a month in support. For example, Qatar and Libya have deposited $50 million in an Arab League Palestinian Relief Fund, while Yemen and Oman together have sent another $11 million. Under the plan, funds began to dribble into Palestinian pockets, but was nowhere near the amount needed to meet the PA's $160 million-plus monthly budget.

**A Single Currency for the Middle East**

A single currency throughout the Middle East will, if accomplished, parallel the present 12-nation Euro-zone of the European Union. The new currency will initially be limited to members of the Gulf nations. "The establishment of an economic and monetary union will create an important regional entity that in 2001 had an estimated combined GDP of about $335 billion, with an average weighted per capita income in nominal terms of about

$12,708, and 45 and 17 percent, respectively, of the world's oil and natural gas reserves."

Perhaps a bit too optimistic in its target dates, any realization of a single currency in the region portends a future MERP, with its natural outcome – regional economic integration.

## FROM IRAQ TO THE WEST BANK/GAZA

At the beginning of 2006, the average daily wage for Palestinians in Gaza, with its 1.4 million population, (there are 1.8 additional Palestinians residing in the West Bank) was $12 a day. Before the Intifada of 2000, 30,000 Gazans crossed into Israel proper each day to find work. Now, only a few thousands do. Unemployment in this strip alone, riding the Mediterranean and bordered by Israel and Egypt, has an unemployment rate of 60 percent. Those with work look after an average of 7.7 dependents.

Overnight, it seemed that the world was coming to grips with the reality of the devastating plight of the Palestinians. In addition to the terrible loss of life in both the Palestinian Authority and Israel, according to United Nations estimates, the on-going conflict between Israelis and Palestinians has led to a doubling of Palestinian poverty and unemployment rates.

"50 percent of Palestinians now live below the poverty line, and that up to 60 percent are unemployed," according to former U.S. Senator George Mitchell who testified before the U.S. House of Representatives International Relations Committee. He said that U.N. relief officials indicate that two million Palestinians are in need of food, aid, shelter, and/or medical assistance.

Congressman Henry Hyde, Chairman of the International Relations Committee, forcefully called for the establishment of a special temporary agency to make investments in the private sector in the Middle East aimed at sustainable job creation. He said investments by this agency should be made only if the following conditions are put into place: "...firm, measurable commitments to economic openness, including intra-regional free trade, so that growth will be continuous."

Chairman Hyde was convinced, as were other senior Congressmen, that a comprehensive economic development program for the Middle East was needed to parallel the 1948 Marshall Plan that rebuilt Western Europe following World War II. He said that the Marshall Plan in Europe dealt with the threat of renewed instability by providing reconstruction assistance and promoting economic cooperation.

Based on a study done after his trip to the Middle East, Chairman Hyde argued, "We sensed that the people who had hope of a better life in economic terms would not resort to violence. We sensed that when people had a stake in their own economic future, they do not adhere to extremist ideologies. We believed that the way towards the future was to liberalize economies, freeing them from the dead hand of outdated regulation, tariffs, and other trade barriers within the region."

The ranking minority member on the International Relations Committee, Congressman Tom Lantos, a prominent thinker and continuing advocate for the Middle East peace process, offered his support for Hyde's ideas, saying that economic assistance could serve as a powerful weapon to fight terrorism. "I am extremely confident that an open, democratic Arab world is destined to prosper with the help of the American Marshall Plan you proposed."

Hyde was quick to make the point that his ideas for a Marshall Plan for the Middle East "were consistent with President Bush's recent statement that a future Palestinian state would require a vibrant economy based on honest enterprise and encouraged by honest government."

Congressman Benjamin Gilman, another senior member of the International Relations Committee believed that a Marshall Plan for the region was a "sound idea," but it must be predicated on a move toward democracy through social and economic reforms. "So too we need a Marshall Plan which focuses on religious freedom and political pluralism....We must provide those societies with the tools to repair themselves socially."

Hyde and others on the House International Relations Committee are leading the way towards MERP. Economics with deregulation, trade with reduced tariffs and quotas, and debt relief and international donor commitments point to a future MERP strategy.

Recent findings continue to plague the social conscience of Middle East nations and the world. Only days before the House of Representatives' meeting, the United Nations Development Program (UNDP) had released its *Arab Human Development Report 2002* which highlighted a wide range of challenges that a Middle East Recovery Program could address. "The mismatch between aspirations and their fulfillment," according to Rima Khalaf, an assistant secretary-general of the United Nations and Director of UNDP "has in some cases led to alienation and its offspring, apathy or discontent," throughout the region. "For the non-oil producing countries, this requires huge investment outlays that are currently beyond their financial means. A Marshall Plan approach can tremendously help in pulling them out of their predicament." The thrust for a Middle East Marshall Plan "can be instrumental to making that shift from a struggling region to a progressing one."

Before coming to the United Nations, Rima Khalaf served as Deputy Prime Minister of Jordan and concluded that it is possible to build "human capabilities through quality education, health and social services, and quality research and developmental activities, promoting creativity and technological empowerment."

The Director of UNDP, in addition, persists using human capabilities, through utilizing the economies and providing equal opportunities to all, especially women. And on the issue of change "…. liberating human capabilities through promoting systems of good governance including the reform of state institutions and activating the voice of people,"can advance the average citizens lifetstyle.

The House of Representatives' International Relations Committee heard her call that "An equivalent of a Marshall Plan for the region cannot be timelier to provide Arab people of the region with hope and bring them closer to their aspirations for a better life."

It was now time to hear from the Israeli leadership. "As a soldier who knows the horrors of war," spoke Prime Minister Ariel Sharon in April 2002, "I seek a peace with every Arab country. We are ready to share our know-how with Palestinians, to help you and be helped by you. I see a Marshall Plan for Palestine - call it the Bush-Sharon plan - to solve your problem of unemployment. Together we can make tremendous achievements."

A bit of optimism, at this point, can be helpful. The reawakening, at least between Israel and Palestine, may be showing signs of a positive turnaround. Trade between the PA and Israel stood at $1.9 billion in 2004, up 37 percent over the previous year. In 2001, trade stood at $1.4 billion, taking a dip the following year and bouncing back to earlier levels in 2003. In 2004, the total amount of Israeli exports to the PA reached $1.6 billion, a 26 percent increase over 2003. The PA is the second largest importer of Israeli goods after the U.S. Meanwhile, Israel imported $300 million worth of goods from the PA in 2004, a jump of 36 percent over the previous year.

Of course, all of these impressive improvements were to shift following the parliamentary election of Hamas in early 2006.

## TIME FOR ACTION

"We need a Marshall Plan for Iraq......Good economics makes for good politics and we have not done well here..... We blundered by failing to promote Iraqi small business and by failing to involve thousands of Iraqis in the reconstruction of their country." Lt. General (retired) Jay Garner; former director of Reconstruction after the April 2003 U.S. intervention in Iraq.

The MERP process will most likely begin in the disputed areas of the Middle East, (in theory, it could start in North Africa and/or Central Asia, but political priorities may suggest otherwise.) For disputed areas, consideration should be given to utilizing significant monies for relocating Israelis from West Bank/Gaza settlements, for renovating their abandoned facilities to be used by returning Palestinian refugees, for assisting in the return of Palestinians to either Israel or to the newly-established Palestinian state, for compensating Israelis for lands and property confiscated because of leaving their original homelands, and for other legitimate purposes.

MERP could readily commence as MENARP - Middle East/North Africa Recovery Program, or indeed as MENACARP - Middle East/North Africa/Central Asia Recovery Program. Some would argue that the latter would be ideal, but pragmatic needs of the day, including financial and political needs, might require consideration of additions for a later time. However, events since 9/11/01 may necessitate changing all approaches.

Assuredly, Iraq because of the continuing conflict could be the central focus of MERP, but I am hesitant with this approach.

Probably, but with uncertainty on my part, I believe that the recovery effort should commence with financial assistance to the Palestinians, then to other Middle East nations, including Iraq and Afghanistan. To anticipate the possibility that a match can be found along the way, it is desirable to anticipate nations of North Africa and Central Asia entering the recovery program.

Consequently, all geographically-eligible countries, including past or present enemies, should be invited at the outset to participate in dialogue with Middle East states to offer statements of need, and then, to await the time and reasons when they will be factored into the providing of assistance.

Administratively, Amman would, at this point in time, be my preferred choice as the seat of the non-US Middle East MERP effort. Fairness dictates that Jordan, while the heart of the organizational effort, would remain a lesser candidate for large MERP funding.

I believe that the recovery effort should commence with financial assistance and guidance to the Palestinians, then to other Middle East nations, including Iraq.

Palestine will be a small nation, with significant and known problems, and it is relatively stable compared with Iraq. Recall, a major lesson since the Oslo accord was that economic progress can only succeed once the parties have ceased fighting. Iraq remains mired in conflict. Yet, no matter where MERP monies are first spent, all eligible countries, including past or current enemies, should be invited at the outset to participate in the crucial dialogue that will move MERP forward.

## ENTER THE "VISIONARY OF GALILEE"

Then there is 79 year old Stef Wertheimer, a creative giant, who knows quite well how business and profits can nourish the peace process. One of Israel's richest men, he has a simple plan to end the Palestinian-Israeli conflict – bring good jobs to the Arab world with an economic infusion modeled on the Marshall Plan. Invest in industry and infrastructure, he tirelessly tells leaders in Israel and abroad so that prosperity can bring peace.

I first met Wertheimer in Casablanca, more than a decade ago at the first Middle East/North Africa Economic Summit. As part of an enormous Israeli group at the conference, he stood out as the calm, but realistic champion of cross-border trade.

A rags-to-riches story, he created one of Israel's biggest industrial empires and used the profits to establish a network of industrial parks that along with his tools business, account for more than one-tenth of the country's industrial product.

He follows the ideology and practice of Shimon Peres' *New Middle East*. Wertheimer is promoting a scheme to build as many as 10 industrial parks across the region, including a billion-dollar demonstration project in Aqaba, Jordan, and a part in Rafah, the impoverished southern tip of the Gaza Strip.

For Wertheimer, the Rafah site would face an Israeli "sister" park across the heavily guarded fence that separates Israel from the Palestinian-dominated Strip. In the end, he expects that this action would lead to the funneling of foreign investment into the region with a single goal: to increase domestic output thus raising living standards for the Palestinians. For this patriot, the cost of one industrial park, he proudly states, is less than half the cost of a fighter jet.

Wertheimer parallels the evolution of the 1948 Marshall Plan with the present conflict. He doesn't want the funds to go to governments but directly to the development of infrastructure and industries, with possible oversight by the United Nations or the World Bank, "The best approach is to present a package that includes the ending of Israeli occupation and a Marshall Plan for economic cooperation," he declares.

"You can't have peace with a poor neighbor" he says, noting the income disparity between Israelis, who average $18,000 a year, and Palestinians, who average $1,800.

Wertheimer, a self-made millionaire who dropped out of school at 14 argues that "the only way to make peace is to make Palestinians successful."

He regards job creation in the region as a weapon in the war on terror. "People are dangerous, when they have nothing to lose." At the height of the Palestinian uprising in 2002, Wertheimer appeared before the U.S. House of Representatives foreign relations committee to propose a new Marshall Plan that would  eventually  embrace  the

Palestinians, Lebanon and Egypt. "It should have less government, less politics, no more free meals. Instead of giving people fish, teach them how to use hooks."

And in May 2006, Warren Buffett, the U.S. investor, plunked down $4 billion to buy 80 percent control of Wertheimer's company. This was Buffett's first purchase outside the U.S. and provided a psychological boost to Israel's financial community and lifted the Tel-Aviv Stock Exchange.

Eitan Wertheimer, the founder's son, summed up the mood when he told Ehud Olmert, the Israeli prime minister, that Mr. Buffett's declaration of confidence in Israel would come to be spoken of in the same light as the *Balfour Declaration.*

## MOVING FORWARD

Inclusion of all MENACA nations at the outset would demand (a) a signed statement from each entity that it will recognize the rights of all members to exist (including the State of Israel and the Palestinian state.), (b) cancellation of all acts of aggression against another member nation, including terrorist acts, boycotts, etc., to qualify as a potential recipient of U.S. assistance, and (c) renunciation of violence and terrorism, economic boycotts, and other acts detrimental to the economic and political stability of the region.

The bill presented to the House of Representatives and to the Senate should be all-inclusive of the 28 nations that might someday become partners, and should call the legislation, the *Middle East/North Africa/Central Asia Recovery Program.* Alternatively, should the mood of the moment only wish to consider a *Middle East Recovery Program,* so it shall be. However, the record should indicate that a more appropriate, expansive effort should also include the nations of North Africa, plus those of Central Asia, Pakistan, Afghanistan, and until she becomes a full-fledged European Union member – possibly Turkey.

With extensive borrowing, assessing, and evaluating of Public Law 472 from the Legislative history of the *Foreign Assistance Act* that went before the House, (Report No. 185-March 20, 1948) and from the Act that went before the Senate, (Report No. 935-February 26, 1948), guidelines should be carefully scrutinized for application and utilization in the *Middle East Recovery Program (MERP)* legislation. Concepts of institution-building and governance, which will assuredly be open to debate, alteration, and change should be discussed. Crystal ball gazing encourages this exchange.

Equally appropriate to the proposed *Middle East Recovery Program* is the study of the introduction to the *Foreign Assistance Act of 1948*, which stated: "An Act to promote world peace and the general welfare, national interest, and foreign policy of the United States through economic, financial, and other measures necessary to the maintenance of conditions abroad in which free institutions may survive and consistent with the maintenance of the strength and stability of the United States."

It might be expected that the figures their experts work up can in many cases be questioned, or that they may not leave much to be desired in allowing for regional, as opposed to nationalistic development. But rather, the remarkable fact might be that they are able to agree upon anything at all definitive.

The conference should attempt to arrive at estimates of need as a function of each country's net balance-of-payments position with the United States and to arrive at a total figure for combined countries. It can be expected that this group will add up the individual country estimates of requirements and present the totals as to the need for the entire area. This procedure, however could result in overstated national requirements where national economic ambition is inflated instead of relating to members of a closely-coordinated economic group.

## THE PRACTICAL VS. THE NAÏVE

*Appendix I* and *II*, at the end of this book provides a detailed description of the proposed *Middle East Recovery Program*. *Appendix I* contains the possible language for MERP, detailing the 17 steps in its evolution, while *Appendix II* provides a general analysis of the process. I have tried my best to suggest a meaningful and practical wording that could be the basis for debate and rewriting.

Throughout, I have pondered the huge differences, in both time and place, between a Marshall Plan for western European governments, and MERP for the broader Middle East nations. Western Europe in 1948 was historically democratic, while many in today's broader Middle East are ruled by despots. Nevertheless, many of these despots seem poised to embrace at least a portion of democracy and might need only a little encouragement, say, in the form of MERP.

MERP is an integral part of introducing democracy to the Middle East. No, not alone, but central to its happening. Once the dollars are there for MERP, let's hope that there will be an enticement for change.

MERP alone cannot do it. Democratic winds occur when the people within each of the nation's borders want the freedom that they can define and accept as the future route. Yes, our government can emerge and support these hopes. However, neither the U.S., nor any other country, can impose its ideologies on other citizens, nor will any amount of funding affect these changes, if resisted by the masses.

Shifts towards democracy do not occur overnight, they require time to be tested before final implementation. However, the changes can be incremental, phased in over time. We'll get as many countries as possible, and those who qualify will get involved in MERP. And these member nations will be so successful that other countries will see the necessity of joining versus the isolation and economic decline that would follow from being on the outside looking in. That is the essential nature of the MERP models.

MERP can succeed, but significant obstacles to its passage must be dealt with. For example, even in a period of disastrous U.S. budget deficits and record tax cuts, MERP is affordable and must remain a necessary priority. Also, the leaders in the broader Middle East need to convince themselves that MERP is not a threat to their power and influence, but is a means to provide a future with higher living standards, improved health and education, and increased prosperity for all citizens.

Lastly, when our standing in the world appears to be at one of its lowest points; when so many people across the globe hate and mistrust our government, and, by proxy all U.S. citizens, the U.S. must "step up to the plate" and make the offer and then carry out MERP.

\*   \*   \*   \*   \*   \*   \*   \*   \*   \*   \*   \*

## A ONE-TRILLION DOLLAR INVESTMENT

In 13 years, the US has mounted six major nation-building efforts, five of which were in a Muslim nation; this on top of costly military actions followed by occupation.

Although nation-building, according to the Rand Corporation, "is not principally about economic reconstruction; rather it is about political transformation" ultimately investing in the well-being of strife ridden countries is required.

The history of nation-building is mixed; assuredly, the monies consumed must be weighed against the benefits derived. Some comparisons are:

| | |
|---|---|
| Germany-1946-47 | $ 11.5 b |
| Bosnia-1996-97 | 4.5 b |
| Japan-1946-47 | 4.1 b |
| Afghanistan-2002-03 | 3.2 b |
| Kosovo-2000-2001 | 1.4 b |
| Haiti-1995-96 | 1.0 b |

A *Middle East Recovery Program* (MERP) necessitates funds for ending the conflicts throughout the region; assisting nations to reconstruct and evolve strong economies and industries; providing for employment and raised living standards, assisting in the resolution of nagging long-term issues, such as costs of resettlement; possible refugee compensation in lieu of the right of return; the proper training of leaders and security personnel; costs of democratic election procedures; the introduction of democratic principles into rebuilt schools and universities; and a host of major, costly construction, and infrastructure projects for roads, bridges, water and sewage works, etc.

Estimating costs is fraught with error. Assuredly, once the history books are written it will be easier to assess expenditures as receipts are in and accounts are balanced. To provide accurate information in advance is risky and filled with both misjudgment and miscalculation. Nevertheless the effort is required.

As a reminder, the post World War II Marshall Plan (officially, the European Recovery Program) orchestrated US (unilateral) expenditures of $17 billion US (in today's dollar value roughly worth about $100 billion US). From 1948-52, funds (only $13.5 billion was actually spent) were used by 17 Western European nations, including former war enemies, neutral nations, and allies. Adding to the $6 billion given prior to the end of WW II, one can calculate a cost near $150 billion on today's market.

And it worked. Not only leading to industrial rebuilding and ultimately to prosperity but as importantly, it forged the way for regional economic integration – the present day European Union of 27 nations.

The emerging Soviet threat became the warning system to the U.S. that apparently persuaded the nation and Congress to support the European Recovery Program. In comparison, the present-day threat of terrorism is the button that will encourage the acceptance and passage of MERP.

### Afghanistan

The military campaign was swift and victorious. In addition to the loss of life, on all sides, the past and continuing costs for this response to being attacked continue.

Unfortunately, the nation-building program in Afghanistan, more than five years after the response to 9/11, has not pursued an effective format. This approach assuredly should not become a working model for aid throughout the Middle East. While the military, primarily

U.S., developed important road and bridge projects and helped rebuild scores of schools, irrigation systems and health clinics in nearly one dozen provinces, this approach was ill-timed, was ineffective for the long term, and may fail to accomplish its intended goals.

Afghan officials and donors estimated that the government would need at least $10 billion to rebuild its shattered economy.    The World Bank representative identified six priority areas for development: education, roads, power, rebuilding of government buildings nationwide, water, and sanitation in the cities, and rural development.

(The United Nations Development Program estimated that the effort in Afghanistan would cost upwards of $6.5 billion for the first 30 months.)

Many critics said that the Pentagon's new plans fell well short of a pledge by President Bush to work "in the best traditions of George Marshall."    Rather than getting out there in a leadership role and saying "We need a Marshall Plan, and fighting for it, they've taken a minimalist approach," said Joel Charny, Vice President for *Policy with Refugees International.*

The United States and its allies put 25 times more funds and 50 times more soldiers, on a per capita basis into the post conflict Kosovo than into the post conflict Afghanistan. As noted by a Rand Corporation report: "Whereas Yugoslavia was a strong state broken up by internal tensions, Afghanistan has been a weak state pulled apart by its neighbors." In fact, Afghanistan is a country that has had more than 23 years of conflict.

The post 9/11 US response included *Operation Enduring Freedom,* whose chief objective was the elimination of al Qaeda. That program began on October 7, 2001.

At a Tokyo donor's conference in January 2002, countries pledged significant financial assistance for reconstruction to Kabul. More than $1.8 billion for the year 2002 was offered, with $4.5 billion over a five year cycle. A few of the pledges were:
. United States: $297 million in 2002
. Japan: $500 million over 30 months
. EU: $500 in 2002
. Saudi Arabia: $220 million over three years
. World Bank: $500 million over 30 months

The approximate amount per capita in Afghanistan for 2002 was between $150 and $180, excluding illegal poppy cultivation and narcotics production. Realizing that Afghanistan ranked 169th poorest of the 174 nations listed by the UN, it is not surprising that between 60 and 80 percent of the population live below the international poverty threshold of $1 a day.

The average life expectancy is a little above 40 years, and over 50 percent of its children under the age of five are malnourished. Infant mortality, life expectancy, and literacy rates are among the world's lowest.

More than one year after the US attack on Al Qaeda, only 2 percent of per capita external assistance was given in Afghanistan. (In Bosnia it was $1,390 and $814 in Kosovo.)

A foreign aid bill which passed the US Senate in September 2004 foresees spending $929 million in Afghanistan in 2005, down from the $1.2 billion in 2004. In response to which Deputy Secretary of State Richard Armitrage added while in Kabul: "The only possible change that might occur in the next four years of George

W. Bush is to accelerate even further our assistance and support for Afghanistan."

Today, much of the US aid goes towards training Afghanistan's fledgling national army, a force designed to replace warlord militias currently being demobilized and to allow the currently 17,000 US troop hunting Taliban and Al Qaeda rebels to go home.

Years of civil war, compounded by Taliban rule and drought, have devastated Afghanistan. Virtually all the country's institutions and much of its infrastructure were destroyed.

Agriculture remains a way of life for 80 percent of Afghanistan's people. With US funding, production nearly doubled by 2006.

The health situation of Afghans was among the worst in the world. Roughly one in five Afghan children died before the age of 5, and the number of mothers who died due to pregnancy complications is one of the highest in the world. Today, the US provides health services to more than 2 million people, 90 percent of whom are women and children. US funds are used to assist in polio vaccinations for 9.9 million children and for malaria treatment.

As if a mini-Marshall plan, US funds were injected into Afghanistan's economy. Short-term jobs were created for 3 million of its citizens; $7 million was set aside for small-to-medium size loans to help Afghans start their own businesses; and US aid was used to help convert the old currency to a new one by training staff, transporting money, and providing counting machines.

By 2006, the US had paid for the rebuilding of roads to clinics and markets and reopened the Salang Tunnel, high in the mountains, which has reduced travel time dramatically. President George W. Bush revealed his strategy in working towards Afghanistan's stability and economic growth: "We'll continue to support reconstruction, economic development and investments that will help educate and build the skills of the Afghan people."

President Bush, following his 2007 State of the Union address, plans to ask Congress for $10.6 billion in aid for Afghanistan, primarily to beef up the country's security forces, with $2 billion for reconstruction projects.

## *Iraq*

While most analysts predict that the Iraq war, occupation and rebuilding efforts will cost the U.S. taxpayer $1 trillion, others calculate the figure to be closer to $2 trillion. The higher sum would amount to $6,600 per American man, woman and child, or $18,000 per household; costing taxpayers $2 billion a week. For every additional year the U.S. keeps troops in Iraq, it will add $200 billion to tax bills. We're paying $380,000 for every extra minute we remain in Iraq.

For the 12 months ending September 30, 2006, spending on the Iraq War alone ran at an average rate of $8 billion in a month, according to the Congressional Research Service. (Since 9/11 spending on the military outside the regular budget process, primarily for the wars in Iraq and Afghanistan had totaled more than $400 billion.)

Army estimates believe that for every 10,000 soldiers added to its force, would cost about $1.2 billion. By the end of 2006, the Defense Department asked Congress for $100 billion more in war spending that will push fiscal 2007 costs near $170 billion. Their estimates for the four years of war in Iraq total roughly $350 billion.

In addition, the Center for Strategic and International Studies estimated that total foreign claims on Iraq had run $383 billion. Her foreign debt reached $127 billion, including an estimated $12 billion debt to Russia and a $47 billion debt to banks and governments from the Gulf Cooperation Council nations. Unpaid interest runs at an estimated $47 billion. (Iraq has not made payments on its foreign debts since the mid-1980s).

Soon after the Coalition invasion of Iraq began, estimates for reconstruction were introduced (as of March 31, 2003):

1. *U.S. Congressional Budget Office* estimated
   a. $250,000 per soldier; with 100,000 troops a total of $25 billion/year.
   b. Humanitarian aid at $500 per head, for a total of $2.5 billion.
   c. Rebuilding infrastructure - $25 billion.
   d. Construction of hospitals, schools - $100 billion.
2. *United Nations* estimates-Oil-for-Food Program
   a. existing $2.5 billion – food, medicine, etc.
   b. goods - $ 6.5 billion.
3. *United States*
   a. Tomahawk Cruise Missile - $600,000 per missile - (had already used 500 missiles).
   b. transport U.S. troops to Iraq and back – $30 billion, plus $ 15 billion for extras.
4. *United Kingdom*
   a. budgeted war effort - $ 1.6 billion plus recently added estimates of $1 billion.
   b. short war – estimates of $ 4.5 billion – equal to the building in the UK of 25 hospitals.

In all, the Bush administration planned to

accomplish an ambitious reconstruction effort in Iraq, such as:

*Major Infrastructure* – Umm Qasr Port fully open to cargo traffic; all major roads, about 2,780 miles, repaired and fully open; 10 power plants rebuilt; electricity restored to 75 percent of pre-1991 level.

*Health* – Referral hospitals functioning in 21 cities; maternity care available to 100 percent of population.

*Local Government* – interim institutions offer "transparent local governance."

*Schools* – 100 percent school enrollment; 25,000 schools functioning at "standard level of quality; school supplies distributed to 4.2 million children."

*Economic Governance* – Central Bank and Ministry of Finance fully operative;

*Housing* – Rehabilitation of nearly 20,000 houses "nearing completion."

Most of these objectives were never fulfilled.

The pre-re-election days of 2004 saw $180 billion authorized by Congress for both military and reconstruction needs.

Assuming that the continuing costs will be at least over a five-year period, the $250 billion might easily approach 1 trillion dollars, all in the outlay for one country – Iraq.

Although it can be expected that the military costs of occupation will be reduced with the passage of time, there is also no guarantee that other nations will make significant contributions towards this nation-building effort. Just look at the October 23-24, 2003 donor's conference in Madrid.

The United Nations/World Bank gave a cumulative assessment of Iraq's reconstruction needs, in billions while the Iraqi Governing Council appealed to wealthy nations to help raise the $55 billion needed for rebuilding Iraq.

| | |
|---|---|
| Infrastructure – from 2004-07 | $ 24.2 b |
| Health, education, employment | 7.2 b |
| Agriculture, water | 3.0 b |
| Other | 1.4 b |

The Coalition Provisional Authority estimated needs, in areas not covered by the UN/World Bank assessment, in billions:

| | |
|---|---|
| Oil | $  8.0 b |
| Security and Police | 5.0 b |
| Environment | 3.5 b |
| Culture | .9 b |
| Other | 2.0 b |

Seventy countries and organizations participated. The U.S. appropriated $20 billion (2/3$^{rd}$ to be spent in 2004, with $1 billion for Afghanistan) while other donors would appropriate $13 billion. This meager support is reflected in the breakdown by nations; for example -

Japan proposed $ 1.5 billion for the year 2004;

Saudi Arabia proposed $1 billion

United Arab Emirates proposed $200 - $250 million

Kuwait proposed $500 million

European Union/individual European countries (excluding Germany and France) proposed $800 million and;

The World Bank/IM Fund proposed $9 - $10 billion.

Congress approved an additional $87 billion supplemental aid package for Iraq, but tinkered a bit with the portion set aside for reconstruction. Of the $20.3 billion requested by President Bush, Congress nipped and tucked about a dozen projects to bring the total down to $18.4 billion. For example: on Law Enforcement Bush requested

$1,217 million and Congress gave him $1,167 million. On Justice, Public Safety and Civil Society Bush requested $1,843 million and Congress gave him $1,318 million.

Reconstruction projects were also cut by Congress:

a. Electricity-requested $5,675 million; Congress approved $5,560 million

b. Oil Infrastructure-requested $2,200 million; Congress approved $1,8890 million

c. Public works projects-requested $3,710; Congress approved $3,557 million.

d. Water resources – requested $875 million; Congress approved $775 million.

e. Transportation-Telecommunications-requested $835 million; Congress approved $500 million

f. Roads, Bridges, Construction-requested - $470 million; Congress approved $370 million

g. Health Care-requested $850 million; Congress approved $ 793 million.

h. Private Sector Development-requested $353 million; Congress approved $153 million.

i. Education, Refugees, Human Rights-requested $300 million; Congress approved $280 million.

As expected, a new infusion of funds was approved by Congress in September 2007. $63 billion were made available for military operations in Iraq and Afghanistan. $99 billion was appropriated for military personnel, $126 billion for operations and maintenance, $81 billion for weapons procurement, and $73 billion for research and development.

With this latest addition of money Congress authorized about $500 billion for the wars in Iraq and

Afghanistan and other anti-terrorism efforts since the September 11, 2001 attacks.

## Palestine

"Where there was once a peace process, there is now little peace and even less process," according to Richard Haass, in November 2004. Haass, the former U.S. State Department chief policy and planning executive in 2001-03 and presently President of the New York based Council on Foreign Relations.

Impressively, the Palestinians have received more aid per-capita than those aided by the 1948 Marshall Plan. The funding has increased since the beginning of the violence. Palestinian assistance from international sources, over a 9 year period, and prior to Arafat's death, amounted to more than $4 billion. The amount per Palestinian was estimated to be $1,330 or $161 for each year.

On December 5, 2001, an Italian sponsored "Extraordinary Initiative for the Reconstruction and Development of the Palestinian Economy," was approved by the Council of Ministers of the European Union at its Laeken European Council meeting. Underlying this major idea was the hope that the prospect of a future of shared prosperity might spur the parties engaged in the conflict to take a decisive step forward and embark upon the final negotiations for the constitution of a Palestinian state.

The EU time frame was 10 years, with the first five being the most critical.  Giving a new impetus to the dialogue on regional cooperation, the total funding required for the initiative was estimated to be around 6.2 billion euros (approximately $7 billion today) for the first five years as follows:

Millions of euros
    Production....................... 1,510 M
    Infrastructure............... .. 2,750 M
    Social and humanitarian........1,140 M
    Training, technical assistance and scientific
    cooperation......................    800 M

Leonid Palanov, an independent Swiss, and truly committed world citizen, spent considerable private capital in newspaper advertising with his "Middle East Peace and Cooperation Agreement." MEPCA (a revised, though supportive form of MERP) would assign the role of the leader to the international community and asks it to provide financial, military and organizational resources."

MEPCA utilizes strategies outlined in the Clinton-Mitchell plan, Bush's "Road Map," the Geneva Accord, the Arab Proposal of 2002, and various UN resolutions.

A persuasive and independent conflict-resolver, Palanov suggests that the EU, US, and moderate Arab countries (a mini-Marshall Plan in itself) should create a fully funded trust-fund administered by an independent team of financial professionals, organized as a non-profit corporation with the purpose of:

    a.  financing the design and implementation of the Peace and Cooperation Agreement;

    b.  compensating for financial losses suffered by displaced settlers and Palestinians as a result of the events prior to, during, and after the implementation of the Agreement, based on the replacement value concept; to be completed within 3 years.

    c.  providing on-going humanitarian aid to both parties during the transition period;

  d. reimbursing the Israeli government and businesses for losses suffered as a result of the implementation of the Agreement;

  e. assisting the new state in creating the necessary infrastructure, without creating welfare-like dependence, and in establishing democratic, transparent institutions.

The author of this fascinating proposal argues that "all financial considerations are resolved within 36 months of the creation of the Palestinian state."

Furthermore, Elmer L. Winter, Chairman of the Committee for Economic Growth of Israel proposed in the summer 2002, a *Middle East Economic Development* (MEED) Plan through the economic development of the area – based on the creation of 320,000 jobs for Palestinians.

Winters does not neglect the benefits of these efforts for Israel. For example:

. Israel will become a full member of the nations of the world.

. Foreign investment will flow into Israel.

. There will be an expansion of R & D in Israel.

. Tourism will expand.

. The UN will get off Israel's back.

. Israeli firms will expand throughout the Middle East and move further into world markets.

. U.S.-Israeli government relations will expand, as well as European nations.

. Israel will be able to convert some funds presently used for military protection to improving the quality of life for its citizens.

An equally ambitious and creative analysis of the ongoing conflict comes from the Aix Group. As a participant at their initial conference in Arles, France, I found their recommendations refreshing.

Their 2004 Economic Road-Map assumes that a viable two-state solution will embody:
. The Palestinian state will have the power to define its economic objectives and strategies and to implement them freely, within the parameters of a bilateral, permanent agreement.
. Economic cooperation will be conducted in good faith and mutuality, free of any intention to dominate another nation's economy.
. There will be a clear, unambiguous agreement on borders;
. The Palestinian state will have full economic jurisdiction over its external borders with Jordan, Egypt and Israel, meaning that the Palestinian state and Israel will implement trade, labor and other regulatory policies in a manner congruent with normal relations between sovereign states.
. The Palestinian state will feature contiguity within the West Bank and efficient connections with Gaza.

*The Aix Group* urges the creation of a Free Trade Area (FTA) consistent with World Trade Organizations protocols. The Group believes "that a FTA between a Palestinian state and Israel is likely to be feasible and efficient, as well as to offer exploitable development opportunities. A bilateral free trade agreement would provide the Palestinian state open access to the Israeli market, which will continue to be a key trading partner."

The Aix plan would allow the Palestinian state to diversify its trade relations and implement development policies conducive to economic growth and prosperity. Of course, the pendulum today suggests separation, not integration, making the Aix plan in opposition to Israeli policy.

\*\*\*\*\*\*\*\*\*\*\*\*\*\*\*\*\*\*\*\*\*\*\*\*

The renewed optimism following Arafat's death was clearly present on December 14, 2004 when the United States, Europe, and several Arab countries supported a four-year package of $6 to $8 billion to the Palestinians should their January 9, 2005 elections prove successful. Afterwards, further aid was promised.

This donor's aid package would have been the largest per person international program since the Marshall Plan. (The Palestinians are already the world's largest per capita recipients of international aid, getting about $1 billion for 3.5 million inhabitants, or nearly $300 per person, per year.)

Initial aid from the U.S. was disbursed on December 28, 2004, with $20 million going to the interim Palestinian leadership to help finance economic reform. These funds were the first direct budgetary support from Washington to the PA since the summer of 2003 – to be used for projects such as electricity, and water and sewage improvements in the West Bank and Gaza.

After the January 9, 2005 election of Abbas the U.S. pondered increasing its direct aid to the Palestinians. On February 1$^{st}$, Bush channeled $350 million to rebuild infrastructure in Palestine, paying salaries and shoring up support from moderate Palestinian leaders.

Condoleezza Rice, in her first trip as Secretary of State tried to convince Europeans to persuade Arab countries to increase aid to the Palestinian Authority. One possible use of funds, giving $100 monthly stipends to poor Palestinians and retirement benefits for 1,000 members of Palestinian militia groups.

Then on December 7, 2005, President Bush signed a new National Security Presidential Directive announcing that the State Department would be the leading agency for "reconstruction and stabilization assistance for foreign states and regions at risk of, in, or in transition from conflict or civil strife." Only nine days earlier, the Office of the U.S. Secretary of Defense released a report on stability operations.

"This policy directed that stability operations become a core mission for the United States military-a dramatic departure from traditional U.S. military culture. Its purpose was to focus the military education and training toward postconflict stabilization, thereby assisting the new office at the State Department. This was the "coup de grace" according to George F. Oliver, writing a Marshall Foundation chapter on "Relevance of the Marshall Plan to Modern Faled States."

"Military involvement may be necessary to stop a bloody conflict, but peace and stability will last only if follow-on efforts to restore order and rebuild are successful. The world has found through bitter experience that success often depends on the early establishment of strong local institutions such as effective police force and a functioning justice and penal system.  This governance capacity is critical to establishing the rule of law and a free market economy, which provide long-term stability and prosperity."

Retired Colonel Oliver emphasizes, "The signing of these documents demonstrates that the United States is once again taking the task of nation building seriously. Although President Bush has avoided saying that America's actions in Iraq were mismanaged and poorly planned, the signing of these public policies indicates that as a nation we can do better.  Indeed, America has done better." Time is running out for the administration to prove it commitment.

A month earlier, the Bush administration created an independent foundation to promote democracy throughout the Islamic world, the non-profit *Foundation for the Future*. It initially provided more than $55 million, arguably the first step of a reinvented Marshall Plan, with another $35 million promised by Qatar, and with Bahrain and Jordan on board with additional pledges.

The Foundation's charter indicates that it will provide "financial and technical assistance to local non-governmental organizations, academic institutions, professional associations" and undertake activities that "contribute to the strengthening of freedoms and democracy."

## ONE TRILLION DOLLARS

The $1 trillion price-tag is based on knowns and unknowns, for both military and reconstruction expenditures, for the present and beyond, that will determine the predictability and accuracy of restoring the Middle East of Iraq, Afghanistan, Lebanon, and a future state of Palestine. Not taken into account are possible additional funding requirements for other nations, i.e., Israel, Syria, Iran, Egypt, Uzbekistan, and other future potential hot-spots.

## IRAQ

Iraq has a highly predictable cost, which by 2006 was amounting to about $100 billion a year, or just under 20 percent of total US military spending.

MILITARY

A. Invasion costs........................$ 150.0 B.

B. Continuing military costs............   70.0 B.

C. 140,000 troops in 2004 @

$250,000/soldier..................... 35.0 B.
D.  Transporting troops to and from.......30.0 B.
E.  Feb. 2005 additional requests....... 80.0 B.
F.  Extras................................... 15.0 B.
NATION-BUILDING
A.  U.S. estimates-humanitarian-$500/p... 2.5 B
B.  Rebuilding infrastructure.............. 25.0 B
C.  Construction-hospitals/schools...... 100.0 B
D.  Election-institutional governance.... 2.5 B
                        SUBTOTAL    $ 510.00 B


(ESTIMATED) IRAQ SUBTOTAL        **$ 1.0  T**
            OVER FIVE YEARS


### AFGHANISTAN
MILITARY
A.  Invasion costs .......................... 10.0 B
B.  17,000 US troops in 2004 @
       $250,000/soldier.................. ........ 4.0 B
C.  Transporting troops to/from .............3.0 B
D.  FEB.2005-training-security ...............1.7 B
E.  Extras ....................................... 3.0 B
NATION-BUILDING
    A.  United Nations Develop Program -
       Estimates for first thirty months.......10.0 B
                        SUBTOTAL    $ 31.7 B


(ESTIMATED) AFGHANISTAN SUBTOTAL
            OVER FIVE YEARS    **$ 80.0 B**
(In January 2007, the President announced
intentions of asking Congress for another $10.6 b.)

Linda Bilmes was assistant secretary at the Department of Commerce from 1999 to 2001, and now teaches budgeting and public finance at the Kennedy School of Government at Harvard University. In August 2005, she calculated the Trillion-Dollar war as follows:

. Funds already spent on operations
  in Iraq and Afghanistan..................... 258.0 B
. Running costs of the war over the
  next five years – Operations(military
  and contractor pay, equipment and
  weapons, fuel, etc.)....................... 345.0 B
. Additional costs of recruiting and
  retaining armed forces personnel....... 5.0 B
. Aid to frontline states (Jordan,
  Pakistan, Turkey and others)............ 10.0 B
. Replacement of military hardware
  (vehicles, weapons, helicopters, planes).. 100.0 B

TOTAL                                   $ 460.0 B

. Veterans costs, (based on age 23,
  life-span of 45 more years, and claims
  filings similar to those after 1991 Gulf War)
  Health care and benefits (including
  Medical, education, housing loan)......... 90.0 B
. Long-term disability pay to
  soldiers and their dependents............. .225.0 B

TOTAL                                   $ 315.0 B

Deficit Financing Costs (Interest)
(Assumes current and projected
spending is financed on a five-year

replacement cycle at an interest
rate of 4 percent) ...........................        220.0 B

Economic impact of a $5 increase
    in price of oil
(March 2003-July 2010)..................        119.0 B

TOTAL COST                                **$ 1,372.0 B**

      Reporting in the *New York Times* in August 2005, she said: "The human cost of the more than 2,000 American military personnel killed and 14,500 wounded so far in Iraq and Afghanistan is all too apparent. But the financial toll is still largely hidden from public view and, like the suffering of those who have lost loved ones, will persist long after the fighting is over."

      "The cost goes well beyond the more than $250 million already spent on military operations and reconstruction. Basic running costs of the current conflicts are $6 billion a month – a figure that reflects the Pentagon's unprecedented reliance on expensive private contractors. Other factors keeping costs high include inducements for recruits and for military personnel serving second and third deployments, extra pay for reservists and members of the National Guard, as well as more than $ 2 billion a year in additional foreign aid to Jordan, Pakistan, Turkey and others to reward their cooperation in Iraq and Afghanistan. The bill for repairing and replacing military hardware is $20 billion a year, according to figures from the Congressional Budget Office."

      "But the biggest long-term costs are disability and health payments for returning troops, which will be incurred even if hostilities were to stop tomorrow. The

U.S. currently pays more than $2 billion in disability claims per year for 159,000 veterans of the 1991 Gulf War, even though that conflict lasted only five weeks, with 148 dead and 467 wounded. Even assuming that the 525,000 American troops who have so far served in Iraq and Afghanistan will require treatment only on the same scale as their predecessors from the Gulf War, these payments are likely to run at $ 7 billion a year for the next 45 years."

(On February 5, 2007, the White House unveiled its $2.9 trillion budget. It called for $145 billion for the war in the year starting October 1st, mostly for Iraq and Afghanistan, on top of a new request for an additional $99.6 billion to pay for the war in 2007. These estimated figures would bring the total costs of the Iraq-Afghanistan wars and reconstruction in excess of ½ trillion dollars since 9/11 and the attacks against the Taliban. The administration did not include any new supplemental appropriation for Iraq and Afghanistan after 2009.)

One of the earliest cost-benefit comparisons was made by Steven Davis, Kevin Murphy, and Bob Topel of the University of Chicago on the eve of the 2003 invasion of Iraq. They concluded that the cost of pursuing a containment strategy was $258 billion to $380 billion: "This dwarfs any reasonable estimate of US war costs," they claimed. Their anticipated price tag or the war, which they considered conservative, was $125 billion. Soon after they revised their figures to more realistic figures: "Their estimated war costs have increased to a range of $410 billion to $630 billion."

Another study of Iraq war costs by Linda J. Bilmes of Harvard University and Joseph Stigitz of Columbia University concluded that an oversized $2.2 trillion, probably a gross overstatement, would be needed, all assuming that the US would be out of Iraq by 2015.

Even by this simple yardstick, if the American military presence in the region lasts another five years, the total outlay for the war could stretch to more than $1.3 trillion, or $11,300 for every household in the United States.

### LEBANON

Following the summer 2006 attack against Hezbollah militants within Lebanon, a wrinkle in reconstruction aid quickly appeared. Hezbollah announced its intent to offered hundreds of millions of dollars in aid, most of it apparently from Iran, to rebuild Lebanon's roads, bridges and homes shattered by the Israeli bombings. A reaction and counteroffer seemed necessary from the U.S. and Europe to overcome fears that, unless they provided significant financing, support for Hezbollah, Iran and Islamic militancy would grow substantially. Donors nations were determined to offer more than twice as much money per family as Hezbollah did to those that had lost homes.

Since 2001, the United States has provided over $14.2 billion in aid to Afghanistan.

U.S., Europe and Gulf state pledges -
For rebuilding infrastructure,
clearing unexploded Israeli bombs,
restoring social services................ $ 940 M

BREAKDOWN included:
United States.....................          $ 175 M

European Union................     54 M
Qatar............................     300 M

Estimates for rebuilding structural damage..  $3.6 B
Estimates for personal belongings, indirect
  losses incurred by such things as factory
  closures, higher insurance premiums, and
  reduced tourist revenue....          $ 10.0 B
(In January 2007, led by Saudi Arabia and the U.S.,
international donors from more than 30 nations pledged
$7.6 billion in aid for Lebanon.)

## PALESTINE
Added to these huge expenses are additional costs.
Considering the Israeli-Palestinian conflict, and including
the growing funding for the August 2005 withdrawal of
Israeli settlements from Gaza, I estimate further
expenditures:

NATION-BUILDING*
   A.  US estimates-humanitarian
      $500/person for 2005................   $1.0 B
   B.  Re-settlement of refugees @
      $500/person .........................   1.0 B
   C.  Elections and institutional/governance  .5 B
   D.  Internal security reconstruction........   .7 B
   E.  Water and sanitation costs.............   .5 B
   F.  Health....................................   .2 B
   G.  Education-schools.....................   1.5 B
   H. Rebuilding infrastructure........ ...   4.5 B
      West Bank to Gaza Road – 1.0 B
      Gaza seaport -          .6 B
      Airport -            .3 B

Electric power grid -          .6 B
Housing -                       1.0 B
Job creation -                  1.0 B
Economic development zones
SUBTOTAL                        9.9 B
(ESTIMATED PALESTINIAN SUBTOTAL)-
5 YEARS ........................     **$ 30.0 B**
* Most of these figures are interpolations from the 2005
Rand Report - *Building a Successful Palestinian State.*

### ISRAEL

Will Israel seek and receive outside funding to participate in the shifts of the broader Middle East, especially in terms of the future state of Palestine?

The U.S. has agreed to extend the terms of loan guarantees it gave Israel in 2003 through to 2008. Israel has yet to use $3 billion worth of the guarantees which allow it to raise money on international markets with Washington's backing These guarantees were set to expire in 2006, but the deadline has been extended to 2008.

Who will pay for the costs of the Gaza and future withdrawals? Israel has asked the U.S. for $1.6 billion in assistance related to its Gaza Strip disengagement. The request encompasses the transfer of Gaza military bases ad development of the Negev and Galilee, areas likely to absorb most of the thousands of settlers who will leave Gaza and part of the northern West Bank. (It appears that no U.S. funds requested will go directly to the settlers.)

GAZA DISENGAGEMENT
SUBTOTAL                        **$ 1.6 B**

## A PRE-MERP FUNDING FOR THE PALESTINIANS

In the spirit of multilateralism, the G-8 countries in July 2005 promised $ 3 billion for the Palestinians (before the election of Hamas which resulted in their domination of the Parliament) to rebuild the infrastructure of a future state. The message is clear, the international community means business and they want to put the Israeli-Palestinian conflict behind them, knowing that the money must be accompanied by political commitments (recall the failure of the post-Oslo accords.)

This funding suggests an eventual *Middle East Recovery Program,* with steps along the way to ensure compliance. First, the Palestinians must work to truly implement all the obligations placed on them by the international community. The PA must complete the unification of its security forces, and the illegal militias must finally be dealt with.

Part of the MERP funding should be spent on creating a social security retirement fund for those officials and officers who should be sent home. Additional monies should be used for whatever it will take to implement law and order on the streets of Palestine.

In addition, MERP funds should be used for connecting the land of Gaza with the West Bank. MERP allocations should be used to build a passage between these two territories in order for goods and people to traverse with as much unimpeded movements as possible. For example, a short link from Gaza's Eres crossing to Zikim, south of Askelon, would enable Palestinian goods to be transported anywhere in Israel and the West Bank. MERP monies could help build a rail link from Kiryat Gat to Tarkumiyeh, near Hebron, some 15 miles could enable a direct link to the West Bank. Without MERP funding, the Palestinian territories will remain a bottomless pit.

## AND MORE TO COME

The future, at times, is predictable. It appears unlikely that other nations of the broader Middle East will remain unchanged. A neighbor's experience, when broadcast on the airwaves, is a potential signal that past forms of government may be on their way out. For example, on May 14, 2005, events in Uzbekistan, with the massacre of more than 500 citizens, suggested the inevitability of shifts. Of the 28 governments in the broader Middle East, some will fail their people and be overturned. President Bush has promised both moral and financial support to these brave citizens seeking freedom and a greater control over their destiny. MERP must be ready to serve them.

On May 19, 2005, speaking to the International Republican Institute, Bush continued his gradual reversal from a central commitment of the 2000 presidential campaign, that he would never use the U.S. military for what he called "nation-building." Showing renewed flexibility he now said that members of the armed forces are "also undertaking a less visible, but increasingly important task: helping people of these nations building civil societies from the rubble of oppression." He was now celebrating the military's participation in actions that are normally considered civilian. Additionally, with an initial $24 million set aside, he talked about a proposal to create a new civilian *Active Response Corps* to help newly formed governments build institutions, including courts and tax systems.

Will the nation-building monies come from international donors, the UN, the World Bank, or exclusively from the United States? Although the US could choose to "go-it-alone" the economic costs would be overwhelming. In the end, even if other rich nations contribute significantly needed resources to rebuilding a future Middle East, it can be expected that the US will bear the brunt of the costs.

The U.S. can expect to spend at least $1 trillion, nearly 10 percent of the nation's yearly gross domestic product – the nation's output of goods and services produced by labor and property located within the United States – to resurrect the broader Middle East and win the war on terror.

The United States in 2006 is in a difficult financial situation. The government spent $650 billion more last year than it raised in revenue, at the same time financing the deficit largely by borrowing from foreign central banks, mainly those of Japan and China. And one year earlier, the US spent nearly as much on its military as all other nations in the world combined.

Whether resistance to this MERP proposal will win out is beyond my ability to predict. If we do appropriate this huge amount of money, from a near $12 trillion annual economy, will sacrifices be required? The simple answer is I don't know, nor do I believe anyone knows, but free of war and defense build-ups in the Middle East, the argument is easier to make.

As generally agreed to in his first term, President Bush argued that "the road to Jerusalem passed through Baghdad." Before and following 9/11 he resisted discussing any peace-process with Israel and the Palestinians. Supported by key members of the administration, his strategy appeared to be that only with a regional democratic transformation, starting with Iraq and reaching across to the corrupt and terror-inspired Palestinian Authority, could resolution occur in the West Bank and Gaza.

In his June 24, 2002 speech setting out a two-state solution – usually referred to as the "Road Map," Bush declared: "In order to achieve peace and for a Palestinian state to be established, a different leadership is required. I call upon the Palestinian people to choose new leaders who do not compromise on the issue of terror."

Arafat is gone as is Sharon, and new leaders are in place. Hamas controls parliament and Ehud Olmert is the new prime minister of Israel. Administrative and economic reform have been promised. Now to the funding battle for reconstruction and reform.

The United States remains the world's richest country. Yet, financial support is best measured by how well we give of our national income to the neediest of the world. In that respect, the U.S. clearly fails. We are the stingiest of the Group of Seven industrialized nations. For example, the percentage of U.S. income going to poor nations is a pitiful 0.14 percent of our wealth. Britain's contributions stand at 0.34 percent with France's at 0.41 percent. Norway and Sweden further shame the US by spending 0.92 percent and 0.79 percent respectively.

In 2004, the Bush administration cited the federal budget as the reason for its cutback in donations. Of course, the government was able to find $87 billion for the fighting in Iraq, but only a bit more than $15 billion was provided for development assistance. The government spends $450 billion annually on the military and $15 billion on development, a 30-1 ratio. Jeffrey Sachs, the UN director of the *Millennium Project* said that the U.S. has become "all war and no peace in our foreign policy."

It is embarrassing today to acknowledge that to help rebuild Europe after World War II the U.S. gave a generous 2 percent of its national income.

It is time to open the discussion and to open our hearts. Apathy will not do. U.S. security is the most pressing issue of the day. Action is demanded.

Finding and securing approval for these significant costs will be both a challenge and assuredly a fight. There will be tension in  Congress, in the arena of democratic/republican politics gearing up for the 2008 presidential election, then in international geo-politics, and ultimately with the American public.

(The Marshall Plan was implemented despite the American public's opposition. Present leadership will be tested. Will it go ahead with what may be an unpopular program because it's the right thing to do?)

The arguments will first focus on the wisdom in the MERP proposal. Ultimately, it will then turn to expenses and whether the U.S., with or without the global participation, can afford spending up to $1 trillion. To secure the support to spend such monies amidst cries to lower growth in federal spending will put further pressures on funds available for defense, foreign aid of reconstruction in Iraq, funding for resolution of the Israeli-Palestinian conflict including settlement payments and right of return payouts, for homeland security, and the continued  fight against terrorism, etc. It will, like the 1947 Marshall Plan, be a hard sell, both domestically and abroad.

The right of return issue can be implemented in two forms: explicit and implicit. The explicit right of return is when some Palestinians are able to return to their property within the new borders of the new Palestinian state. The implicit right of return is when Palestinians are being financially reimbursed for their property which remains outside the borders of the new Palestinian state, or when they receive financial assistance to resettle in another country. A poll indicates that large numbers of Palestinians would be willing to accept such financial reimbursement.

It is time to cease the discussion and open our hearts to getting to the source of funding for the region. Apathy or preoccupation with other matters will not suffice for here we have the number #1 issue of the century. Action is demanded. The question now turns to the affordability of MERP

Let's face it, the U.S. is losing its economic power. When World War II ended, the U.S. had 50 percent of global GDP; today it has less than 25 percent. Of course, with a $12 trillion yearly economy, we remain strong and rich.

When George W. Bush first ran for president, the budget was in surplus at $236 billion. Today, the annual deficit is more than $400 billion. In addition, the current-account deficit is about 5.5 percent of the nation's GDP.

Complicating the stretch of finances, the U.S. today imports about 12 million barrels each day, more than half the amount it consumes, further exacerbating the Treasury's capabilities.

Nevertheless, the U.S. and supportive nations of the world must work to build up trade with enlightened Muslim nations. Trade is the primary mechanism to promote prosperity.

Since abject poverty remains a key part of the solution, war and instability only increases poverty while cross border trade is the surest way to get parties involved.

The singular assumption is that terrorism slips as wealth rises and becomes more evenly distributed across the cities of troubled nations.

Between the end of World War II in 1945 and 1947, the United States had already loaned or given nearly $6 billion (today equal to more than $60 billion) to save the starving and unemployed in Europe, both friend and foe. Working with existing regional organizations, the Marshall Plan was the natural next step. The restoration of Western Europe's economy with the eventual evolution of the European Economic Community clearly vilified the U.S. role in its foreign-aid developmental effort.

Transparency, accountability, and corruption remain critical issues in the Middle East. In 2006, an audit of American financial practices in Iraq uncovered irregularities including millions of reconstruction dollars stuffed casually into footlockers and filing cabinets. Released by the Office of the Special Inspector General for Iraq Reconstruction, their findings support the argument for a greater adherence to the rules and procedures used in the transfer and spending of foreign funds.

How were the transparency and accountability issues of the Marshall Plan funding handled, and what lessons can be passed on to the present proposal? Comparison are necessary.

Let's learn from the Marshall Plan and with pride, open our wallets to permit a more meaningful outpouring of funds that can parallel the great accomplishments of the recovery program following the end of World War II.

MERP can now move the process to a higher level and emulate the wonders and successes resulting from the 1948 Marshall Plan. As John Kerry aptly implied during his

October 2004 presidential debates with George W. Bush, you need a military strategy for engaging in war, but more critically you require a detailed plan for peace.

A peace plan, post-killings, needs to shift gears and focus on diplomacy, politics, and critically economic/trade efforts, initially funded by outside sources with aid and management skills. Once the military action fades, hopelessness can convert to promises for a better way of life.

It isn't going to be easy, but we are apt to forget that passage of the 1947 Marshall Plan wasn't easy either. If people will start focusing on the positives instead of the negatives, MERP can become a reality a lot quicker than one might think.

# CHAPTER V

## THE REBIRTH CONTINUES - ECONOMIC INTEGRATION

"The effort to increase regional economic cooperation is not - as some seem to feel - a favor to any particular nation. Shared prosperity will create a more broadly felt stake in peace and deny nourishment to the violent extremists who feed on deprivation. Increased commerce and investment will diminish the mistrust that has long divided governments and prevent sectors from working together for their mutual benefit and that of their societies."

**Madeleine Albright**

Following the scourge of the Israeli-Palestinian violence which began on September 29, 2000 and the horrific loss of life during Intifada II, the often heard phrase "Oslo is dead, long live..." had captured the attention of the media. Certainly, the Oslo Agreement of 1993, was severely wounded with deafening accusations of dishonesty, naivete, and betrayal during Intifada II. However, the proper response was not to bury the Oslo Agreements, but rather, to absorb lessons learned from it, and eventually to reinvent it.

World leaders were already exasperated because of the Israeli-Palestinian conflict when terrorists attacked the U.S. on September 11, 2001. In the aftermath of the attacks, the Middle East conflict took on new dimensions as U.S. resolve to eliminate terrorism spread into other capitols of both Arab/Muslim and non-Arab/Muslim nations.

President George W. Bush reluctantly stepped into the Israel/Palestinian conflict with his Road-Map to peace, along with England's Tony Blair.   In doing so, the president, according to Dennis Ross, the former Middle East negotiator under President Clinton: "created a new basis for the international community to address the Middle East peace. Palestinian reform now became the focal point for activity, with emphasis on creating transparency and accountability in the Palestinian Authority."

Thirteen years ago, an enterprise of integration was conceived as possible for a Middle East/North Africa population approaching 300 million.  Today, with Central Asia, Afghanistan, Pakistan, and possibly Turkey added into the equation, the combined population of the region would reach one-half a billion.

Revitalization in the form of better health care, increased access to education and housing and repair of infrastructure will lead the rebirth of the region. The question is how best to achieve these goals? Can an institutional framework be created, with a proper form of governance, to discharge such weighty responsibilities?

Enactment of a recovery program and its implementation will go a long way towards upgrading and restoring the spirit of past agreements, and to bring a better quality of life throughout the Middle East/North Africa and Central Asia (MENACA). A carefully monitored economic recovery program promises to increase the level of employment, provide for new infrastructure, and in general, to pave the way for    cross-border trade and regional economic integration.

Likewise, the scope of activity and evidence of its success will encourage nations of MENACA who do not participate from the very beginning to reassess their position, and sooner, rather than later, join in this great experiment.

Many in the past have recommended institution-building and forms of governance to pave the way for openness – the sharing of ideas and opportunities, dreams and realities, all without the significant financial assistance of  MERP. This funding is called for to guarantee  the progress towards cooperation demanded as a        condition for aid. If the EU in the last four decades is any sort of model, MENACA countries will proceed ever closer to economic integration.

Integration in the EU had demonstrated its efficacy. Economic isolation and trade barriers between contiguous and neighboring nations are no way to curb conflict or to improve standards of living. The cost of disengagement is poverty and misery. Being part of a geographic region necessitates free trade agreements that naturally flow from bilateral and multilateral accords. Integration opens up windows for win-win residuals.

Globalization, though imperfect, has led to a better quality of life throughout the world. Crossing borders with trade, joint-projects,   financial sharing, etc., is a natural benefit of any     recovery program as witnessed by the Marshall Plan. The establishment of a European Economic Community, or common market, led to record   prosperity and created stability rarely seen on that continent over the past thousand years. In the same way MERP can serve to jumpstart economies while it fosters stability.

The world is on a course to globalize future cross-border trade by forging institutions to encourage regional economic integration. Natural barriers separating countries, long the means for controlling the interchange between peoples of different nationalities, are rapidly being dismantled. No portion of the globe, it seems, is without some   form   of   regional   economic   testing   and experimentation, which has already been put in place by many governments, or is being considered.

Bilateral trade even succeeds during periods of intense conflict. The 2000-2005 Intifada II did not impact on the successful bilateral trade between Israel and her two existing peace treaty partners --Egypt and Jordan. Israeli exports to Egypt rose 10 percent since the beginning of 2000, totaling $55.3 million, compared with $50.2 million in the corresponding period of 1999.  Imports of Egyptian goods rose 4.3 percent totaling $19.6 million, compared with $18.8 million over the same period.

The potential for more regional cooperation is enormous. For example, Israeli exports to Jordan doubled since the start of the year 2000, totaling $36.4 percent, compared with $18.5 million in the same period of 1999. At the same time, imports from Jordanians rose 79 percent to $30.5 million, up from $18.8 million.

Cross-border trade between Israel and Jordan rose over 20 percent despite the political upheaval in the region.

According to the Israel-Jordan Chamber of Commerce, in the first eleven months of 2003, imports and exports totaled $87 million, compared with $70 million in the same period of 2000, with the total for the year close to $100 million for the first time. Israel imported $39 million in goods (mostly finished textiles) from Jordan and exported $48 million (mostly industrial inputs) to Jordan.

The increase of trade was due to manufacturing, especially textiles, and the expansion of Jordanian factories in Qualifying Industrial Zones (QIZ). Under the QIZ agreements, factories are committed to buying Israeli inputs totaling 8 percent of the products' value, and they receive duty-free treatment for exports to the U.S. in return.

King Abdullah II of the Hashemite Kingdom of Jordan came to Washington, D.C. and signed a free trade agreement with the United States only days after the September 11, 2001 terrorist attacks. It was the first such treaty that the U.S. has signed with an Arab nation, (and also the first American trade accord to include labor and environmental protections within the main text.)

Possessing few geographic advantages, Jordan, a sandy, near- landlocked nation with few natural resources and a small, though well-educated population, has shown nations of the region how to succeed. First, under King Hussein, and later with the present king, numerous challenges were met and policies were altered.

Jordan has reformed its economy by lowering trade and other goods trade barriers. King Abdullah approved the opening of many service industries to international investment and encouraged regional relationships via partial free trade accords with Syria and Lebanon. An innovative Qualifying Industrial Zones (QIZ) program (which has created 25,000 jobs for its citizens, accounts for nearly half of all new jobs in Jordan) allows the U.S. to offer duty-free treatment to the products of 35 Jordanian-Israeli factories in seven industrial parks. The U.S. free trade agreement and Jordan's entry into the World Trade Organization has also helped Jordan gain membership in the global village of trade.

Jordan's foreign investment has grown twenty-fold in the past five years, from the average of $14 million each year between 1985 and 1995, to over $300 million a year since 1997. Her exports directed to the U.S. rose from $16 million in 1998 to $72 million at the turn of the new century. (Egypt-with a population 12 times Jordan runs the risk of being bypassed by this tiny country, which has already exceeded Syria, Tunisia, and Lebanon in exports to the U.S.)

In a promising move in January 2005, Egypt and Israel agreed upon a rare trade cooperation deal.   The two countries and the U.S. signed a protocol to set up seven special zones, where goods would gain free access to U.S. markets provided that 35 percent of their products came from cooperation between Egypt and Israeli companies.

Egypt and the E. U. initialed a trade partnership agreement that will pave the way for an interactive bilateral relationship. Under the terms of the accord that was signed in 2001, tariffs on EU exports are to be gradually reduced over a 15-year transitional period.  This signing is further evidence of integration and will be   another component in the evolution of the triangle of the Jordanian-Israeli-Palestinian Trade Agreement.

Total bilateral trade between Israel and its two existing peace partners, Egypt and Jordan, reached $158 million in the year 2000, a 36 percent jump over 1999's total of $116 million. Thus, in spite of the violence between

Israel and the Palestinians, cross-border trade can still succeed. Imagine the possibilities if there was stability throughout the region!

A counter argument to regional cooperation was heard from the Palestinian Media Center with claims that former President Clinton's failed strategy for securing peace in the region was only a "mirage designed to trick their governments into prematurely establishing economic ties that would help Israel break out of its regional isolation. This has had the added repercussion of promoting not only anti-Israel sentiment of countries that have established economic ties with Israel, but has also promoted anti-American sentiment in all countries of the region, as demonstrated by the grass-roots popular boycott of American products in many states....."

At Cairo's MENA Economic Conference in 1996, Egypt's President Mubarak emphasized that   regional cooperation does not revolve around Israel; that there is plenty of room for consolidating inter-Arab ties and Arab relations with other countries. (Mubarak almost cancelled the meeting out of anger and disappointment that Israelis elected Netanyahu as prime minister instead of Peres.)

For the Middle East, the question above all others is: Does peace bring stability and prosperity, or is it prosperity that encourages peace and stability? No matter how one answers that question, however, it has become clear that the peace process cannot and should not primarily be driven by economics. Rather, economics can best be employed as the dynamic crutch to sustain self-sufficiency, and thus self-pride. Economic action  is most effective in reaching its goals when placed in a proper political context. Similarly, when pushing a political settlement, it is necessary to know the economic direction that one wishes to pursue.

Shimon Peres' *New Middle East* concept following the Oslo 1993 accord signing on the White House lawn was based on cross-border trade as the glue to sustain peace. Today, most experts believe that his approach was over-ambitious, naïve, and impractical.

## ECONOMIC REFORM IN THE MIDDLE EAST COMMUNITY

While structural and macroeconomic reforms have helped streamline several Middle Eastern nations, the region is still searching for     sustained growth and productivity. Although a number of countries have embarked on economic reforms over the past years, the growth-rate of these economies has been disappointing, barely keeping pace with population growth. On a per capita basis, people have not seen their incomes grow, indeed in some cases, incomes have even declined.

The *Arab Human Development Report* 2002, produced by the United Nations, was prepared by Arab intellectuals. It warned that Arab societies were being crippled by a lack of political freedom and by increasing isolation from the world of ideas that nourishes creativity. (Released in both Arabic and in English, this report was downloaded from the Internet one million times.)

In 2003, the same group produced their second report, dealing with the Arab "knowledge deficit." They didn't hesitate in treating the highly sensitive issue of how Islam and its current spiritual leadership may be restraining modern education.

The 2004 *Arab Human Development Report* deals with the issue of governance in the Arab world and the legal, institutional, and religious impediments to political reform.

Countries throughout the Middle East have    failed to adjust to the decline in oil revenues and associated financial remittances. Even in those instances where there has been reform, there has been little growth and investment opportunities.

Furthermore, slow growth has resulted in the inadequacies of a private sector that shies away from global integration and is underdeveloped. Private sector investment as a share of total investment in the regional economy is 40-45 percent lower than other parts of Africa and particularly low when compared to the 75-80 percent in Latin America and East Asia. It is time for the gradual and selective integration of the Middle East/North Africa and Central Asia nations into the world economy.

"While oil income has transformed the landscapes of some Arab countries, the region remains richer than it is developed. Per capita income growth has shrunk in the last 20 years to a level just above that of sub-Saharan Africa. Productivity is declining," as reported by the *Arab Human Development Report* authors of the 2002 study.

Secretary of State Powell's last visit to North Africa before leaving office brought him to Rabat, Morocco on December 10, 2004. Foreign ministers from the Arab world met to advance political change. Powell spoke of efforts to make "participation in political and public life more inclusive." Nevertheless, representatives from the 20 Arab states turned the near four-hour meeting into discussions on economic integration and development, and the Arab-Israeli conflict.

## ONE LESS OBSTACLE – USURY

All three of the Abrahamic religions frown on usury, but Christians and Jews long ago found the means for circumventing this apparent obstacle. Although many Muslims still believe that charging or paying interest is wrong, with the passage of time this issue is being neutralized.

Until the past few years a significant portion of Muslims were excluded from dealing with Western banks which all pay interest on deposits and make charges on loans. Middle Eastern companies skirted this problem through *sharia* - approved financial services established in the 1970s. In 2004 a *sharia* - compliant bank, the Islamic Bank of Britain was created. It provides Islamic versions of traditional services-deposit accounts, personal loans, and mortgages.

In addition to prohibiting banking interest, the *Koran* prohibits "making money from money" and investment is considered immoral. Now, deposit accounts operate like unit trusts, with funds invested on the depositor's behalf and a share of the profits replace interest payments.

*Sharia* committees have been established to monitor that no funds are used by questionable sources, for example, for pornography, consumption or sales of alcohol, or for usurious, non-Islamic banking.

Mortgages and loans can now be taken out on a "hire-purchase" scheme where the bank purchases items on the customer's behalf. The customer then pays the bank a series of installments until the cost, plus a profit for the bank has been achieved.

These schemes are considered by some experts as foolish and potentially troublesome. But for the average Muslim citizen, concerned with violating the dignity of the *Koran*, it remains the best approach today.

## FREE TRADE IDEOLOGY

Does free trade mean, for example, that firms from Israel have a right to sell whatever they choose to sell in Jordan? No, free trade allows governments to block imports on grounds of public policy; and on the other hand, free trade accords argue that such bans must not amount to arbitrary discrimination or disguised restrictions on trade.

Skilled workers tend to benefit more from free trade than unskilled workers. The disparities in skill among the peoples of any given community can be great, and many may be disadvantaged until they learn to be more productive.

However, average income usually rises under free trade since unemployment can be expected to decline. People terminated in any industry should easily find employment in new or expanding industries, so personal income at the macro-level will sustain upward momentum, at least in theory. However, there is no absolute certainty that average incomes throughout the Middle East/North Africa and Central Asia will increase by shifting to a free trade model.

Likewise, the theory of free trade assumes that people are paid salaries based on the demand for their services, not upon the industry in which they are employed. Jumping, during this transition period, from one industry to another will not automatically guarantee equality of wages. The same task, if done in two different industries, will pay two different salaries, and if done in two different countries, will pay as additional two different salaries.

Recent experience in Central Europe, suggests that the costs of structural improvements are great; old facilities must be torn down and new ones built, infrastructure has to be constructed and other costly projects begun.

Consequently, free-trade accords with countries of dissimilar living standards, differing wage scales, and varying cultures, as in MENACA, do not readily adapt to one another in a short time period. The community will initially be hard pressed to service the needs of the weaker nations as free-trade agreements proliferate.

If free trade areas (where partners agree to eliminate tariffs on trade among themselves) are to help world trade, they must try to be nondiscriminatory. Entry should be granted willingly, not grudgingly. Members should commit themselves to reducing their external, as well as internal barriers to trade.

Is the world better off being grouped into a series of economic trade regions, especially with the increasing demand for environmental and worker protections included in many new agreements?

The stresses and strains within economic unions override nationalist feelings - where so many people seem so remote that they identify with local ethnic groups, often adding friction between neighboring nations and within the boundaries of existing countries.

For many in MENACA, integration has rarely if ever been a driving force moving political and economic relations. Traditionally, MENACA countries have remained separate entities, sinking alone. It is time for a dramatic shift.

## EARLY ATTEMPTS AT INTEGRATION

Even before passage of the European Recovery Program following World War II, talk of economic integration in the region was a worthy topic. If the objective of the program was not solely relief, then assuredly it was designed to revive agriculture, industry, and trade so that affected nations might eventually be self-supporting. One of the few visionaries was Under-Secretary of State for Economic Affairs (under Marshall) William L. Clayton, who recommended a European economic federation nearly ten years before the European common market was created in 1958.

The European Union's Treaty of Rome was preceded by the visionary Treaty of the Arab Market in the mid-1950s. (The dream for an Arab Common Market was revived at the Arab Summit in Cairo in 1996.)

At a meeting of the Council of Europe in Strasbourg in September 1967, former Foreign Minister of Israel Abba Eban suggested that Israel and its neighbors should explore the European Community idea as a precedent for their own relationships. Little happened.

On December 23, 1973, at the Geneva peace conference, speaking on behalf of the Israeli government, Eban again called for movement in this area, "The ultimate guarantee of a peace agreement lies in the creation of common regional interests, in such degree of intensity, such entanglement of reciprocal advantage, in such mutual human accessibility as to put future wars beyond rational contingency." Again, little happened.

When Jordan's Prince Hassan bin Talal, the former crown prince and King Abdullah's uncle visited Washington, D.C. in June 2006, he recalled Eban who advocated the Benelux concept for Israel, Palestine, and Jordan, or independence within a large economic union.

## WARTS AND ALL - THE EUROPEAN UNION MODEL

The European Recovery Program made the economically vital EU possible by zeroing in on the creation of a harmonized, economically independent, internal market for countries that had miraculously crept out of the ashes of a horrific and destructive war.

In great part, one of the frequently unspoken elements in the creation of the European Economic Community (EEC), later the Economic Community (EC), and now the European Union (EU), was the principle of self-containment. In other words, the devastated nations of Europe were committed to economic resurgence supported by a set of laws that ensured no single nation within its web would ever be powerful enough to assert its will or muscle on another member state or states.

The "idea broker" behind the creation of the European Economic Community was Jean Monnet. He was "convinced that ideas marched into politics only by reaching key people; his job was to find those people and use them; to pass the proper proposals through the proper offices over the proper tables to get the effects he wanted."

The French plan for postwar reconstruction was called the *Monnet Plan*. In turn, the French would propose that the victors release their grip on Germany's steel production if Germany freely shared its coal resources with France. Thus the *Schuman Plan*, named for Robert S. Schuman, then French Foreign Minister.

The Suez Canal crisis of 1956 brought a new reality to the governments of France and the United Kingdom.

When U.S. President Eisenhower decided not to support their call to protect the Canal from a takeover by Egypt's Nasser, on November 6th, the German chancellor Konrad Adenauer said that "France and England will never be powers comparable to the United States.....Not Germany either. There remains to them only one way of playing a decisive role in the world: that is to unite Europe.....We have no time to waste; Europe will be your revenge."

Thus was born the six-nation European common market. A reawakening by leading member nations of the Middle East should also conclude that being separate they will stall, but united brings opportunities to compete globally.

Those expecting an easy transfer of the EU model should consider the changing dynamics of those times. Post WW II Western Europe followed a plan of rejuvenation which led to the creation of a High Authority, later the Commission of the European Union in Brussels based on:

a.  the containment of Germany against future aggressions;

b.  the containment of the new "enemy" - the Soviets;

c.  overcoming post-war poverty and encouraging economic growth (in great part to counter the Soviets by receiving U.S. aid in the form of the European Recovery Program); and

d.  establishing a laissez-faire policy along with institutions and skills required to perpetuate economic expansion.

A cautious and deliberate study of the evolution of the European Union can provide an essential model for the development of a Jordanian-Israeli-Palestinian Trade Agreement (JIPTA), a Middle East Free Trade Agreement (MEFTA), a Middle East/North Africa Free Trade

Agreement     (MENAFTA),     a     Middle     East/North
Africa/Central     Asia     Free     Trade     Agreement
(MENACAFTA), and finally the ultimate Middle East
Community (MEC).

Shortly after the end of the Second World War,
several countries in Europe, at the behest of the UK. and
with the prompting of the Marshall Plan, began to
cooperate with one another to the advantage of their
economies. France and Germany, out of industrial
necessity, created the impressive European Coal and Steel
Community.

BENELUX countries were made more efficient as
Belgium, The Netherlands, and Luxembourg were added to
the great cross-border market experiment allowing their
citizens to freely move and work in their contiguous sister
nations. These governments believed that the moment had
arrived to initiate a new path in  reconstructing Europe.

The story of interdependence by two neighboring,
and formerly embattled nations, the German Republic and
the Republic of France, is illustrative of how the sharing of
economic benefits with a "win-win" result (an incentive
that should be often repeated within the MEC) would be the
glue for expansion of the concepts of regional economic
integration. (It should be remembered that the present and
ongoing success of the EU was not based on emulating the
structure of the BENELUX nations, but upon the forceful
determination of the leaders and governments of Germany
and France).

At the outset, the goal of the emerging European
Coal and  Steel Community (ECSC), was to transfer control
of the basic materials of war (coal, iron, and steel) away
from each national government to common institutions.
Economic expansion, rational distribution and production,

and safeguarded employment within the industry were all part of the plan. With the creation of ECSC, agreements abolished duties and quantitative restrictions on trade in coal and steel between the founding six member nations who signed the Treaty of Rome in 1957 and eliminated restrictive practices such as cartels (a must in the formation of the MEC).

Germany, France and Italy would soon ascend the European Economic Community along with the Benelux nations and sign the Treaty of Rome. Another nine nations would eventually join the Community. Transformation of the European Community included the Single European Act, amending the original Treaty at the end of 1992. The Maastricht Treaty, signed in the glorious city of Maastricht in The Netherlands, further amended the founding constitution in 1994, with a Single European currency commencing in January 2002, and social and political considerations being pronounced for the future history of the European Community. (Forty-seven years after formation, the jigsaw remains incomplete, a reminder to the impatient when fitting the pieces in place within the Middle East/North Africa/Central Asia region.)

The European Community (EC) then changed its name to the European Union (EU), and  became the model for all grandiose theories on regional trade, social, and political accords.  It is critical to note that the EU owes much of its success to the fact that the institutions and skills required for economic growth were in place even though the physical stock of capital and infrastructure were devastated by war.

Attempts to emulate this impressive   achievement will be difficult, especially in a broader Middle East, due to the divergent cultures, histories, economies, and conflicts.

(Recall that the continent of Europe was in a continual state of war for one thousand years.)

One must keep in mind, too, that the Marshall Plan and its successors have not been static documents solving all problems, but sophisticated frameworks within which change was not only possible but required. The present 27 member nations of the EU, (ten states ascended in 2004) with two more in 2007, have a combined population of more than 450 million people who consume one-quarter of the world's goods. But the EU has been reborn time and again as a viable model for other global efforts at economic integration, social and political issues aside. The EU's magnetic power has been seen in repeated attempts to glorify its creative spirit, in overcoming strong national and cultural forces, in generating economies of scale and, in hearing its name repeated as the preferred alternative for future regional economic attempts of integration, harmony, and profit.

The first miracle of the Marshall Plan was the revitalization of Western Europe; the second was the impressive evolution and success of the European Union (EU). After nearly five decades following its creation, the world has an appropriate historical laboratory for governments to study and dissect, in order to incorporate ideas and procedures into their own efforts based on distinct needs and unique regional accords.

A collective, regional approach accelerated European recovery, leaving in Thomas C. Schelling's view, a model of "successful multinational cooperation to achieve a common goal" as one of the Marshall Plan's lasting legacies.

What is behind this fascination? Is it justified? And what are the pitfalls of any non-critical and hasty acceptance of this model?  Some governments of the world contemplate the pros and cons of the EU model and are, perhaps naively, positively impressed with these arguments:

*With size comes strength*. Evidence -- the European Union, now twenty-seven nations, has   become a suction - cup drawing both foreign direct investment and creating profits, especially since the implementation of the Single European Act at the end of 1992. Contiguous and surrounding nations, from both the European Free Trade Association and from other central and eastern European areas are rushing in with membership applications (a preview of events in the Middle East for nations not neighbors to Israel) anticipating clout that will be derived from the sheer size and global influence of the EU. Combined, these outlying nations, if integrated with the EU nation-states, will have a total population of more than one-half a billion people. (A fully expanded region including Israel and its contiguous nations, Arab states in North Africa, the Persian Gulf area, plus Iran, Central Asia, Afghanistan and Pakistan and, based on her destiny with membership in the EU, perhaps even Turkey, would be host to a  population in excess of  500 million.)

*The quest for unity unites others.* Evidence -- not since Napoleon's push to unite Europe has anything so ambitious been attempted, and today the EU's gross domestic product accounts for 25 percent of world output.  Statistics readily impress global nations who are seeking ways out of poverty and low productivity. (Likewise, a prospering MEC would generate opportunities for international trade, set a path for increased consumer spending and raise the standard of living for all. For example, the proximity of rival ports at Eilat and Aqaba, the need for sharing the Dead Sea and the Jordan-Yarmuk water systems, the large-scale potential for tourism, rapid growth of electronic communications -- all these point to a particular intimacy of relations that can evolve among the people of JIPTA.)

*There will be quantum leaps in technology and research.* Evidence -- the EU and member governments have released billions of dollars for  megaresearch programs. With new EU directives, revised tax laws permit greater expansion into the venture capital markets and substantial increases in foreign direct investments. Regional integration has allowed for the combining of people, talents, ambitions, and resources to assert a unique and determined leadership in science and technology, all promising to raise the living standards of its member populations.

*Regional integration helps build global markets.* Evidence -- for most of the EU's life, strong economic ties with other nations have been building around the world, all with determination and confidence. For example, shortly after Spain and Portugal joined the European Community on June 22, 1987, EU adopted a policy paper outlining an overall, coordinated strategy for  strengthening relations throughout the EU. Latin America adopted a policy paper outlining an overall, coordinated strategy for strengthening relations throughout its region building natural links based on history, common language and cultural bridges and networks. (A prospering MEC will reach out to the world, with the power to export affordable products.)

*Foreign direct investments will flow.* Evidence -- The World Bank and other authority institutions decry the poor level of foreign direct investment (FDI) in MEC countries. The first requirement is to encourage overseas FDIs indicating a positive attitude in investment. Foreign investors look for more than financial incentives when deciding how to disburse their speculative money. The want to invest in countries with open societies, stable governments and solid infrastructures.

*Devastation can turn to profit.* Evidence -- as nations seek ways to move out of poverty and to          leave the so-called Third World behind, the recent history of Western Europe is a most attractive  model. After the devastation of World War II and as late as the early 1980s, many experts thought the EU had no future. Now, many wonder what lies ahead in the EU's push for new markets and profits. Leaders from around the world remain amazed at the marvels of European reconstruction and revitalization as they ponder their own decisions for tomorrow. (Might a parallel result occur throughout the Middle East/North Africa and Central Asia?)

*Regional economic agreements can counter other regional trade accords.* Evidence -- the agreement between Canada and the United States in March of 1985 to "explore all the possible ways" of reducing trade barriers is illustrative of the economic forces of the day. The two governments concluded a free-trade agreement on October 4, 1987, only months after the Single European Act was proposed in the European Community.  Shortly thereafter, the Mexican government sought a free trade accord with the United States (Canada would participate). The result was the North American Free Trade Agreement (NAFTA), which went into effect on January 1, 1994.  At that time, this three-nation, combined force of 380 million people, with an estimated $7 trillion market made NAFTA the world's largest regional trading bloc.

It is doubtful that this powerful trade agreement (some consider it a trade treaty) would ever have been negotiated had there not been a mighty European Union to stimulate bold action. Can these accords, with their promises of reducing waste and upgrading efficiencies and profits, become an incentive to the formation of trade agreements among nations in the broader Middle East?

Some in the Middle East perceive that the U.S. is no longer an "honest broker" of peace in the region since the failure of negotiations at Camp David in December 2000, (President Bush's Road-Map plan remains stalled as he moved into his second term in 2005.) It is appropriate to turn to the European Union for leadership in integrating the southern and eastern rim of the Mediterranean.

The EU remains the dominant regional political and economic power, it has developed a culture of peaceful conflict resolution and negotiation, it maintains considerable military strength based on the collective potential of the EU member states, and it maintains strong cultural ties with the societies of the MENA region.

After all, the EU has been a consistent voice for regional economic integration since before the Madrid Conference in 1991 and immediately following the first Gulf War.

The issues of containment, threats to security and peace, widespread poverty, and rampant corruption remain central challenges to the creation of a Middle East/North Africa/Central Asia regional community. The community's establishment would help to cope with rising forms of religious extremism and disturbances resulting from limited water resources and skyrocketing increases in population.

Peace treaties are but pieces of paper when contrasted with the power of economic interdependence that achieves a rising living standard and a longer and healthier life. With or without MERP, the glue of interdependence brings people and nations closer together, forming a binding force for success. The desert of gloom and deprivation might then be overcome.

*The Barcelona Declaration* envisaged a partnership between the 15-members of the EU (now 27) and the 12 nations of the southern and eastern Mediterranean. In the November 1995 declaration, the EU agreed to the "acceleration of the pace of sustainable socio-economic development, improvement of the living conditions of the populations, increase in the employment levels and reduction in the development gap in the Euro-Mediterranean region, encouragement of regional cooperation and integration."

This partnership had high hopes of deepening ties among the countries of the Mediterranean but became enervated because of the second Palestinian Intifada and September 11th. For the last 10 years, the European Union has carried out its own engagement strategy with the Barcelona process. However, EU officials privately admit that this program has little to show for the $13 billion it has spent.

The economic/trade breakdown of the Middle East/North Africa region during rapid globalization, can be seen as "one of the four major crises of the Arab world, others being the Six Day War of 1967, the Iranian revolution, and Saddam Hussein's hegemonic posture in 1990," according to Fouad Ajami in his insightful *Foreign Affairs* article "The Arab Inheritance."

When interested countries first meet to discuss MERP, early goals will be to identify concrete means of achieving and maintaining peace through a series of confidence-building measures. The commitments each country makes should reduce the likelihood of hostilities while promoting national and regional economies. The founding members should look to create additional sources of income and to raises   the  standard of living in their respective countries through cooperative initiatives, such as joint industrial parks and the sharing of resources. At the outset, poorer nations will require a greater share of aid and assistance.

## THE ECONOMIC SUMMITS

In the last 13 years we have learned that a successful Middle East peace process depends not only on sufficient aid (MERP) but also satisfactory political solutions. The MENA Economic Summits were part of the economic vision of a New Middle East, so carefully articulated by Israel's Shimon Peres, that would create an atmosphere on which a political resolution of  stalemate might be shaped.

As early as October 1993, according to Dennis Ross, President Clinton's Middle East negotiator, Shimon Peres was "storming ahead" to forge a peace treaty with Jordan and proposed that Jerusalem and Amman jointly host an international conference of several thousand CEOs who would be "ferried back and forth between the two cities." The purpose would be "to capture international imagination and demonstrate that the Middle East was now open for business."

This was an idea whose time had arrived, though  a bit naïve  in its approach.  Peres, was ultimately supported by  Prime Minister  Rabin who remained overly cautious. Rabin was concerned that any coordinated business with the Palestinians must be preceded by the termination of terror into Israel and full-recognition of Israel's right to exist.

The assassination of Yitzhak Rabin in 1995 within days of the close of the MENA meeting in Amman devastated the peace process. Afterwards , Bibi Netanyahu was elected Prime Minister, narrowly defeating Peres. Peres's vision of the *New Middle East* lay in tatters.

With passage of the Oslo Accord in 1993, the potential for regional economic integration had been reborn. It was reported that the late King of Jordan, HM Hussein II had in January 1994, approved the convening of an economic integration regional conference between Jordan and Israel to detail the future of a "Middle East Commonwealth." (This was six months before the historic meeting on July 22, 1994 between President Clinton and Prime Minister Rabin in Washington.) The concept was promising but the faded as a peace treaty had not been signed early enough to have the conference in Jordan (a second economic summit was rescheduled and held October 1995 in Amman, Jordan, once again reinforcing the recent King's determination to play a primary role in the evolution of a community of regional nations.)

Shortly after King Hussein's announcement of the planned Economic Summit in January 1994, Israel's Abba Eban again called for forming a community between Israel and Jordan based on the European model. The European model had similarly begun with three small countries who agreed to open their frontiers and not to sign alliances without each other's agreement. Eban years later recalled "The western powers were willing to give Germany sovereignty on the condition that they join a community with community obligations which would dilute nationalism."

Echoing phrases from the post-Nazi era, Eban argued: "If Israel, Jordan, and the new Palestine were members of a community in which none of them could do anything in terms of security without some agreement from the others, boundaries were open, and, above all, economic investment…. proliferates," then Palestinian interests could be realized without being a threat to Israel's security." A triangle of three interactive nations could well become the emerging tiger of the Middle East.

(Abba Eban's recommendations are very distant from those of the recent Israeli government. Prime Minister Sharon continued his hard-line policies towards the Palestinians and whether it be maintaining settlements in the West Bank or building fences around the occupied territories, Sharon would probably had scoffed at Eban's proposals, as undesirable and unworkable.)

Morocco's King Hassan II, then jumped into the void by accepting the challenge and responsibility to sponsor the first of four annual regional economic meetings. By this act, Arab/Muslim North Africa would be included in all future interactions along with the Middle East, a strategic move that would benefit nations of the southern Mediterranean rim and, in particular, Morocco.

The U.S., Israel, and Arab regional nations began to anticipate the coming of a new era of cross-border economic integration. It was conceivable that the Marshall Plan's call for cooperation among recipients could be massaged and appropriately altered, and then transplanted to yield economic integration that might include the 20-plus nations of North Africa and the Middle East.

(Five Central Asian nations, Afghanistan, Pakistan, and perhaps Turkey were added in this model following a second invited briefing that I gave at the U.S. Department of State after September 11, 2001.)

When it was decided by the State Department that economics could be a major factor in the success of Middle East stability, nations from around the globe found funds (illustrative of the continuing potential for MERP) to support the first phase of the process, one that would lead to the economic summits all on the way to a promising and decidedly controversial regional economic community. The plan would   commence with a Jordan - Israel - Palestine Trade Agreement (JIPTA).

## CASABLANCA - MENA I

This was what an Arabian nights dream would have been about. Coverage by the world's media was the catalyst for spending on a lavish celebration, toasting the possibilities for the future. At one point an Arab-English *Sesame Street* was negotiated and US public television was preparing for this open dialogue and entertainment. It was described as a commercial, educational, and political victory.

Recent, critically important books (by  President Clinton, Israel's Beilin, U.S. Middle East envoy Ross) have emphasized the political dimensions of the efforts to resolve the region's conflicts, but until MENA I, little had been written on the trade/business challenges. Similarly, little research had been done on the subject.

Hosted by Morocco's late King Hassan II, the Middle East/North Africa Economic Summit was held in Casablanca from October 30 to November 1, 1994, 13 months following the signing of the Oslo accord on the White House lawn. At the opening plenary session, His Royal Highness said: "In working together with this conference, we assume a responsibility for which we are accountable before many generations to come. Only an unshakable faith and a sound vision of the future can ensure the victory of life over despair."

Co-sponsored by the U.S. Council on Foreign Relations and the Switzerland-based World Economic Forum, and heavily funded by the U.S. government, nearly 1,800 political leaders, business senior-executives, and a handful of economists and other academics from 61 nations were present, including all Arab nations except Syria, Iran, Iraq, Yemen, Sudan, and Libya.

It was a magical meeting. Pageantry was everywhere to be found. Returning to my hotel on a bus from the final banquet, I noticed that as we rounded a fountain in front of the hall, we were riding atop oriental rugs. For me, this was an ultimate Arabian nights tale. The Casablanca Summit, sponsored jointly by President Clinton and Soviet President Boris Yeltsin, had a similar energizing effect as the meetings held in Madrid, 13 years earlier, called for by George Bush, the present president's father. Multilateral economic linkages were proposed as the forerunner of economic cooperation. One-time adversaries sat together to discuss joint-ventures that would help to undermine the remnants of the Arab boycott against Israel.

It may not have been Jericho, but walls came tumbling down in Morocco's capital.

The concluding *Casablanca Declaration* (read by a close friend, Andre Azoulay, the highest ranking Jew in the kingdom and chief advisor to the King), in part stated: "The participants....explored how best to accelerate the development of the region and overcome, as soon as possible, obstacles, including boycotts and all barriers to trade and investment."

Warren Christopher, then U.S. Secretary of State declared at the Summit, "The time has come to dismantle the boycott entirely," to which one delegate added, "We are witnessing a royal funeral of the boycott." Crown Prince Hassan of Jordan echoed the feeling of most in the Great Hall of the Royal Palace that "the New Middle East needs new things .. our vision is of a Middle East without barriers, with free movement of peoples and goods."

An Executive Secretariat was established, thanks to the *Declaration* in Rabat, Morocco's capital, in part as a way of showing appreciation to King Hassan II. The Executive Secretariat Mostafa Terrab, an M.I.T., Ph.d. and sponsor of my newly formed Center for Middle East Business Studies at Rutgers Business School, was to serve as coordinator and facilitator and to work with a Steering Committee comprised of government officials and the U.S. Council on Foreign Relations.

David Kimche, president of the Israel Council of Foreign Relations proclaimed that the Casablanca Summit was a critical turning point: "The seed was sown for a new era in the Middle East. It remains to be seen whether that seed will grow into a strong and healthy plant."

A giant step was taken by holding the Casablanca Economic Summit in 1994. It defined the possibilities of a regional cooperative to harmonize relationships across borders of neighboring nations. Some Middle East governments were nudged by the U.S., some were more supportive at the outset than others. In the end, the process began a call for institutional structuring and governance that was then officially on the table.

I made a presentation at the Casablanca Summit in which I argued that the dream of stability could begin, first with a Jordan-Israel-Palestine Trade Agreement (JIPTA), then a Middle East Free Trade Agreement (MEFTA), followed by a Middle East/North Africa Trade Agreement

(MENAFTA) (For obvious reasons, Central Asia and its neighborhood was not on participants' minds at that time.) The goal was to show that citizens from differing cultures and nations could enter into business agreements and joint-ventures, some projects as profitable, others as reinforcing community needs.

I was scheduled for an early breakfast seminar; twelve people attended. I had only one hour to convince those at the table that cross – border trade and regional cooperation was the best path to follow. The model was distributed indicating a plan for the integration of economies.

Over a final cup of coffee, each attendee in turn responded to my model. Most Arab participants appeared supportive, but some were puzzled or argumentative. Two of them were unwilling to accept that my descriptive drawing of the model placed Israel in the center of JIPTA, suggesting hegemony. My response was that JIPTA, an acronym, required a vowel, and "I" – the vowel – representing Israel, was placed in the center between Jordan and the Palestinians.

Realizing that the truth is often misperceived, I was willing to revise the model. In a final draft of the chart, I would move Israel to the side, noting also that JIPTA, with an English spelling would certainly be different in Arabic.

One tall, young man, dressed totally in white, with a turban, demanded to know why I referred to "The Palestinians," not "Palestine," in my chart. All other 22 country listings gave the name of a nation. My response was quick: "Palestine does not yet exist as a country." I held firm in the final version.

The atmosphere at the Summit created its own momentum. Casablanca announced to the world that

Middle Eastern and North African trade accords were viable and potentially profitable for its 300 million consumers.

Long-term, a Middle East/North Africa Economic Community (MENAC) would reward the initiators of the Casablanca Summit for their insight and courage to move peace and prosperity across borders that were once thought to be ironclad and impenetrable.

Aside from the overpowering list of corporate and political participants, I studied the list of attendees to see how many academics were present. To my surprise and continuing puzzlement, there were only four.

(And to think that I almost didn't attend. The registration fee for this three-day summit was $1,500. I was able to cover the hotel and flight, but my dean was unwilling to pay the hefty registration fee. Thanks to a colleague's friendship with Les Gelb, then President of the *Council on Foreign Relations* in New York City, this huge sum was waived for me and for the remaining three annual conferences. But, to my dismay, the dean would only support my participation as a speaker, not merely as a participant. Thanks to the intervention of Lester Pollack, my name was brought to the top of the list to give a paper at the summit.)

## AMMAN - MENA II

If the Casablanca Economic Summit was germinal, the Amman meeting one year later indicated a determination among the participating nations to continue movement towards regional cooperation.

For three days, from October 29 to 31, 1995, optimism filled the air. The second Middle East/North Africa Economic Summit was held under the patronage of the late King Hussein bin Talal, ruler of the Hashemite Kingdom of Jordan since May 1953.

It was clear that this small country could ill-afford the extravagances of Casablanca. The King, a most somber man, held the Summit in a serious fashion (although Crown Prince Hassan, the younger brother of the King, would actually be the dominant representative at the meeting.) At the opening Plenary session, His Royal Highness King Hussein said: "The international community is able to contribute to the rehabilitation of the economies of the region at a minimum cost. To achieve this result, there should be a clear and common outlook for the future which we seek for the region, in partnership and through cooperation with the international community. Each one of us will have a distinctive role to play in making our subregion an active participant in the regional and world economies…May God help us to achieve that which brings benefits to our peoples, and may God bless you all." We all applauded as the CNN cameras rolled.

The goals of this summit were to facilitate the expansion of private-sector investment in the region, to cement a public-private partnership that would ensure that end, and to enhance regional cooperation and development.

The summit inaugurated a new phase in the peace process: transition to the possible integration of the infrastructures of Israel and the Arab states (clearly a byproduct flowing from MERP.) In other words, the creation of systems of long-term interdependency and cooperation including Israel, a first giant step toward any regional integration effort.

Nearly 1,600 participants networked throughout the great hall seeking partners for joint-ventures and exchanging words of creativity and support. (While 12 people heard my presentation in Casablanca, now 15 attended my talk in Amman.  I was convinced, perhaps wrongly, that CEOs and business presidents were too busy to hear brilliant remedies from an academic.)

*The Amman Declaration* called for:

A.  A Bank for Economic Cooperation and Development in the Middle East and North Africa to be established in Cairo, with initial capitalization of $5 billion (it never came to pass).

B.  The establishment of a Regional Tourism Board-The Middle East-Mediterranean Travel and Tourism Association-to facilitate tourism and promote the region as a unique and attractive tourist destination.

C.  The establishment of a Regional Business Council to promote cooperation and trade among the sectors of the countries in the region.

D.  The formal inauguration of the Economic Summit Executive Secretariat, located in Rabat, Morocco to work for the advancement of the public-private partnership, to promote contacts, to share data, and to foster private sector investment in the region.

As a complement to the regional institutions, set up by the *Amman Declaration*, the Steering Group of the Multilateral Peace Negotiations (established at the 1993 Oslo Accord signing) decided to establish the REDWG Monitoring Committee Secretariat. Located in Amman, it was to be a permanent regional economic institution, and, I had hoped, the possible forerunner of a headquarters for the Middle East/North Africa Community. All participating parties agreed that REDWG would promote and strengthen regional economic cooperation.

At the opening plenary Yasir Arafat demanded that Jerusalem be the capital of the future Palestinian state. Israel's Prime Minister Yitzhak Rabin said "No......," which was echoed by Israel's Foreign Minister Shimon Peres. Throughout, television cameras and Barbara Walters captured their debate for the U.S. viewers. The audience remained calm and was determined to ride out the political session before turning to matters of business and trade.

Finally, Rabin said: "No one will come here because of our winning smiles....They all want to make money." (Six days following his participation in the Amman Economic Summit, Rabin was assassinated. The future for peace and prosperity in the region was in grave jeopardy.)

At MENA I in Casablanca, participating nations articulated the reasons for regional integration, but left it to MENA II to translate them into reality. It was clear that unless and until the intentions of the parties were better coordinated and an institutional structure was created, the wheels toward integration would spin haplessly.

The Summit formally ended with a huge banquet. Over a thousand people packed the lobby awaiting the festivities. It was hot; drinks were served (no alcohol). An hour passed before the CEOs and corporate presidents from around the world began a climb up the steps towards the dining room.

On the top of the landing, Crown Prince Hassan spent about 10 seconds greeting each participant: "Shalom....Salam.". When it was my turn, he gazed down at my security badge and noticed Rutgers University." He followed by inquiring if I knew how many academics were present at the session. I responded that a quick perusal of the list of participants indicated perhaps four university professors. We shook hands and away I went into the dining area.

The Crown Prince, sitting with Rabin, Arafat and other dignitaries, greeted the audience again, and then he stated to his dismay that only a handful of academics were in attendance and that this was a disappointment to him. He then asked that: "the professor from Rutgers University please stand up."

I was shocked, somewhat embarrassed, but pleased to know that at least a member of the royal family recognized the role of an academic at these summits.

By the end of the dinner, walking across the room to say goodbye to a friend, I noticed the wave of a hand asking me to approach. It was that of the Crown Prince. Of course, you don't say no to such a request and when I approached, he turned and said to me: "Chairman Arafat this is the professor I had mentioned."

Arafat and I talked for about 15 minutes. During which he invited himself to come to my university to give a lecture. I was expecting an unpleasant conversation, for the PA leader had just returned from a meeting of the United Nations in New York City where Mayor Guiliani had Arafat escorted out of Lincoln Center (the mayor was making a political statement prior to an election campaign.)

I said to Chairman Arafat that I would love to see him at my university and that I would pursue the invitation. For security reasons my administration rejected the idea.

And to think that I almost missed the Summit. On the day of my flight from New York, for the first (and hopefully last) time I had a kidney stone attack. Refusing to surrender to this inconvenience I had the hospital physician insert a stent until my return. Fortunately, my wife Ellen was with me throughout the week. With no apparent complications, I then proceeded, once back in New York City to have the stone blasted away. A hardship certainly, but the compensation was attending the Summit in Amman.

## CAIRO - MENA III

Egypt sponsored the Cairo meeting from November 12 to 14, 1996. It was downgraded from an economic summit, which by definition required heads of state in attendance, to an economic conference. This event included fewer Americans, Europeans, and Israelis, resulting in participation of about 1,400 representatives from 87 nations.

Rabin had established a special relationship with President Mubarak. But with his death, a cautious president awaited the naming of a new prime minister in Israel.

Mubarak almost scrapped the next economic meeting altogether after the May election of Israeli Prime Minister Netanyahu, whose policies were viewed to have slowed the region's peace process. Mubarank did not attempt to hide his hope than Shimon Peres, by now acting Prime Minister, would be elected Prime Minister of Israel following the assassination of Rabin.

Consequently, one of the central messages that Mubarak sent in his opening comments was that regional cooperation need not and did not revolve around Israel; that there was plenty of room for consolidating inter-Arab ties and Arab relations with other countries.

The common theme "Building for the Future, Creating an Investor-Friendly Environment" was illustrated in Mubarak's opening address when he said that economic dividends of peace would not be forthcoming without progress in the Arab-Israeli peace negotiations. In a departure from the previous summits, MENA III saw political pressure being brought to bear on Israel, rather than on the participating Arab states.

"If you lose peace, everyone will be the loser. If we put the peace process back on track, everyone will gain." Prime Minister of Egypt Ganzouri said later in the closing session.

Participants stressed in the *Cairo Declaration* the crucial importance of the development of the Palestinian economy. They noted with concern that the already weak Palestinian economy was suffering from restrictions, and that border closures hindered the daily movement of Palestinian labor and trade.

With pride that so much could be achieved with minimal participation from the Israelis, the Egyptian government announced that during the Cairo session, business people had closed deals worth an astonishing $6.8 billion. A major statement by Warren Christopher (his last visit to the Middle East as Secretary of State) was made for the Middle East Development Bank's charter. The Bank was expected to begin operation in Cairo by the end of 1997, aiming to be a catalyst in supporting private-sector projects, promoting regional projects and dialogue, and focusing on the region's growing infrastructure needs. Plans for its creation were soon cancelled and also my hopes for a filter of funding via an impressive reinvented Marshall Plan.

Mostafa Terrab, the Executive Secretariat of MENA in Rabat, Morocco had urged me to write a book on an economic regional community in time for the Cairo meeting. As a gesture it was to be distributed to all participants. Unfortunately something went wrong with the printing process and the books only arrived on the closing day. Copies were distributed. (Having been to numerous international meetings, the weight of papers encouraged many to discard them as they returned to their rooms. In fact, I was witness to about 100 executives tossing their copies of the volume into waste baskets in the center corridor. I in turn, and my friends, followed them to reclaim many of the books from the trash. I still have some of these copies as souvenirs.)

## DOHA - MENA IV

MENA IV was held in Qatar's capital Doha from November 16-18, 1997. Participants were not excited about this meeting. The mood had changed completely and there was a significant drop in attendance.

It would be, in fact, the last of the consecutive annual economic meetings. Qatar's Emir, His Royal Highness Sheikh Hamad bin Khalifa Al Thani opened the conference (once again the Summit concept has been discarded and replaced with Conference) with a strongly worded attack on Israel, criticizing the hard-line policies of Israeli Prime Minister Netanyahu, which he said were threatening the region's stability, "The Middle East peace process, unfortunately, is going through a critical period and is being hindered by the intransigence of the Israeli government and its unjustified backing away from the peace agreements it signed." He said, "The Israeli government must be aware that its actions will undermine the peace process and expose the region to a danger of unpredictable dimensions." While a number of Arab states chose to boycott the conference, nearly 1000 people still participated.

It was now the turn of the new U.S. Secretary of State: "I am here in Doha...because America keeps its word," declared Madeleine Albright as she addressed the opening plenary session following the Emir. Declaring that the peace process was in jeopardy, she dazzled the delegates, by stating, "It would be helpful if all the leaders of the region would keep commitments they have made."

Secretary Albright had held a private session one hour before the start of the Doha meeting with about 25 CEOs from the U.S. to test out her planned comments at the opening plenary. It was an amazing interaction. I was an observer sitting on the sidelines. She held forth, shooting straight as did the corporate leadership within the room. This dress rehearsal for her made a lasting impression on the participants.

Klaus Schwab, president of the World Economic Forum, who for the fourth consecutive year organized the conference, noted that even at the end of the twentieth century, the MENA region is being held hostage by politics. "I hope Doha will be a turning point … .the region is being bypassed on the global investment highway," he stated. Citing some depressing statistics, he attempted to drive home the need for achieving economic and social progress in the region. Total GDP had remained almost stagnant since 1980, he said, while the population had grown by an alarming 28 percent annually. Sixty percent of the population was under 25 years of age and 40 percent less than 14 years.

Even with a small attendance and a dour mood, Qataris declared the event to be a great success, claiming that $12 billion worth of contracts and memorandums of understanding had been signed, compared with the final $10 billion at the previous years' Cairo meeting.

On the last day, Shimon Peres of Israel made an appearance. Two receptions were held prior to his speaking at the closing session. He delivered one of his most impassioned, clear, and optimistic speeches. Many in the conference hall had tears in their eyes. The applause, from Arab, Israeli, Moslem, Jew and Christian alike, was deafening.

Dennis Ross was convinced "opening the Middle East for business might catalyze far-reaching reforms and build a stronger stake in peace in the Arab world." Shimon Peres saw the global economy becoming increasingly interconnected with fewer borders and barriers to information, investment, and economic growth. He envisioned a "new Middle East" and grew, according to Ross, "obsessed with convincing Israel's neighbors – including the Palestinians – of the economic benefits of peace."

**IN TRIBUTE**

The four consecutive MENA meetings (1994-1997) provided a meaningful platform promoting economics and trade as the impetus for moving the region forward.

What these important meetings provided was a framework that advanced the cause of regional cooperation. JIPTA – when and if it is realized – and its offshoots will learn from the Economic Summits and Conferences. The writing of history books may hopefully support the claim that the impetus for a future economic bloc was a direct outgrowth of these four sessions. Without them, cross-border trade, alliances, joint-ventures, and investments would have remained theories only.

The legacy of the MENA meetings are a display of commitment during the ups and downs of the Israel-Palestinian peace negotiations. Economic meetings designed to encourage meaningful cross-border activities have proven to be a viable and major source for hope throughout the region. "Oslo is Dead" is still heard throughout    the region, and no alternate political or economic substitutes are on the drawing board. Eventually, for stability to exist in the Middle East, economic interactions and regional trade must be resurrected with or without a Middle East Recovery Program. The Middle East should  not  reject  this  opportunity  to  enrich  future generations  who  are  entitled  to  share  in  the  world's prosperity.

By the end of 2006 the world was in its most prosperous year in human history. The World Bank released its optimistic report indicating that global growth had "accelerated sharply" to a rate of approximately 4 percent.

The developing world led the way in this economic surge, with 6.1 percent growth in the year. The evidence indicates that all developing areas are growing faster in the present decade than they did in the 1980's and 90's.

A spectacular decline in poverty occurred in East and South Asia. In 1990, there were 470 million people in this region living on less than $1 each day. By 2001, that figure had been reduced to   271 million living in extreme poverty. By 2015 it is projected to be only 19 million people facing these conditions. The Middle East can and must share in these impressive gains.

The change in strategy is working. Globalization, free-trade accords, and regional economic integration are contributing significantly to these impressive numbers.

If "Oslo is Dead," I ask, then what are the alternatives?   Whether the post-Arafat era ushers in stability, a reduction or elimination of suicide-bombings, and/or an acceptance of Israel's right to exist, somewhere along the way the Palestinians must face the negative prospects of "going it alone." A welfare-state must ultimately fend for itself to succeed. Yes, the global community by necessity will pour funds into the newly created Palestinian state, but with time self-sufficiency is required. Sooner or later, the Oslo-concept of regional economic integration will resurface.

Richard Haass, President of the *Council on Foreign Relations* remains cautious about regional trade in the area. In the fall 2006 he argued: "Trade within the Middle East will remain modest because few countries offer goods and services that others want to buy on a large scale, and advanced manufactured goods will have to continue to come from elsewhere. Few of the advantages of global economic integration will come to this part of the world, despite the pressing need for them."

While deciding which half of the glass one admires, optimists and pessimists inevitably clash over the dilemmas of life. From Madrid, via Oslo I and II, and then from engagement with the four annual economic conferences, the path towards the end of conflict in the region was outlined. But outlines are not solutions, good intentions are not actions. It was not that simple.

Post-Oslo economics provided Israel with the chance to flex her muscles and enter the global economy; prosperity followed bringing with it foreign investors and business partners. It showed others that Israel could conduct business in Israel even amid security tensions. If allowed, this story could be repeated throughout nations of the broader Middle East, with Israel serving as proof that new monies will be invested if solid economic agreements are in place.

Palestinian separation from the Israeli economy is an alternative. Some prominent Israeli leaders argue that Israel must disengage from a future Palestinian state. This does not imply that Israel is immune to the needs of Palestinians; in fact, they are seeking alternative and creative solutions for getting the Palestinian economy and living - standards upgraded. For example, in June 2005, the Portland Trust, a foundation that aims to revive the Palestinian economy in order to strengthen the Israeli-Palestinian stability came forward with a program.

This project, initiated by Israel's Brigadier General Eival Giladi theorizes that the Palestinian economy will not be integrated into the Israeli economy. He wants loan guarantees for the Palestinians and is pushing for an international project to build 150,000 housing units in Gaza, in the post-disengagement era.

Separation efforts are wrong solutions. The state of Palestine's economic future is integration with the Israeli economy. Recall that in 1994 the *Protocol on Economic Relations* – also referred to as the *Paris Protocol*, cemented the Israeli and West Bank/Gaza economy. It formed a customs union and imposed common, though Israeli, tariffs. The result is that Palestinian goods are traded duty free. In other words, Israeli and Palestinian goods receive preferential treatment in each other's markets, relative to the goods of other nations. Indeed, 13 years ago, the *Paris Protocol* transferred control over much of the Palestinian economy from Israel to the Palestinian Authority.

The Israeli and Palestinian connection is necessary. Israel is the main trading partner of the West Bank and Gaza, accounting for 80 percent of Palestinian trade. Jordan remains its second largest trading partner, representing a mere 2.4 percent of exports, while Egypt is ninth, representing only 1.0 percent.

In "The Missing Peace," former U.S. Middle East negotiator Dennis Ross points out: "We can offer guarantees on security; financial assistance to demonstrate the material benefits of hard decisions; and political and international support to bolster the legitimacy of the decisions, all of which may be important in helping each side cross historic thresholds. But we cannot create the will for such decisions. And it is foolhardy to try to impose such decisions."

This argument was repeatedly made at the Arab foreign ministers meeting in Rabat, Morocco. The conference was dedicated to advancing political change in the region. As one of his last appearances before leaving the State Department, Secretary Colin Powell spoke of the effort to make "participation in political and public life more inclusive." Each of the 20 foreign ministers responded with talk about economic development and the ever-present thorn in debate -- the Palestinian-Israeli conflict. Washington's earlier call for democratization was not shared by the Arab representatives who preferred to concentrate on economic and social reform.

"The Death of Oslo," mantra cannot conceal the fact that the 1993 agreement provided a venue and an opportunity for business transactions and incoming investments, in addition to providing for significant loans and gifts to the Middle East from around the world. MERP will bring opportunities to secure the future, for Israelis, for the Palestinians, for the citizens of Iraq, and for all other peoples of the region whose governments choose to participate.

A fair question often asked of me is: When will the decline curve reverse towards rebirth? I don't know. Decline is not a straight line down and rebirth is not a straight line up. The precise date is hard to fix, but in truth it is not critical.

As a perennial optimist, I believe that the upward slope for this decade began to take shape in the aftermath of Arafat's death. In January 2005, this process began. A new President and government was formed in Palestine, Iraq had an impressive election, Syria began its withdrawal from Lebanon, President Mubarak discussed a new form of elections for Egypt, and Saudi Arabia promised a more open society. Finally, at the Arab League's March meeting in Algiers, plans for a regional economic community -- parallel to the European Union -- were announced, calling for implementation by 2015. Of course, some or all of these promising events can fail.

What has been learned from Oslo more than a decade later, is that the point of reversal must come from within the nations involved not imposed by other powers. Whether it be in the future state of Palestine, Iraq, Afghanistan or elsewhere in the region, war must end before any    shift towards economic integration and recovery can take hold. The lesson of the Marshall Plan was that it succeeded after the battles had terminated and the killing had ceased. This applies today in the Middle East.

Jumpstarting the recovery process with aid from MERP can serve as both a motivator and    catalyst. The recipients of the aid will, by design, allow free trade, free markets, and cross-border cooperation to stamp out tightly-guarded protectionist policies. A recovery plan to energize and commit the senior players in MENACA to unify for economic well-being is far more desirable than the present condition: desperate nations embroiled in violence, terrorism and oppression.

Following the death of Yasir Arafat in November 2004, King Abdullah II of Jordan stated: "For lasting peace, Israel must be fully integrated into the entire region, from Morocco to Yemen." His words project future possibilities for a region of nearly 500 million people longing to provide an improved way of life for their children and grandchildren.

The U.S. must not go it alone. Multilateral cooperation will strengthen rather than weaken the U.S. According to Colin Powell's State Department advisor and confidant Richard N. Haass, history, "is largely determined by the degree to which the major powers of the era can agree on rules of the road ---and impose them on those who reject them."

President Bush must be careful that his U.S. strategies in the broader Middle East do not run roughshod over small nations. Haass argues that democratic reform should, "be handled with sensitivity and perspective....",(by which he implies the U.S. should butt out of other countries affairs.)

A counterrevolution may be in the making. Haass' arguments can become pivotal, "....neither the United States nor anyone else should insist on any single or particular model of democracy or market."

President Bush in May 2005 called for patience in assessing the progress in the Middle East toward democracy, and that it could take years for newly free countries to establish the institutions necessary for stability and prosperity. "No nation in history," he said, "has made the transition from tyranny to a free society without setbacks and false starts....What separates those nations that succeed from those that falter is their progress in establishing free institutions." On May 18, 2005 he announced his proposal to create a new civilian *Active Response Corps* to help newly formed governments build these institutions.

Perhaps the ultimate model for an Islamic common market will be based on the October 3, 2005 meeting of the *First World Islamic Economic Forum*. It called for the establishment of an Islamic common market and floated a series of initiatives to boost business cooperation among Muslim nations.

A declaration was issued at the end of the three-day meeting in Kuala Lumpur and urged the 57 governments of the Organization of the Islamic Conference (OIC) to facilitative trade and business environments. Delegates called for governments to "consider the establishment of an Islamic Free Trade Agreement through regional and sub-regional FTAs in a step-by-step, time-bound process that would ultimately lead to an Islamic common market." The forum gathered over 500 delegates from 44 nations.

Not to be denied an American initiative for the region, in his goal of reform for the area, President Bush has targeted 2013 for launching the *Middle East Free Trade Area*. The precise timing is less important than the call for, and ultimate support towards this economic integration.

# CHAPTER VI

## THE MODEL

"...Contrary to conventional wisdom on both sides of the aisle, the consequences of withdrawal (from Iraq) need not be catastrophic to American interests in the region. Secretary of State Condoleezza Rice; the national security adviser, Steve Hadley; and Gates need to develop a secondary track, simultaneous with a military withdrawal, centered on new economic and diplomatic initiatives in the Middle East to re-establish America's credibility and purpose."

**John Deutch**
**(former Deputy Secretary of Defense)**

The Middle East seems to be in constant flux and turmoil, so it is not surprising that any attempt to resolve the Israeli-Palestinian conflict has, since September 11, 2001, had implications for North Africa, Afghanistan, Pakistan and Central Asia.

President Harry Truman understood there could be no more effective way to stop the spread of Communism than to help rebuild the war-ravaged states of western Europe.

In an admirable attempt to emulate Truman, in words if not thus far in deeds, President Bush delivered a speech in 2002 in which he argued "that militant Islam and other destructive, radical ideologies can be discouraged within Afghanistan only with the building of a safe, functioning civil society." At the time, Bush vowed to lead an international effort to rebuild Afghanistan on the Marshall Plan concept.

The analogy between Afghanistan and Europe is imperfect, for Europe, before World War II, was a set of vastly different countries than Afghanistan. Nations of the European Continent possessed a modern industrial economy, complete with populations trained and equipped for dynamic economic progress.

A plausible and closer parallel to post-1945 Europe was envisioned on June 24, 2002 when President Bush insisted that, "Things must change in the Middle East." Turning to the Palestinian-Israeli conflict, he was borrowing once again from the principles of Marshall when he declared, "Today the Palestinian people live in economic stagnation made worse by official corruption. A Palestinian state will require a vibrant economy where honest enterprise is encouraged by honest government. The United States, the international donor community, and the World Bank stand ready to work with Palestinians on a major project of economic reform and development." Palestinian aid was on the agenda of the White House, with a vision of jobs, border-crossings for employment, and perhaps even eventually, integrated economies.

Just as the Marshall Plan acknowledged the need for closer cross-border trade and business activity between competing states, should a Middle East Recovery Program (MERP) be initiated, movement would have to be decisive towards regional economic integration. Assuredly, this will be difficult. Numerous brakes will need to be applied to ease tensions that derive from clashing cultures, traditions, and economics. Discord and mistrust are likely.

I will not attempt here to point fingers or attach blame for the present conditions in the Arab/Muslim or non-Arab/Muslim world. If the malaise of the Middle East is caused by its resentment over decades of suffering under Western hegemony, people must stop focusing on past injustices and work to ensure a prosperous future.

Some people point to globalization and the selective poverty it has brought as the primary culprit for the Middle East's economic downtrend. Yet there is evidence that globalization has succeeded when lower trade barriers have been put in place. As argued by *The Financial Times* writer Martin Wolf in his book "Why Globalization Works": "Never before have so many people – of so large a proportion of the world's population – enjoyed such large rises in their standard of living." Free trade reduces world suffering, and its contagion needs to spread throughout the Middle East.

The eminent Middle East historian Bernard Lewis, writes that the Middle Eastern "combination of low productivity and high birth rate makes for an unstable mix, and by all indications the Arab countries, in such matters as job creation, education, technology, and productivity, lag ever farther behind the West.... According to United Nations statistics, Israel's per-capita GDP was three and a half times that of Lebanon and Syria, twelve times that of Jordan, and thirteen and a half times that of Egypt."

The Middle East/North Africa/Central Asia
(MENACA) region may not be the poorest on earth, but it
ranks close to the poorest. Only the oil money that flows
through Arab economies belies    the region's underlying
poverty. Half a billion people within its boundaries are its
victims.

With the United States as the innovator and
provider of most of the monies for MERP, poverty could
begin to be eased, if not eradicated. But if the Marshall
Plan teaches us anything, it is that the U.S. must not be seen
in the region as attempting to impose its will on others.

Were MERP to be established, were it to exercise
its charter, were it to encourage cross-border economics,
what can be shared and what steps should be taken to avoid
duplicating the excess production (usually unprofitable
agricultural items) of already deplorable economies? By
necessity, work in each country will require identifying
each nation's international trade policy, encouraging work
with existing key institutions, mastering negotiations
procedures and agreements, and learning to resolve disputes
efficiently and peacefully.    Solutions will be found in
present-day economies and in the yet-to-be-discovered
potential of 28 nations.

Before, during, and following enactment of a
Middle East Recovery Program, regional economic
integration accompanied by free-trade will succeed because
it is the only reasonable alternative. Regional economic
integration can squash the seeds of hate and discontent and
restore optimism for a future dedicated to restrained
neighborliness.

With or without MERP, the incentive to establish
both bilateral and multilateral free trade agreements, and
ultimately an economic community in the region will

provide its own rewards. This first step can be done without a great deal of U.S. aid. (It remains to be seen whether some of the governments in question will be willing to participate with westerners to accomplish their rehabilitation. Some may not.)

Regional economic integration, possibly commencing with a *Jordanian-Israeli-Palestinian Free Trade Agreement (JIPTA)*, may indeed be the most emotional and controversial issue than the acceptance and eventual passage of MERP itself. Initially, a monetary package of recovery aid, akin to MERP, may for many citizens be easier to digest, for there will be funds directed towards heightening living standards, a goal that few could rationally reject.

If, on the other hand, economic integration is instituted before MERP, a significant segment of populations throughout the region might reject the plan outright, afraid that more openness might actually encourage terrorism and biological/ chemical warfare, increase hatred, accelerate migration, and minimize cultural differences. These fears could possibly destroy the nation-building potential of MERP. MERP might be seen as an avalanche of free funding to be spent selfishly within a country's boundaries, free of the responsibility to interface with neighbors who may share the same feelings. Firmly defined borders to contain rather than integrate; to separate rather than interact, might be called for throughout the region.

However, it is important for MENACA countries to consider that were the European Recovery Program to have stalled and were economic integration not pursued over the past five decades, the European Union would probably have required generations or more to achieve its myriad of economic successes.

But time is not on the side of MENACA. MERP can provide the wealth, ideas can be contributed by all, but only cross-border interaction, followed by regional integration will lead to greater stability.

**Figure 1** describes in the simplest model the five levels for a Middle East Community, incorporating entities of the Middle East, North Africa, Central Asia, and Pakistan, Afghanistan and possibly, Turkey. Israel becomes one of the three founding members of the triangle, including Jordan, and the Palestinians.

**Figure 2** alternatively, Iraq replaces Israel (Israel shifts into the Iraq space) as any nation can be substituted with another. (A country whose first initial is not "I" would by necessity dissolve JIPTA as an appropriate acronym.)

**Levels** progressively advance, first with new nations ascending to membership, then with the expansion of integration. For example, at the outset free trade accords that dominate economic transfer and cooperation, and provide for the free movement of goods, capital, and services. Ultimately, as the economic community evolves, new rules may also allow for the free movement of people within the region. Achievement of the latter freedom may take several decades, perhaps even longer, perhaps never.

\* \* \* \* \* \* \* \* \* \* \* \* \* \* \* \* \* \* \* \* \*

# FIGURE 1

## CREATING A MIDDLE EAST COMMUNITY (MEC)

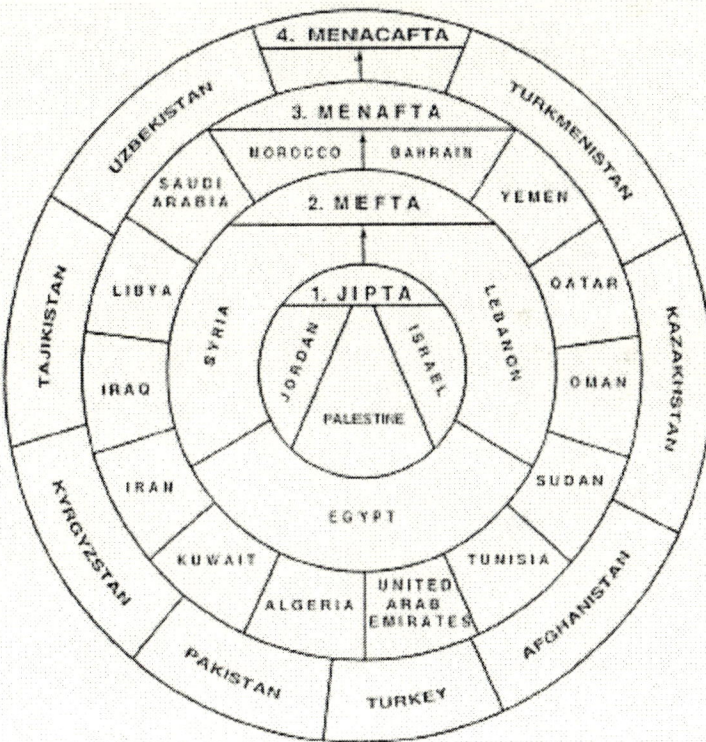

# FIGURE 2

# CREATING A MIDDLE EAST COMMUNITY (MEC)

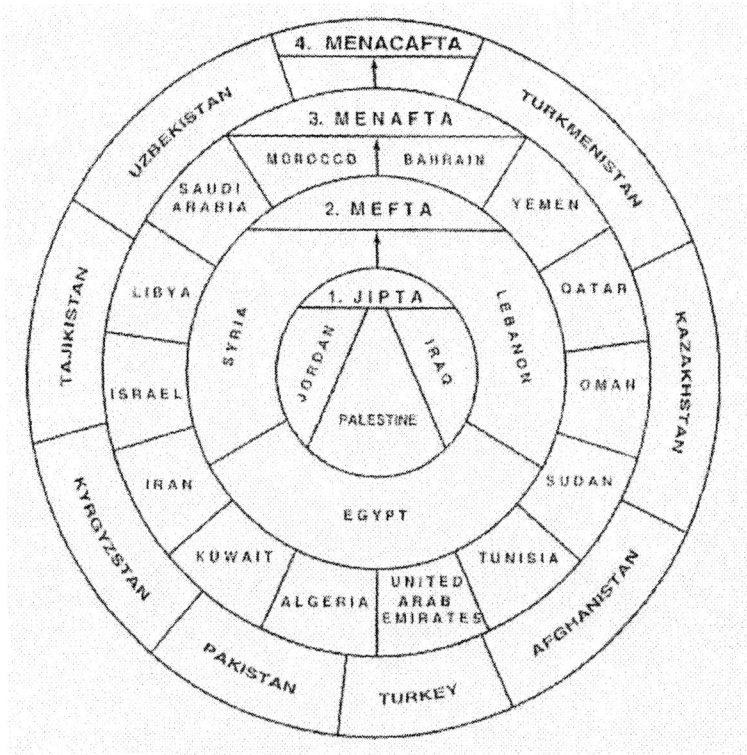

## LEVEL ONE

JIPTA envisions a *Jordanian-Israeli-Palestinian (Free) Trade Agreement* that would function to reduce and ultimately eliminate tariffs and quotas within the "triangle."

JIPTA identifies the first step in the process of bilateral trade (2 nations)- extended to multilateral trade (more than 2 nations.) Commencing a dialogue to materialize into an open trading community of capital, goods, and services between peoples and governments of these three entities can illustrate, to the region and to the world, that interdependence can be strengthened by establishing tariff -free imports and exports.

The PA is evolving its own trade links with the common market in Europe. With time and the creation of a post-Arafat Palestinian state, all of these progressing economic structures, possessing rules of origin and tariff and customs regulations, can combine to serve as the model for a workable and productive JIPTA.

The previously-established (in 1995), but presently inactive Middle East/North Africa Economic Secretariat, based in Rabat, Morocco, could be reactivated and then charged with commencing the process of institution building and governance throughout the region (assuming Morocco becomes a member nation from the extended North African area) to encourage and facilitate others to join in a larger free trade area, and eventually establish a community that someday will stretch its freedoms. (As an alternative to this Secretariat, a new organization can be established in one of the JIPTA states, recommended by this author, in Amman, Jordan. (Headquarters in Israel is unrealistic for political reasons, and Palestine is too fragile and evolving.)   Sub-offices, responsible for discharging rules and regulations of integration, with determined government accountability, will be created in each new member nation, all reporting to the home office.

## LEVEL TWO

The ascendance of other contiguous nations to JIPTA countries, that is Lebanon, Syria, and Egypt, could create the *Middle East Free Trade Agreement (MEFTA)*. MEFTA would be established once three or more national bodies within the broader Middle East region form trade accords with each other. It would encourage and administer the free movement of capital, goods, and services, but not people, the latter reserved for the institutional creation of a community should that come to pass.

## LEVEL THREE

A *Middle East/North Africa Community (MENAC)* would emerge from a purely economic relationship (then hopefully, but not necessarily, social and political relationships). Although an institutional structure could begin, as with the formation of a Secretariat, it is best to await a systematic trade agreement with at least three countries, such as Jordan-Israel-Palestine. Once the "triangle" is committed to creating an effective model for the free movement of capital, goods, and services, a mechanism for governance and regulation for a larger entity would be required.

With as many as 20 nations, "size" will inevitably become a challenge and systematic organizational life will be urgently needed. Forms of governance, standardization of procedures, centralized rules and regulations, etc., will become mandatory to minimize chaos and the potential for inertia.

Ascension of some of the countries added to the original three, or perhaps six, will be justified as proof of progress as economic growth becomes evident among the members of the founding nations.

**LEVEL FOUR**

With potential membership set at 28 nations, a *Middle East/North Africa/Central Asia Free Trade Agreement* would be created *(MENACAFTA)*. In the end, at least in theory, were all the countries to join, with a combined population exceeding one-half billion people, MENACAFTA would test the forces of the free movement of capital, services, and goods. As nations beyond the region agree to participate in trade accords with Middle East Free Trade Agreement (MEFTA) countries, a change would be required: renaming the authority or secretariat MEFTA, to recognize inclusion of a non-Middle East MEFTA, change would be required: renaming the authority or secretariat MEFTA, to recognize inclusion of non-Middle East members. Each new member would enjoy equal rights.

It would be naïve to assume an early membership of 28 countries. It took the European Union about forty-eight years to go from its founding Treaty of six nations, to its current 27 nations, even though most of the nations possessed numerous common - characteristics. This overlap will not be the case with MEC.

*   *   *   *   *   *   *   *   *   *   *

Progress in fulfilling these expectations of regional cooperation will require:

.   *CONSCIENCE*: Individual conscience must be the guiding light for citizens of MEC. Personal notions of right and wrong and how best to fulfill dreams of freedom and prosperity shall hold high value in determining requirements of the community. Inevitably, conflicts between society at large and individuals will evolve. Individual citizens should not be pounced upon by any regulation or directive coming from officials. Acceptance will evolve constructively and productively only when openly debated and understood. The final decision factor will be individual conscience, which can counter the needs of society, but which must be protected and be permitted to express itself. Individuality within the group must be supreme. Others must not impose a value system that will be counterproductive and create a lack of goodwill. Individuals, when confronted by others, could cause guilt and rapprochement among members of the group, who tomorrow become the next oppressed individual.

.   *CONSENT*: Popular consent will be a critical force in sustaining interest in the goals of MEC. It is imperative that a permanent communication network be open to the citizenry, not merely to officials of the government and politicians serving its institutions. Officials who attempt to rush veiled decisions past its citizens may initially succeed, but such action will eventually return to haunt them. Consent to govern is the only winning avenue to change, short of revolution, which requires coercion.

.   *CONFIDENCE:*   Individual confidence is the prerequisite for a successful MEC, for economic growth, for upgraded social welfare programs, for political security, and for the maintenance of cultural sovereignty. But confidence is not an inherent right -- it must be earned through clear thinking and a willingness to change, with the continuous cycles to follow.

The ultimate goal is economic unification founded on a single governmental authority and administrative system. Existing problems can best be mastered when potential MEC nations move forward along the paths that lead them to unity. Many people take the view that without integration, it will not be possible to secure peace, democracy, law and justice, economic prosperity and social security, and to guarantee them for the future. Unemployment, inflation, and inadequate growth have long stopped being merely national problems; nor can they be resolved at national levels. Through the power of unification at the community, these barriers can be overcome. There is no greater motivation for MEC unification than the desire for peace.

\* \* \* \* \* \* \* \* \* \*

For JIPTA, and later other regional free trade agreements (FTAs) to become attractive, the following primary issues must be addressed:

A potential thorny problem is the low value-added economy in the Palestinian Authority (and undoubtedly also the Central Asian nations, Pakistan, and Afghanistan). Under JIPTA, free trade would only apply to goods that have a minimum share of domestic content – made in a specific country - (such as 40 percent.) Trade preferences given to Israel, in which the share of domestic value-added in goods is large, could be much more valuable than those accorded to the West Bank and Gaza, where only a few such goods exist. This may not seem problematic for several traditional exports (such as agriculture and shoes) where the share of domestic value-added is large. In textiles, however, some form of derogation would be needed.

JIPTA has the same weakness as the current system with respect to border closures. To reduce this problem will entail reducing special privileges accorded to Israel. This can be done without losing access to the Israeli market by reducing the tariffs that apply to third parties. If tariffs are set to zero, free trade with Israel would not entail any costly preferences. Indeed, there would no longer be a preferential relation.

JIPTA would remove tariffs on third parties, whose prices would then come under the influence of lobby (pressure) groups, with potentially very high costs to consumers. One solution is to use some commitment mechanism to bind these rates. The World Trade Organization provides such mechanisms through potential trade agreements with other parties (in particular, the US, the EU, and other Arab countries) or by establishing free trade zones.

Moving to JIPTA would involve renegotiating the Paris Economic Agreement between Israel and Palestine.

In the post-Arafat era, the issues of who controls Jerusalem, settlements in the Palestinian Authority, and the geographical separation of the West Bank and Gaza complicates such an economic agreement.

*     *     *     *     *     *     *     *     *     *

Throughout the twentieth century, countries in the Middle East have been involved in conflict, especially but not exclusively with Israel.

A tightly developed, structured policy for JIPTA/MEFTA/MENAFTA/MENACAFTA and ultimately MEC, will mean the creation of a Community which will simultaneously evolve the centerpiece into a framework of peace in the region rendering any war between participating countries improbable.

In the context of the MEC, a stable economic order can be created within the region, and through joint Community efforts of an international economic policy, performance of the regional national economies will contribute to social justice in the nations of the area. With internal cohesion, these states can assert their political and economic independence from the rest of the world. They can win back influence in the globe and can gain a proper place in the brotherhood of nations.

## THE MIDDLE EAST COMMUNITY TREATY

The foundation and support for MEC rests with its Treaty, to be negotiated by its founding members. By design, it should be general and brief, allowing the exceptional issues to be dealt with later by a predetermined governing body, thereby not restricting future opportunities by minimizing flexibility or attending to a larger audience than the immediate situation calls for.

In developing a final treaty, creators of this document must take into account existing national policies, work effectively with existing institutions, negotiate agreements and work to resolve evolving disputes.

The Treaty, once completed and signed, with its lofty status will have primacy over any other structural or legislative detail, including separately negotiated trade alliances. Challenges to the treaty and its obligations will be addressed by a Court of Justice, which will rule in specific cases and interpret law for the future. Amendments will flow, as they should, but the Treaty, the Constitution of the Middle East Community, should remain the guiding light of MEC. The Constitution should strengthen the commitment to regional security; eliminate all forms of terrorist threats; encourage greater  conflict containment; improve health, housing, and educational opportunities; seek a rising standard of living; and promote equal opportunity for all. The Treaty needs to emphasize that wherever people live within artificially-created borders, neighbors on the other side of the boundary do indeed enrich community life, no matter what their past history or animosities.

(Rejection of the proposed EU Constitution by France and The Netherlands in the spring 2005 raises questions of comparison. To begin with, I believe it was a terrible mistake to call these suggestions for altering the original Treaty of Rome a "constitution." It was ill-advised and inappropriate. More importantly, an EU constitution coming before its citizens-whether by referendum or parliament-45 years after its organizational founding was a mistake. The MEC proposed constitution will be introduced at the very outset, during a period of optimism and high-hope.)

MEC will become the test-run for the larger community, an agreement modest enough to make experimentation more manageable at the outset. In addition, all trade accords, such as JIPTA, should focus on unique characteristics for relationships involving specific nations and identify in advance  many, if not most, of the elements for the concluding Treaty.

Creating a larger entity by linking up multiple countries will afford freedom of movement beyond national borders. This means, in particular, freedom of movement for workers to purchase and/or sell needed services, goods, and capital.

These fundamental freedoms under a founding MEC Treaty will guarantee entrepreneurs freedom of decision-making, and workers freedom to choose their place of work (but with no guarantee of a job offer), and consumers the freedom of choice between the greatest possible variety of products. Freedom of competition will allow entrepreneurs to offer their goods and services to an incomparably wider pool of potential consumers. People can seek work and change their place of employment according to their own needs and interests throughout the entire territory of the Community. Consumers would be able to choose the cheapest and best products from the far-greater wealth of goods that will result from increased competition.

## NOT A SOCIAL CONTRACT

In the historical usage of the phrase, a "social contract" would be controversial in MEC. Under the traditional principles of a social contract, the individual is obligated to alienate himself, with all rights and freedoms surrendered to the greater society.

MEC must constantly be on the alert to avoid this sort of social contract, which would be counterproductive and would violate the primary and critical needs of all citizens. What may be considered good for society may not be good for the individual. Thus, each person has a responsibility to argue and defend that which he considers sound and productive in fulfilling one's interests and needs, as long as they do not impinge on the rights of others, nor adversely affect the nation's well-being. No one should be coerced by any form of authoritarian government even if he is misdirected or behaving as a child. With personal freedom comes personal responsibility.

The creation of a regional trade agreement and also a treaty should reflect the will of its people. This subtle variable can play the greatest role in how successful nations develop as they attempt to coordinate their goals and objectives. For nations of MEC, a will is needed to take risks, by individuals and governments; both by regional leadership and the collective community. People long suspicious, with a state-dominated approach to day-to-day living will be hard-pressed to evolve a self-generated motivation to join the market economy. The drive, the intensity, the get-up-and-go mentality that has been a boon to capitalist countries the world over may flourish throughout the MEC, given a chance.

Attitudes, by way of education and through mass communication must be reexamined over and over again. Old attitudes must be tested for bias, and resistance and complacency must be overthrown if the citizens of the Middle East are to be successful in pursuing economic prosperity. The Tsdreaty will influence those attitudes. Without the direction of a treaty, management of MEC would only stir resentment and heighten tension.

Once the people of a nation make the commitment to accept the treaty via the mechanism of a referendum, and to move in the direction of MEC, educational programs will be needed to reach people throughout the region, preparing them for the tradeoffs that will follow, many of which will be difficult, especially at first. Only then can more decisive steps achieve a higher living standard for all.

A fundamental value of the MEC Treaty must be provisions for economic security and nonviolence. The Treaty must render the future predictable for community citizens and their institutions.

Although bureaucrats would first create mini-rules as found in trade accords, and evaluate the results of their actions before jumping ahead towards a full-fledged treaty, that process might tear at the heart of community support. It would be best to make some inappropriate, or even poor, judgments in the initial version and come back with future amendments than to prolong the debate for years.

Any Treaty will be binding. It shall serve all members equally and be the organizational foundation, the constitution bearing witness to all decisions, and be the basis for all interpretations. Initially, it shall possess Objectives, Activities, and be Non-discriminatory. A possible scenario on these proposed, primary subjects might be:

### I - *Objectives*

The Community will establish a host of trade accords and a common market, and progressively, bring together the economic policies of member nations to promote a harmonious development of economic activities throughout the Middle East Community. The Community should also pursue a judicious and balanced expansion of membership, increased stability, and an accelerated raising of the standard of living as well as closer relationships among the countries belonging to it.

### II - *Activities*

To achieve the objectives of the Middle East Community, activities shall include, as provided in the Treaty:

1. The elimination of customs duties and of financial restrictions on the import and export of goods among member nations, and of all other measures having equivalent effect;

2. The establishment of a common customs tariff and of a common commercial policy towards nations outside the Middle East Community;

3. The abolition of obstacles to the freedom of movement, initially of goods, services, and capital, with a longer-

term objective to include people, among the member nations;

4. The adoption of common and coordinated policies in the spheres of agriculture, transport, water, energy, health, education, monetary policy, tourism, research and development, goods standards, and so on;

5. The institution of a system ensuring that competition in the common market is not distorted;

6. The application of procedures by which the economic policies of member nations can be coordinated and disequilibria in their internal and external balance of payments remedied;

7. The development of a common set of laws of member nations to the extent required for the proper functioning of the common market;

8. The creation and funding of a permanent Middle East Community Social Fund in order to improve employment opportunities for workers and to contribute to the raising of their standard of living;

9. The establishment of a permanent Middle East Community Development Bank to facilitate the economic expansion of the Community by opening up fresh resources;

10. The association of overseas nations and territories in order to increase trade and to promote joint economic and social development.

### III - *Non - discrimination*

Within the scope of application of the Treaty, and without prejudice to any special provisions contained therein, any discrimination against people, goods, capital and/or services on the grounds of nationality and/or religious preference, shall be prohibited.

*    *    *    *    *    *    *    *    *    *

There should be no threat to the future of the nation-state with the formation of a Middle East Community Treaty. Countries are more sophisticated than ever in their formation with a sense of political and social purpose. Under the Treaty, the only initial significant shift will be the surrendering of some sovereignty of a nation's economic independence; other social and political concerns may follow. In the end, the nation-state will survive and prosper.

Richard Haass, President of the Council on Foreign Relations, effectively deals with the electrically charged issue of sovereign rights. He points out that a state qualifies as sovereign if it means to enjoy supreme political authority and a monopoly on the legitimate use of force within its borders; is able to control its borders and regulate what goes in and out of its country; is free to adopt the foreign and domestic policies it wants; and is recognized as sovereign by its peers. In MEC considerations, this criteria will be used.

In addition, no organizational structure can better deal with the governments of large societies within their boundaries than an economic community. It has been and it shall remain the primary objective of global trade, defense, and internationalism, to have nations negotiate, unite, and break apart, all based on needs and desires of its citizens and the parties in control of the government. The nation-state model works and should be perpetuated.

This Treaty creates a level of solidarity in the definition of freedom, for the continuing exercise of freedom by some is sometimes lost at the expense of others. For this reason, if the MEC Treaty is to endure, it must always recognize the solidarity of its members as a fundamental principle, and share both the advantages and the burdens equally and justly among its members.

The Treaty should fulfill the needs of a broad membership of the contiguous nations touching the boundaries of Israel and beyond. These concepts can be applied to two or more nations and even expanded away from the traditionally defined lines of geography of the Middle East.

Obviously, the larger the membership base the greater the need to create the organizational institutions of the Court, Secretariat, and so forth. In its infancy, alternative institutions will have to be established, but a long-term commitment should involve a full-fledged superstructure, that bows to subsidiarity - when feasible, activities controlled by sovereign nations - to minimize the growth and power of empire-building and empire-controlling.

## STRUCTURE OF THE MIDDLE EAST COMMUNITY

If the various free-trade agreements and the MEC institution are not of a people, as well as for it, you have at best a useless community bureaucracy, and at worst a dictatorship of the technocratic elite. Governments of the Community's individual nations and the Community itself, must move closer to the people, not further away from them.

Nations of the MEC should have respect for the separation of powers among the branches of government, and the full development of an independent judiciary. Historically, there remain significant problems in this area, especially in some Middle Eastern nations where the judiciary owes too much of its power and presence to the executive branch of government. A weak legislature and judiciary only encourages intrusion, by non-supporters, into the process of democracy and harms the prospect for consolidating political and economic liberty.

The model for a MEC structure might come from the European Union (EU), one that has been studied, put into practice, and revised numerous times over the decades. While not all EU tests and experiences have been successful (or are applicable to the MEC); while ocean-sized differences urge caution in adapting their regulations and structure; while world changes necessitate new strategies indicating that not all is efficient, it would also be foolhardy to discard the model without sound reason, for decades of insight can save this regional bloc considerable time and money.

*   *   *   *   *   *   *   *   *   *   *   *   *

Although the North American Free Trade Agreement (NAFTA) is a simpler model, it failed (by design) to prepare for economic efforts beyond free-trade accords, as well as other equally critical interactions of a social and political nature. Arguably, however, NAFTA is a sound template for the formation of JIPTA and other regional free trade accords, as a first step towards MEC. Similarly, JIPTA is a trade accord for three entities, and although the comparisons may be few, both JIPTA and NAFTA represent economies of disproportion. Imagine the enormity of the GDPs of Israel and the U.S., each sitting on a border with a third-level economy, Palestine and Mexico, respectively.

NAFTA, which possesses many of the principles of the European Union, implanted innovative concepts never before witnessed in any trade or economic treaty. For example, the supplemental (side) agreements negotiated at the last moment to ensure Congressional passage introduced labor and environmental cooperation requirements, unique in global negotiations.

The U.S.-Jordan Free Trade Agreement signed in September 2001 is the first trade treaty to incorporate issues of environment and worker rights at the outset of negotiations, as contrasted with NAFTA, which added such issues as supplemental items. (The US-Jordan FTA may well be the model for the framework of the JIPTA/MEFTA/MENAFTA/ and MENACAFTA process.) Jordan in 2003 exported about $900 million in goods to the U.S., up from virtually nothing five years ago.

Another sign of the post-Arafat improvement in relations was the December 2004 signing of a free trade accord between Egypt, Israel, and the United States. It allows for the duty-free import of certain Egyptian goods by American buyers, such as cotton underwear and knit shirts and pants, as long as the items contain some Israeli input.

This agreement, perhaps a significant model for future efforts of cross-border trade with Middle East nations, stipulates that all Egyptian goods produced initially within seven specific "qualified industrial zones" will be exempt from American import tariffs as long as they contain at least 11.7 percent Israeli content, such as buttons or zippers for Egyptian textiles.

The result of this powerful trade effort is significant and must not be underestimated. The textile industry in Egypt employs a million people and accounts for more than one quarter of all industrial production. The U.S. takes half of Egypt's textile exports -- $470 million in 2003, and that number should triple with this agreement. The accord is expected to create 250,000 jobs each year.

## BEFORE STARTING

*Beware of Pyramid Building*

There were about 18,000 bureaucrats within the European Union before the ascendance of 10 new countries in May 2004, overly busy with, meetings, and the passage of copious rules and regulations, many beyond need. MEC must avoid uncontrolled growth of personnel. Expansion for the sake of filling a vacuum and/or in efforts to produce accountability could conceivably lead to disillusionment and, hence, be a threat to the accord's purpose and long-term existence.

The number of employees must be kept to a minimum (I noticed upon my first visit to the Rabat, Morocco-based MENA Secretariat in 1995, that it was operational with a staff of only four) with increases in personnel to be rigorously justified. Ministers, as issues become more hotly contested, will be called forward to meet and debate. The number of sessions must be pertinent and not scheduled simply for show. Legislation will be needed and regulations and directives will be required. But they should be concise, relevant, professional, and free from rancor. The language for these laws shall be kept parsimonious, thus enabling all literate people to comprehend their intent.

Those responsible within the MEC should work hard to defray costs and sustain only a skeleton of manpower when possible. Frugality is far superior to waste; it is an approach that commands respect and honor.

*Beware of Excessive Lobbying*

Lobbying may be ignored by leaders as the MEC rushes through its formative years, but it nevertheless will be there, dutifully seeking ways to service special-interest groups.

Effort must be expended to guarantee that any rapid proliferation of special-interest lobbying does not lead to political paralysis. Lobbying cannot be allowed to disrupt any of the MEC's functions. Knowledgeable advocacy by a wide range of public and private interest groups can be a valuable tool for the MEC, if properly handled.

Since a primary goal of the Treaty will be to make goods and services more competitive in world markets, community officials are going to be receptive to informed opinions from outside, including corporations and trade associations.    Diverse viewpoints can provide valuable insights into a proposal's merits as well as its potential impacts on the competitive positions of Community businesses.

Lobbying will be considered a natural extension of community operations. Lobbying may be well suited to the MEC's extremely fluid political environment, which probably will be characterized by a multitude of competing ideologies and interest groups, and a constantly shifting pattern of institutional alliances and rivalries.

## THE HOUSE THAT MERP HELPED BUILD

In the end, a structure of governance should evolve out of the MEC process. The institutions of MEC might include: a high authority, such as a Secretariat; a final decision-making body, The Council of Ministers; a primary body to create rules, regulations and law, with representatives chosen from the populace and based on open and free elections, The Parliament or Congress; a body to interpret legal order, The Court of Justice; and a watchdog of Community funds, The Court of Auditors; and local Centers composed of functional operating units covering the activities of the Community.

## CENTERS OF THE COMMUNITY

Functional operating units, or Centers, will cover a full-range of activities for the Community and will eventually be spread across participating member nations. It can be assumed that a designated responsibility will be more attractive to some nations than others. Therefore, preference of assignment should be based, when possible on strengths of request for housing the center in a particular country. (It should be obvious that headquartering a Center in a stated nation does not imply favoritism towards that nation or its people.)

As free-trade agreements and MEC unfolds, these Centers will take on their own life, with directors reporting to the President of the Secretariat. In addition, the evolution of these Centers will be determined by recommendations made by the Council of Ministers and the Parliament (Congress) to the Secretariat. Ideally, no country will be home to more than one Center, but this may not be practical during the formative years of the Community as initially, there may be far more Centers than participating nations. At all times, each Center will have an executive committee with representation from every member nation. Suggested Centers are:

Agriculture - providing support and equity programs, research and development, and irrigation;

Banking and Financial Services - cross-border banking, provisions for loans, securities, investment strategies;

Telecommunications - planning and development of enhanced networks and professional training programs;

Research and Development - regional technology plan, regional laboratories for the advancement of science;

Energy and Environment - plans for environmental impact in building power stations, pipelines, and electric grids, etc;

Education - upgrading quality of regional education;

Standards - dealing with barriers toward regional usage;

Health and Housing - border controls on animal and plant products, hospitalization facilities, and pursuit of adequate housing;

Industrial Cooperation and Trade - encouraging cross-border activities, and joint-projects with reduced government involvement;

Water and Desertification - desalination, water-sector training, enhancing water data, waste-water treatment, and desertification projects;

Transportation - developing regional upgrades in infrastructure of roads, ports, railways, and air transport;

Tourism and Culture - efforts at regional development and sharing of tourism and culture programs;

Social Rights - protecting the needs of workers, refugees, men and women, and children; and

Security and Terrorism - confronting nations, leaders, and perpetrators with direct punishment for terrorist and biological/chemical/nuclear attacks.

The governance and structure of any large body must eventually come to grips with the ethnic and other differing characteristics of its population. One area where this often appears to be dramatized is in the lack of shared representation. Excluding people, for whatever reasons, because of race, religion, nationality, or other irrelevant background factors, should not be tolerated within the MEC.

Governance must be open to all interested and qualified people -- male or female, and not be restricted to the wealthy or elitists. Perpetuation of past errors only comes back to haunt the oppressors. Due consideration must be given throughout the Community institutions to the sharing of responsibility by differing forces within the population. All voices should be heard and represented. (Recall that the *Arab Development Report (2002,2003,2004)*, and others, show that women remained locked out of professional opportunities.)

As matters presently exist, but more so as borders eventually open to permit the freedom of movement of goods, services, and capital, the MEC's legal system must anticipate how ethnic and religious bias can sweep a nation, and how government accountability in the discharge of responsibility, especially as to the distribution of funding, must be carefully monitored. Educational programs will also be needed to teach people that differences represent a welcome challenge and not an automatic threat. Racial and religious tolerance must be on everyone's agenda.

Appropriately, suggestions and ideas will have to be negotiated by the founding nations of the Community. The "Why" questions must be answered, but the answer to the "How" question is the structure of the Community. "How" represents the mechanism, the means by which the success and failures of the Middle East Community will ultimately be measured.

MERP represents the vehicle for commencing sound, productive, and competently institutionalized and governed free trade accords that could lead to a prosperous, regional economic community of more than one-half a billion people.

The September 11, 2001 atrocity is now behind us. Yasir Arafat and Ariel Sharon are gone. George W. Bush will be President until January 2008 and he promises to support and prepare for a Palestinian state before leaving office.

One year before the end of World War II, leaders from Europe met in Bretton Woods, New Hampshire to plan a future continent of industrialization and economic development. This conference anticipating a future of great need outlined the framework of the World Bank, the International Monetary Fund, the General Agreement on Tariffs and Trade, and much more. A similar approach should be placed on the drawing board even before the end of the hostilities in the Middle East.

The clock ticks on and time may not favor the Middle East. Its nations cannot afford to wait much longer to modify, and then implement the elusive but still appropriate opportunity, the "Road-Map" for cooperation.

Victor Hugo said: "The Future has many names; For the weak it is unattainable; For the fearful it is unknown; For the bold it is opportunity."

# CHAPTER VII

## PRESENT AT THE CREATION

**"The only prize in the end that really matters is the prize of peace we must give to the children of the Middle East."**

**Bill Clinton**

Future events in the Middle East, North Africa and Central Asia are impossible to predict, made even more foreboding by the complexities of the post-September 11, 2001 world. The wars in Afghanistan and then Iraq; the terrorist bombings in Madrid and London; the passing of Yasir Arafat and Ariel Sharon; the Palestinian parliament election of Hamas, the selection of Ehud Olmert as Israel's new prime minister, and the 2006 invasion of Lebanon, are all recent, dramatic events impacting the Middle East.

We are witnesses to the extensive poverty spread across the Middle East, intertwined with injustices, corruption and massive movements of frightened refugees in an area that time seems to have passed by.

The war against terror now has a front in the Middle East (Iraq) and new personalities, new challenges, new issues, and new battles remain to be fought -- both militarily and economically. The next step calls for rehabilitation and reconstruction as means to help reduce the flames of hate. On the front-burner must be the implementation of a broad recovery program designed by the widest coalition possible. What most Arab specialists already knew has now been formally confirmed by "a group of distinguished Arab intellectuals" -- that only an "unbiased, objective analysis" can assist the "Arab peoples and policy-makers in search of a bright future."

The United Nations Development Program (UNDP) along with the *Arab Fund for Economic and Social Development* pinpointed the three powerful reasons the Arab world remains in trouble: (1) the lack of freedom for citizens to speak, innovate, and affect political life; (2) a failure to allow proper women's rights; and (3) a lack of quality education. The UN's multiple reports were equally powerful and direct.

With 22 Arab League nations claiming nearly 300 million people and growing (by the year 2020 their population is projected to be in excess of 410 million), and with regional GDP on the decline, poverty will spread and illiteracy remains high, while the rest of the world moves forward towards a higher living standard. (Presently, Spain's gross domestic product is greater than that of the combined Arab countries.) A massive international aid package must urgently be provided that can begin to reverse this trend.

A 2005 U.S. Census Bureau report challenges and picks away at the often repeated claim that the Arab world is, by its very nature and culture, different from the western world and the United States in particular. This is a myth.

Based on data collected for the year 2000, people of Arab descent living in the U.S. are better educated and wealthier than the average American of non-Arab descent. The Census found that Arab-Americans are better educated and wealthier than Americans in general.

Twenty-four percent of all U.S. citizens hold college degrees, while 41 percent of Arab-Americans are college graduates. The median annual income of an Arab-American family living in the U.S. is $53,300, or 4.6 percent higher than the figures for all other American families. Forty-two percent of people of Arab descent in the U.S. work as managers or professionals while the overall average is 34 percent.

In the past 20 years, no region besides sub-Saharan Africa has seen income per person grow as slowly as the Middle East. At the current rate, it will take the average Arab living there 140 years to double his or her income. U.S. and European citizens double their income every 10 years.

The world's wealthiest nations – the Group of 8 - formally agreed on June 11, 2005 to cancel at least $40 billion of debt owed to international agencies by the world's poorest lands. Now attention can focus on how these countries can expand their economies and produce more jobs. As Richard Haass points out: "Trade also brings all the countries of the world into a web of relationships that are mutually advantageous economically. Trade has an impact on integration that goes beyond the economic."

## The Israeli-Palestinian Conflict Remains a Central Issue

Were nations encircling Israel prepared to sign on to an economic recovery plan, accompanied by a non-aggression pact with Israel, Congress and President Bush would surely be encouraged to respond with financial assistance via MERP. (We should remind ourselves that the October 30, 1991 Madrid Conference, the forerunner to the Oslo Accords, was the product of intensive diplomatic efforts carried out in the region immediately following the Gulf War. It was initiated by President George H.W. Bush.)

Unfortunately, dreams of better times for the Palestinians, encouraged by the signing of the Oslo Accord in 1993, were largely shattered after the failure of the Camp David talks at the end of the Clinton Administration in December 2000. Expectations of an economic rebirth throughout the West Bank and Gaza have evaporated. Indeed, conditions are worse in 2007 than they were in the 1990s, and civil war encircles President Abbass.

Hope has turned to hopelessness. The bright light is to be found in the post-Arafat era. The rushing in by world states to support a new leadership and provide seed monies to the Palestinians (the U.S. soon after Arafat's death and before the PLO January 9, 2005 election promised an aid allotment of $20 million.)

Rather than continuing to harp on a failed Oslo, it is imperative that future movements and recommendations be linked to the realities of the Middle East and the greater region.

Exacerbating the situation is the ruinous violence that began in late 2000 and continues well into 2007. The problem is that the perceptions of justice and compromise differ considerably, sometimes radically, based on history, culture, religion. Trust is at an all-time low. Inevitably, and the sooner the better, the Middle East, must exhaust itself and seek closure, not of its borders, but of its latest horrific, chapter of violence and confrontation.

During his second term as Prime Minister of Israel, which began in January 2003, the late Ariel Sharon, with considerable engagement from President George W. Bush, the United Nations, the European Union, and Russia have sought the means to heat up meaningful deliberations for too long deferred.

As this author sees it, the U.S. will continue to play the primary role in global leadership, albeit sharing it with others. The U. S. may no longer command the prestigious seat as the "honest broker." It has worn thin and others await the chance to emerge as the new mediators searching for the correct fix. There will also be a formula to move forward with financial assistance, all intended to protect the stability of the region, and consequently, the rest of the world.

Others may also offer some aid, but as promised by the re-elected President Bush, he claims to be prepared to move swiftly. The window of opportunity, open briefly, can provide the avenue towards a permanent finale to this crisis of long-standing. The United States can steer the antagonists to end a sad chapter in their tumultuous history by showing that it will commit significant monies of assistance to the region. A Palestinian state will be created in the near future and monies will be forthcoming to support this venture.

## The promise of peace accords with hopes for financial assistance

The Marshall Plan was conceived as an act of humanity and as a strategy to sustain democracy in Western Europe. For its day, it was an expensive, ingenious program of $17 billion (only $13.3 billion was used) that accomplished its objectives.

With only two Arab nations, Egypt and Jordan, having peace treaties with Israel, much work remains to be done. Efforts to return the region to a once glorious past, a past with a splendid history, rich culture, and prosperity, hinge on a negotiated conclusion of hostilities between the governments of the Israelis and the Palestinians. With the Madrid and Oslo meetings of the early 1990s, most of the promises of initial financial aid have been fulfilled, though to middling success. More is coming. The world is determined to play its role, with the U. S. taking a leadership position to deliver the monies to serve as the glue for both short- and long-term stability.

## The Middle East Recovery Program process

MERP will be the world's second most generous regional aid effort (the first was the 1948 Marshall Plan). It will be created to ensure an end to conflict and the resulting misery, to provide the institutional structure and governance for its own evolution, to create successful models and forms of regional economic integration, to share long-term possibilities, and to resettle and compensate refugees and those expelled from their homelands. Win-win situations are on the horizon, once the benefits to the greater societies are understood and supported.

The Marshall Plan, in its formal three-years of existence, identified the venue for rebuilding, reconstruction, and resurrection. It contains lessons for contemporary policy makers. A Middle East Recovery Program, envisioned by the few, voted upon by the many, and carried out by a well-trained and dedicated body of professionals, will reach out to millions awaiting the chance to fulfill their dreams and destinies.

**Participation from nations of the Middle East, North Africa, Central Asia, Pakistan, Afghanistan, and possibly Turkey**

There will be a call to assemble MENACA countries. At a summit of leaders, surrounded by experts and advisors, the responsibility will be laid out to help those who would attempt to help themselves. The models from histories past shall be reviewed, including the wise counsel of Jean Monnet, Harry S Truman, George C. Marshall, all to interact with the visionaries of the present MENACA. The hushed chambers will applaud the gallant heroes who demonstrate their commitment to the Middle East, to a preservation of culture and religion, and to the crossing of borders in peace.

What may be considered naïve or untested by some critics will find a larger audience willing to explore multiple options and models so that front page headlines may one day shift from coverage of destruction to descriptions of stability and development.

**An extensive review of national needs and national contribution**

The summit gathering will deliver homework to the support staffs of the participating countries. They in turn, with forms, outlines, and surveys in hand, will identify existing national needs and resources within their boundaries, along with the necessary supportive data. At all times, counsel will be provided by Washington to guide these decision-makers towards uniformity. A business plan of usage and monitoring will be sought and found.

**Compensating and repatriating Palestinian refugees, funding Israeli settlers leaving the West Bank/Gaza, compensating Israeli Jews for confiscated properties**

It is estimated that some 600,000 Arabs left Israel in 1948 when war started. It is also believed that more than 600,000 Jews were driven from their homes in Arab countries. However, it is mandatory that no cross-trading should occur with one payment to a Jew subtracting for one payment for a Palestinian, or vice-versa. Each case must be evaluated on its own merit.

Certainly, any resolution of this enormous and complex issue, will require huge sums of money. To aid refugees and displaced persons, institutions must be created to move the process forward. Consequently, it can be expected that the MERP Act could include major funds for the noble efforts herein mentioned.

**Qualifying for assistance**

The mechanism can be outlined, first by studying the forms for information and compliance, as submitted to Congressional committees that were involved in the European Recovery Program. This is certainly a monumental task, but needed. They then should be adjusted and revised to meet current needs.

Recommended forms must be circulated to all interested parties, whether they initially qualify or not. Copies should be freely offered to interested nations and agencies of any government to enable the world's bystanders to witness history in the making. Most, if not all sessions of inquiry and study will be transparent, with government accountability, as well as open to cameras and the media.

A series of reports will be prepared for both the U.S. Senate and House of Representatives. Subcommittees charged with these responsibilities will deliver testimony when requested, will hold internal and external meetings to share progress and information, and will prepare final reports for the President.

### A Bill prepared by the President of the United States

The President will have the responsibility for steering the Bill through Congress, all in preparation of testimony, debate, alterations, final vote, and hopefully, passage of legislation creating the Middle East Recovery Program Act.

Working with counsel, advisors and other appropriate committees and specialists, a Bill following Congressional guidelines will be compiled to enter the channels on the way to a vote in Congress.

### Hearings before the U.S. Senate and U.S. House

Hearings will be held by appropriate committees in both the U.S. Senate and House of Representatives. Testimony will be taken, recommendations offered, and compromises made for a final version of the Bill.

### Revision, preparation of final legislation, vote of Congress, and President's signature

Following revisions and required changes from both the Senate and House of Representatives, the final draft will be made, and at the appropriate time, presented for formal debate, vote in Congress, and a Presidential signature.

**Institutionalizing Congressional findings, along with the Administrator and key officials, in the U.S. and the MENACA region**

Once enacted, the Presidential candidate for administrator should be announced. Facilities and the hiring of personnel shall go forward. Special care must be given to the choice of an Assistant Administrator and representatives in the Middle East Community headquarters, and other appointments in nations where aid and project development is to be discharged.

**International cooperation will be sought as partners, including wealthy nations from around the globe**

Unilateralism is no longer affordable, nor desirable. As a guiding spirit, once US Congressional approval is achieved, additional funding will be sought from countries able and willing to participate in what will be the largest humanitarian assistance program in history. Once achieved nation by nation, or via efforts of the United Nations, the sharing of decision-making will be essential, to be negotiated, but in great part determined by the percentage of financial contribution to the total effort.

**Initial funds to be released with transparency and with accounting procedures established, all monitored**

It will be essential that all funds have an accountable audit trail, with full entry of expenditures, listed and reviewed. A timetable and calendar of events for each nation are to be presented on a continuous and evolving basis to the Administrator, who will, along with his advisory groups, decide on the merits and costs of the projects. Approval must be made by the Administrator, or by his or her representative, and transmitted immediately to the coordinator in each nation, as well as to directors in all other participating countries.

**Study of expenditures, along with impact and results are constantly fed back to Congress and the President, to financial sharing countries, and to members of the Quartet and the United Nations**

The impact of spending is, at all times, to be considered paramount to fulfilling the intents, goals, requirements, and obligations of the MERP Act. Visiting teams chosen by the director are to review on-site project development and assess the fulfillment of expectations from proposals to determine whether commitments have been met. Standards of accomplishment should as best as possible, be consistently applied for all nations and projects evaluated. Results will be fed back to the Administrator, to coordinators for each respective nation, and to appropriate United Nations officials.

**Potential new members are to be considered and evaluated, with rapid decisions made for their eligibility and acceptance.**

Ideally, all of the twenty-eight nations of the region will participate in the opening conference designed to solicit support as well as identify recipients of MERP funding. As argued earlier, although all applying nations may not qualify, either initially, or ever (for example, some will have too much wealth and/or some will refuse to establish a peaceful, non-aggression position with Israel), they should all be invited.

Once set in place, eligible nations should receive documentation describing the progress, country-by-country, resulting from inclusion in MERP. Each non-member nation should be encouraged to apply and become eligible for funding. Of course, any nation may join and not receive MERP funding -- this scenario would occur if their resources are sufficient to achieve national prosperity and stability without MERP assistance.

Each country in the region should be given a window of time within which to join, with a set closing date for participation. Whether it be funding from MERP or ascension into a regional economic integration enterprise, every effort should be made to publicize the acceptance for any new member.

**As soon as possible, but no later than one year from implementation of the MERP Act, the Administrator should proceed to advance the principles of regional economic integration in the Middle East and eventually throughout the Middle East, North Africa, and Central Asia.**

Although not dependent on passage of the MERP Act, regional economic integration in the MENACA would be advanced by its passage. Certainly the approach presented here negates any future possibility for economic separation, but instead, encourages unification to evolve win-win situations. Cross-border trade, investments, joint-projects etc., would be the first step to establishing increased exchanges and cooperation. Free trade agreements will evolve, as identified by JIPTA -- the Jordanian-Israeli-Palestinian (Free) Trade Agreement, followed by other nations ascending from the Middle East. The larger grouping, enlarged to include membership drawn from Egypt, Lebanon, and possibly Syria, would be the foundation for a Middle East Free Trade Agreement.

Success will beget success. Late- comers will be anxious to join the community of prosperous nations.

At this stage, MENAFTA would replace all former accords. The Middle East/North Africa Free Trade Agreement, with Arab nations, plus Israel and Iran, could create a Middle East/North Africa Community (MENAC).

Lastly, MENACAFTA - the Middle East/North Africa/Central Asia Free Trade Agreement will include as many as 28 countries and would become the forerunner of MEC -- the Middle East Community. At that time, this model of cooperation would prepare more than one-half billion citizens of these nations for a renewed prosperity in the region that would serve as the glue for stability and the window of future promise.

**Financial aid can be terminated as well as amended, also possibly extended-following proper debate and legislation**

As detailed in the European Recovery Program of 1948, a means should be provided to allow for the cancellation or amending of  financial assistance, to a particular nation, for a specific project, or indeed if judged necessary, the entire program. Hopefully, there will be no need to terminate funding to any country once they have been cleared for ascension.

However, should it be necessary to withhold funding, a mechanism must be instituted, along with conditions and procedures for reducing, or canceling funding.

The promise of success, accompanied by increased prosperity should serve as the catalyst for fairness, honesty, and trust.

-------------------------------------------

The Marshall Plan also brought considerable prosperity to the U.S. Marshall Plan funding, most of which was spent in the U.S., was used for grants (89 %) and loans (11%). A significant amount of equipment and supplies needed for rebuilding Western Europe was purchased from the U.S. resulting in increased U.S. exports to participating nations. The same would apply under MERP.

## MADE IN THE MIDDLE EAST

Speaking at the Casablanca Economic Summit in 1994, Stanley Fischer, then First Deputy Managing Director of the Washington, D.C.-based International Monetary Fund asserted that the "region has great economic potential. To exploit that potential, it is necessary both for countries to follow the right policies and to build an institutional infrastructure to support growth and cooperation." These words of promise were spoken more than five years before the start of Intifada II in 2000, and that optimism is long gone, replaced with hopelessness and despair. The euphoria, once a dream of opportunity, has been downgraded with the notion of a " New Middle East" vanquished as unrealistic, or even undesirable.

An estimated 47 percent of Palestinians are living below the poverty line of $410 a month for a family of six, according to a World Bank report (The Palestinian Authority believes that 58 percent of its citizens live in poverty.) The Palestinian economy has shrunk by 23 percent since 1999, the year prior to the start of Intifada II. Palestinians have grown dependent on annual international aid of $1 billion.

Indeed, during the height of optimism, in the mid-1990s, the Middle East Economic Strategy Group had already proclaimed "Made in the Middle East" as the appropriate symbol of the promise for tomorrow. Arguably, it was and remains a powerful idea whose time must be resurrected. With help from funds of the U.S.-sponsored Middle East Recovery Program, cooperation will come only after considerable argument, after heated debate, and even a few failures. Eventually, MEC will institutionalize itself and move ever so gradually through its stages: initially JIPTA, followed by MEFTA, MENAFTA and MENACAFTA.

Trade agreements will not evolve easily. Accusations of of imperialism and colonization, fear of the loss of sovereignty, and so on, will be repeatedly raised. The pull between protectionists and free-traders will be particularly severe. In the end, though, MERP will justify the free traders.

Based on dire need, MERP will initially direct its attention to the Palestinians. Soon after, it should focus attention in the remaining triangle of Israel (recall that Iraq could be substitute for Israel) and Jordan, to form a loose, cooperative association, thus creating the first full stage of free-trade accords that will be the harbinger of the extended Middle East Community. Indeed, the process started in May 1995, when Jordan and the Palestinian Authority signed their first detailed trade accord, defining terms for shipments across the Jordan River under a preferential tariff system, thereby preparing the way toward the goal of free trade between the Palestinians and Jordanians.

A successful launching of JIPTA will more than adequately communicate to the rest of the Arab/Muslim and non-Arab/Muslim nations that the idea for a common market can be both realistic and productive. If Jordanians and Palestinians illustrate to other contiguous states that they are able to benefit from an alliance with the Israelis, as well as Jordanians with the Palestinians, and the Palestinians with Jordanians, without being swallowed or made to play a secondary role, then others will rush to participate.

It will not be easy to release the energies from differing nations. Many of the countries of MEC are still dominated by state bureaucrats who have only a cursory grasp of modern economics and market realities, and little political will to institute the changes necessary to realize the enormous benefits awaiting those willing to open up their economies and liberalize trade.

The Middle East region could soon be the substitute for China's and India's past, but declining attraction of low wages. It is clear their production costs will climb as increased attention is paid to their environment and the price of energy. In addition, their labor wages are rising at the same time that her population is rapidly aging.

If present-day economists are correct, China and India will see a leap in salaries over the coming two decades. Nations seeking cheap labor will then rush into many of the broader Middle East countries to take advantage of their comparative advantage. Lower costs of labor can jump start the economies of these people and create employment opportunities.

## LEARNING FROM HISTORY

Pitfalls will have to be avoided whenever possible. Lest we forget, prior to the European Union's proclaimed "moment in history," January 1, 1993, the rhetoric in its closing months provided signs of a *block* to international trade rather than the flow of an international trading *bloc*.

With the passage of time and another promise for a "moment in history," the world will also learn how disenchanted many Europeans are with the single currency that exploded on the scene January 1, 2002.

In addition, the rejection in national referendums by the French and Dutch people for the proposed EU constitution in May 2005, illustrates how the public can rapidly turn against government recommendations, especially during periods of economic uncertainly and high unemployment.

As politicians were embellishing lofty visions in the early 1990s, Europe had slipped backward into old habits of increasing state control of the economy, where what one knows frequently continues to play second fiddle to whom one knows. Nations of the MENACA must avoid this trap of too much internal focus that only leads to impotence and failure.

The globalization debates were highlighted in the media beginning in 1999, with the well-publicized street confrontations in Seattle, followed over the years in Washington, DC, Davos, Doha, Geneva, Genoa, Calgary, New York City, Santiago, and Cancun.

Seven years have gone by since the first major anti-globalization protests. The World Bank and IMF met in October 2004, with a major objective of debt-relief for poor nations, including Iraq. The chosen site was Washington D.C., which remained calm, somewhat indifferent, and basically free from the earlier anti-globalization protests. Then, on November 21st of 2004 the world's leading industrial nations, meeting in Paris, agreed to cancel 80 percent of the nearly $39 billion in debt owed them by Iraq.

As part of the present globalization movement, MENACA nations should be alert to both environmental and worker needs. If they are, they will work to protect the public against the protestors. The arguments against the

World Bank, the International Monetary Fund, the 2001 Switzerland meeting of the World Economic Forum, the November 2001 Qatar session of the World Trade Organization, to mention but a few, are symptoms of a growing backlash against the perceived "haves" for stealing the future away from the perceived "have nots."

## POLITICAL UNION

The feature of a MEC that most people will find hardest to visualize is the idea of a Community reaching out to the world with a united mind, and a single will. Though differing by degree throughout the region, member nations represent separate nations. Although it appears that individual states are diminishing in strength, they have not disappeared, nor will they, nor should they. People from different countries display different feelings toward their historic past, their cultures, outside influences, and their issues.

## A WORD OF CAUTION

Institutionally, the MENACA Community will require a home base, established in one country. (Rotation on a pre-set basis is impractical and inefficient.) MEC bureaucrats must center their loyalties on the Community and not on their home-nations.

Every effort should be made to minimize the number of employees who will be needed to run the Community. For example, many people will be required to translate the weighty documents generated during and following deliberations. MEC will encompass only four languages (English, Arabic, Farsi, and Hebrew), an advantage over the EU, which currently accommodates numerous languages.

In the search for a fuller and more united MEC, "deepening" is the process whereby member nations of the growing Community move toward greater political union. The issue will become increasingly complex when the original members of JIPTA begin to add new nations (Syria, Lebanon, and Egypt, perhaps) to their ranks, followed by others. (The further from the core, the wider the cultural and historical differences which will cause additional barriers.)

Nevertheless, numerous leaders from non-Community nations will insist on joining MEC so as not to be excluded from the benefits of the accord, such as those of fair-play on bidding for public contracts, or those for setting industrial standards, to name but a few. Countries already within the framework of MEC may urge keeping out potential competitor nations.

As soon as nations qualify, they should be accepted. To satisfy all parties, and not be hastily rushed into a decision, the Community should create a mid-staging strategy, allowing non-member countries that have applied to participate in decision-shaping, but not decision-making. Non-Community nations at this point would retain their autonomy.

The cost of failure to implement multinational free-trade accords with a long-term goal for the Middle East common market will be high. Arguably, for the first time in decades, the region is urging peace and is committed to sensible economic reform. Starting with the Casablanca-, followed by the Amman, Cairo, and lastly in 1997, Doha Middle East/North Africa Economic meetings, a significant and promising stage in the marriage of business with the peace process evolved. Through hard work in the spirit of cooperation, optimism swelled, only to slowly fall apart. The whole process must be restarted.

There is so much to be learned and saved from these summits and conferences. Failure to initiate the admirable and responsible goals of the MEC meetings might undermine new democracies and weaken future hopes for cooperation. It could also jeopardize efforts to restructure nations' economies along free-market, export-oriented lines. Any commitment by world leaders to the Middle East/North Africa/Central Asia countries should be as profound as those that have been provided to other global nations.

Executives of the Community should be sensitive to excessive control by member nations. Leaders, secured behind their hidden ivory towers, can easily loose sight of the concerns of the masses. Communication is imperative. Eventually, such insensitivity will return to haunt the progress of the Community.

Additionally, should a "superstate" mentality be perceived, an inevitable backlash will flow from the citizenry. Community authorities must disavow attempts at an inflated status, evidenced by the documents (directives and regulations) that emanate from its governing. They must be cautious to avoid a system with an excessive, centralized bureaucracy. MEC nations must learn from the spring 2005 rejection by the citizens of France and the Netherlands over a proposed constitution that in part implied central governance.

MEC Community pioneers ought to incorporate "subsidiarity" into their deliberations. This principle suggests that anything that can be better done at a local, regional, or national level should, therefore, not be done at a Community level. Claiming that the Community should only act when strictly necessary can be debated at length. One nation of the region can claim interference while another can argue for needed Community action. Each government may have its own priorities that it would impose on the others.

In its operation there will undoubtedly be disappointments and failures that will require action. After all, unrecognized problems tend to go uncorrected, and unaccountable institutions tend to be ineffective.

**VIOLENCE AND TERRORISM BEGETS A MIDDLE EAST RECOVERY PROGRAM WHICH BEGETS A QUEST FOR FREEDOM, RIGHTS,  EDUCATIONAL OPPORTUNITY, STABILITY, NEW LEADERSHIP, PROSPERITY, AND COMMUNITY - THE NOBLEST OF GOALS, THE RESULT - A "REAWAKENING."**

The fall of 2000 started the horrific, and hopefully last chapter of the Israeli-Palestinian violence. What is certain is that the consequences for the Palestinian and Israeli citizens were  enormous, both in terms of lost lives and lost opportunities.

Before Intifada II, trade between Israel and the Palestinians was valued at $2 billion a year. It has dried up almost completely since the start of the uprising.

The Palestinian Authority, having lost more than one-third of its gross domestic product, cannot be viable without trade and jobs within Israel. Economic separation, if implemented, will  only lead to a further decrease in incomes, and higher unemployment. Even greater poverty will be the result. Aid promised by Arab nations to the PA, even if fully distributed, would merely replace already-lost income resulting from the current disturbances.

In Israel, the termination of economic relations has resulted in a one-time loss of about 1 percent of its gross domestic product, or approximately $1 billion.

Hatred does not augur well for the integration of economies. Hatred also frightens away outside assistance, even from formerly-staunch supporters. When describing the need for walls in the Middle East, David Makovsky said: "A wall with windows is required. The geography of the region is so intimate that the two states will have to share resources such as electricity grids and water for the foreseeable future. The PA depends on Israel for a third of its GNP, and if regulated properly, economic interaction could continue."

Terrorist attacks against the U.S. in September 2001 remain a defining moment for its citizens and have forever altered attitudes. It will forever alter attitudes of complacency and indifference. Most importantly, assumptions of insulation from warfare have been shattered. TV programs that tune into camps of the enemy will subject Americans to eye-opening encouragement to remain involved, to outline and defend strategies that protect vulnerable borders. Then, our attention will turn to helping friendly governments of MEC, rebuilding the region stone- by-stone and dollar-by-dollar.

Fortunately, history has provided us with an avenue of rescue. Emotions have and can be tamed. The French and Germans, bitter neighbors for more than one hundred years are today wealthy trading partners in a community of 25 other nations, with others to be added. This superb and powerful model of faith, promise and considerable trust must replace any call for separation, isolation, and the termination of economic sharing across borders.

MERP can provide the incentive and financial means to restore the Middle East region to a vitality not seen in centuries. MERP will also encourage the advancement of neighboring nations to form free trade accords and extend a hand for an eventual community. With success stories and continued outreach, as many as one-half billion people out of the world's six billion, can take comfort in knowing that they are represented by an institution ultimately dedicated to political stability, extended freedom, rights for all, improved education, and economic prosperity.

As barriers to internal trade fall, businesspeople and entrepreneurs from all member nations will begin to take advantage of new opportunities and thereby increase the volume of economic activity. Because the level of cross-border business is presently so small within MENACA, the growth rates will be enormous. In the end, MEC will emerge as a dynamic part of the global economy.

MERP monies are essential but will not alone be the solution. What is critical is for the leaders of member countries to change the way they think. It may prove harder to alter attitudes and expectations than anything else. It will take considerable time for many member countries to prosper, especially those that don't find a "big brother" to take them by the hand to communicate the benefits of participation. Backlashes and calls for a return to older ways of life will occur as progress down the road from the present form of economy to a market-free enterprise economy will be slow-moving. Leaders must devote time to building public support for their policies.

Free-trade partners that move furthest and fastest towards a heightened living standard and fuller employment will be those with national identities, a growing and large middle class, and a developed economy that existed before the formation of the Community.

No aspiring nation of the region that wishes to partake of the MERP funding can avoid eventual participation in MEC, for it will be a condition of released monies. By this, a reinforcing, successful example will be set into place before others rush to embrace the model. Likewise, for those nations that have no democratic tradition to help recast their societies, satisfactory reintegration into MEC may take decades and possibly generations. Privatization procedures should be simple, trade arrangements with neighbors should not be dissolved too rapidly, and adequate attention must be paid to reducing external debt.

- - - - - - - - - - - - - - - - - - - - - - - - - - -

In a golden age over a millennium ago, the Middle East was the commercial and cultural crossroads of the world. Jerusalem was, biblically, the center of the globe, and Baghdad shared a place in history. A reawakening may be ahead, with promises of another glorious period for the region. A more peaceful, more prosperous, and more integrated Middle East, can once again take a position among other movers of the global economy.

Innovation is central to the Community's growth, not only for economic growth, but also for future political and social development. Whether of a product, service, or a process, innovation is not a simple, uniform concept. It does not often happen in one place, or at one time. Usually, innovation is a series of small refinements developed over a lengthy time frame.

The billions of released U.S. dollars from enactment of MERP is a supreme accomplishment. Free trade agreements, with all the promises of opportunity, have risk.

Inflation rates may climb excessively, and a high degree of currency volatility is dangerous. Currency fears can impact policy standardization, one of the preconditions for trade integration.   In addition, infrastructures as they presently are, hinder progress on most fronts. Roads, ports, terminals and means for telecommunicating are woefully inadequate and antiquated in most MEC nations. More importantly, the education, health, and social welfare needs are so great in nearly every country of the region, that people left unfulfilled can tumble the entire enterprise. And, without confidence building, trust, utilizing appropriate existing institutions, and negotiating openly and fairly, the endeavor will stumble and fail.

First, will be the distribution of monies from the enacted MERP Act. Then, with time, there will follow the introduction of free-trade accords (bilateral at first, expanded to multilateral) in varying combinations between the three founding JIPTA partners. This step will be the harbinger to a common market. Along the way, fiscal and trade barriers will fall, common standards will be set, educational priorities and avenues will be encouraged, mergers and industrial cooperation will settle in place, services of all types will be made available with equality as the golden rule, healthcare for individuals and health to the environment will surface as priorities, social rights for all will be the banner command, and peace, not seen in ages, will   enshrine itself as the collective force and presence before the world-at-large.

Thanks primarily to the generosity of the people and government of the U.S. and other funding nations, the countries of MENACA will enter a common market. The benefits of such an allegiance will outweigh all the questions, suspicions, and criticisms. In short time, nations of the Community could become colossus, paving the way in this new millennium for a force of unparalleled envy, ensuring a broader, New Middle East, no longer just in name, but in practice.

Nearly sixty years ago, the European Recovery Program rescued Western Europe and initiated what would become the grand European Union, where 450 million people from 27 countries today consume approximately one-quarter of all worldly goods. A Middle East Recovery Program can do the same for more than one-half a billion people, some from Abraham's biblical descent, others from the Silk Route, if there is courage to collectively move forward despite the myriad obstacles. A Middle East Community could pave the way to a prosperous region that will take pride in its accomplishments, both past and present.

To withdraw from the Middle East turmoil is an improbable but theoretically possible choice. To participate without adequate resources is an option that will result in increased anger directed towards the western world. Time is short. Hope can turn to despair, and surely will, should decisive action not be taken now.

Funds must be found to move the process forward. No better alternative exists to redefine the region. MERP will inevitably become the primary route of opportunity.

Perhaps soon these concepts and models will be debated. If not now, then at some propitious time over the coming years, the spirit and will be found to bring the glories of a once promising region to stand along with the other great countries of the world.

For the Middle East Recovery Program, for free trade accords and regional economic integration to have a chance at success, a significant degree of mutual trust among member nations is a prerequisite. Once accomplished, the gains will be economic, political, and decisively humanitarian. Once MERP is set in place, the region will slowly surface and move out of its bunker and move forward to test itself in the open field. At that time the great experiment will gather speed in its rush to reality.

The *Iraq Study Group* report has come and gone. New strategies are in place to alter the situation in Iraq, Lebanon, Palestine and elsewhere. The Administration's *Compact for Iraq* and *Gulf Plus Two* group, recently created, may point the direction for economic cooperation in the region, indicating a drive towards a reinvented Marshall Plan to be followed by a potential Middle East Economic Community.

By election eve of 2008, a majority of Americans expect that U.S. military involvement in the Middle East will become a regrettable citation of the past. Agreed upon by most Democrats and Republicans, by then a new beginning should occur benefiting all sides.

Not today, perhaps not soon, but eventually nations of the broader Middle East will successfully turn, with international assistance, to forging an economic community. Once sufficient stability finds its place across borders of the region, renewed energy and resources will be used to upgrade living standards and bring long-term stability to all.

**"Had I been present at the creation I would have given some useful hints for the better ordering of the universe."**

**Alphonso X, the Learned**
**(King of Spain, from 1252 to 1284)**

# APPENDIX I

## THE MIDDLE EAST RECOVERY PROGRAM ACT

(Roman typeface identifies a proposed entry for the Act, while *Italic* typeface identifies dialogue and analysis to explain the rationales for the entry)

Section 1.     THE MIDDLE EAST RECOVERY PROGRAM ACT

This TITLE may be cited as the Middle East Recovery Program, or more specifically, the Middle East Economic Cooperation Act.

*Prior to the passage and implementation of the Marshall Plan, eligible nations of Western Europe met with a newly-formed Committee of European Economic Cooperation at Paris in September 1947. Members signed a report of the Committee, thus qualifying for participation in the Plan and for receiving assistance.*

*The Middle East Recovery Program (MERP) Act will emphasize two fundamental aspects: (1) that the assistance is economic in character; and (2) that the success of MERP requires cooperation among the countries participating in the program.*

*Initially, MERP is envisioned to include nations contiguous to Israel. But, other Arab/Muslim and non-Arab/Muslim countries (Iran, the 5 Central Asia nations, Afghanistan, Pakistan, and perhaps Turkey), also part of the Middle East (referred to by the U.S. State Department as the Near East) will be eligible. Likewise, all other Arab nations, extending as far west as Morocco, will also be candidates.*

Section 2. FINDINGS AND DECLARATION OF POLICY
(a) Recognizing the intimate economic and other
relationships between the United States and the nations of
the Middle East/North Africa/Central Africa (MENACA),
and recognizing that disruption of those relationships in the
wake of violence and terrorism is not contained by national
frontiers, the Congress finds that the existing situation in
the region endangers the establishment of a lasting peace,
the general welfare and national interest of the United
States, and the attainment of the objectives of the United
Nations.

The maintenance in MENACA nations of -
individual liberty, free institutions, and genuine
independence rests largely upon the establishment of sound
economic conditions, stable international economic
relationships, and the achievement over time of healthy
economies independent of extraordinary outside assistance.

The accomplishment of these objectives also calls
for economic cooperation, including equitable rates of
exchange and the progressive elimination of trade barriers.

Mindful of the advantages that the U. S. and other
trading blocs have enjoyed large regional markets free of
internal trade barriers, and believing that similar advantages
can accrue to the countries of MENACA, it should be the
policy of the U.S. to encourage these countries through a
joint organization to exert sustained common effort as set
forth in the report of the Committee of Middle East/North
Africa/Central Asia Economic Cooperation, which intends
to achieve economic cooperation in MENACA, and which
is essential for lasting peace and prosperity.

It is further declared to be the policy of the people
of the United States to assist in the creation of a Palestinian

state, where Palestinians may live if they so choose; and/or to compensate Palestinians for their decades of displacement. Funds will also be used to pay for the exodus of Israeli settlers out of the West Bank and Gaza Strip. Additionally, there will be discussions and possible actions to compensate Jews forced from their Arab homelands to resettle within the state of Israel. (The increasing plight of Central Asian refugees must be reexamined as a separate effort of the United Nations.)

*The general welfare and national interests of the United States are intimately related to the existence of a healthy MENACA. The great objectives of a MERP cannot be achieved solely by economic measures, and, therefore, political considerations must be included as a shaper of events.*

*In addition, there must be a willingness and ability of the peoples of the participating states to recognize and emphasize their areas of common interest, rather than their points of difference, and to concentrate their efforts upon devising means for closer cooperation.*

*Reference to a "plan for Middle East recovery" is designed to make clear that the recovery program undertaken by nations of MENACA must be a developing, not a static, program.*

*To aid Middle East refugees in their resettlement, whether Arab/Muslim, or non-Arab Muslim, or Jew, is a worthy expenditure of the recovery program. Without this resolution, little progress on other critical issues for development, restoration, and cooperation will be halted. Likewise, consideration can be given to use some assistance funds to compensate Jewish citizens of Arab descent who were forced to flee their homeland following 1948 and until the end of 1967.*

## (b) PURPOSES OF A RECOVERY PROGRAM

The purpose of the recovery program is to aid participating countries by furnishing material and financial assistance. Through their own individual and concerted efforts, the countries will hopefully become independent of extraordinary outside economic assistance within the period of operations, by:

(1) promoting industrial and agricultural production in the participating countries;

(2) furthering the restoration or maintenance of the soundness of MENACA currencies, budgets, and finances;

(3) facilitating and stimulating the growth of international trade of participating countries with one another and with other countries by appropriate measures including reduction of barriers which may hamper such trade.

*Economic cooperation among the participating countries is dependent upon the political realities in those countries. It is therefore critical that the objectives of the recovery program be stated in a manner sufficiently broad to enable the Administrator, when determining the form and measure of assistance to be given to a participating country, to take into consideration the varied factors which will bear upon the success of this undertaking.*

## Section 3. PARTICIPATING COUNTRIES

To include any MENACA entity whose ranking representative signed the report of the Committee of Middle East/North Africa/Central Asia Economic Cooperation.

Participating countries are eligible if they become a participant in a joint effort for Middle East/North Africa/Central Asia recovery and only for so long as each government remains an adherent to such a program. Certain of the participating nations who do not require assistance will, nevertheless, join in the program for the purpose of cooperating with the other countries in carrying out the mutual effort which is inherent in the recovery plan.

## Section 4. ESTABLISHMENT OF MIDDLE EAST/NORTH AFRICA/ CENTRAL ASIA ECONOMIC COOPERATION ADMINISTRATION

(a) There is hereby established, with its principal office in the District of Columbia, an agency of the Government which shall be known as the Middle East/North Africa/Central Asia Economic Cooperation Administration, hereinafter referred to as the Administration. The Administration shall be headed by an Administrator for MENACA Economic Cooperation, hereinafter referred to as the Administrator, who shall be appointed by the U.S. President, by and with the advice and consent of the Senate.

The Administrator shall be responsible to the President of the United States and shall have a status in the executive branch of the Government comparable to that of the head of an executive department. Except, as otherwise provided in this title, the administration of the provisions of this title is hereby vested in the Administrator and his functions shall be performed under the control of the President.

The Administrator will have a status which will put him or her on a footing of equality with the heads of other agencies and departments of the Government, and he or she will have the right of direct access to the President, under whose leadership functions will be performed.

(b) The Deputy Administrator for MENACA Economic Cooperation shall perform such functions as the Administrator shall designate, and shall be Acting

Administrator for MENACA Economic Cooperation during the absence or disability of the Administrator or in the event of a vacancy in the office of Administrator.

The Deputy Administrator is authorized to perform any functions delegated to him or her by the Administrator, or, in the event of a vacancy in the office of the Administrator, he or she will be Acting Administrator.

(c) The President is authorized, pending the appointment and qualification of the first Administrator or Deputy Administrator for MENACA Economic Cooperation appointed hereunder, to provide, for a period of not to exceed thirty days after the date of enactment of this Act, for the performance of the functions of the Administrator under this recovery program through such departments, agencies, or establishments of the United States Government as he or she may direct. In the event the President nominates an Administrator or Deputy Administrator after the expiration of such thirty-day period, the authority conferred upon the President by this subsection shall be extended beyond such thirty-day period but only until an Administrator or Deputy Administrator qualifies and takes office.

*The intent is to assure commencement of operations as soon as possible following passage, even if it may not have been possible for the first Administrator or his Deputy to take office.*

Section 5. GENERAL FUNCTIONS OF THE ADMINISTRATOR

(a) The Administrator, under the control of the President, shall, in addition to all other functions vested in him or her by this recovery program,

(1) review and appraise the requirements of participating countries for assistance under the terms of this program;

(2) formulate programs using United States assistance under this program, and approve specific projects which have been submitted to him or her by the participating countries;

(3) provide for the efficient execution of any such programs as may be placed in operation; and

(4) terminate provision of assistance or take other remedial action as provided.

*The authority of the Administrator to formulate programs of United States assistance includes authority to approve specific projects which may be proposed to him or her by a participating country, to be undertaken by such country in substantial part with assistance furnished under the recovery program.*

*The authority reposed in the Administrator to provide for the efficient execution of programs refers to the effective performance on the part of agencies of the U.S. Government with respect to services rendered by such agencies. Services for approved programs could include procurement, storage, and transportation.*

*The authority to terminate provision of assistance or take other remedial action relates to the responsibility of the Administrator to take appropriate action to assure that assistance under this recovery program is provided only in accordance with its provisions and its stated purposes. Inasmuch as the termination of the provision of assistance undoubtedly would have serious implications with respect to the foreign-policy objectives of the U.S., it is not contemplated that such action would be taken without consultation with the Secretary of State. Moreover, in*

*some circumstances, certain action by the Administrator,
or by other agencies of the Government, might be more
appropriate than termination of the provision of assistance.
Accordingly, the Administrator may provide for, or
recommend to the President or to the appropriate agency of
the Government, the taking of such other action.*
(b)

In order to strengthen and make more effective the
conduct of the foreign relations of the United States -

(1) the Administrator and the Secretary of State shall keep
each other fully and currently informed on matters,
including perspective action, arising within the scope of
their respective duties which are pertinent to the duties
of the other;

(2) when the Secretary of State believes that any action,
proposed action, or failure to act on the part of the
Administrator is inconsistent with the foreign-policy
objectives of the United States, he or she shall consult
with the Administrator and, if differences of view are
not adjusted by consultation, the matter shall be referred
to the President for final decision;

(3) whenever the Administrator believes that any action,
proposed action, or failure to act on the part of the
Secretary of State in performing functions under this
title is inconsistent with the purposes and provisions of
this title, he shall consult with the Secretary of State
and, if differences of view are not adjusted by
consultation, the matter shall be referred to the
President for final decision.

*To strengthen and make more effective the conduct
of foreign relations of the U.S., the Administrator and the
U.S. Secretary of State will work closely together. Should*

*there arise matters of conflict between the two of them, the*
*President shall serve as final arbiter.*

## Section 6. NATIONAL ADVISORY COUNCIL

In order to coordinate the policies and operations of the representatives of the U.S. and of all agencies of the government which make or participate in making foreign loans or which engage in foreign financial exchange or monetary transactions, there is hereby established the National Advisory council (hereinafter referred to as the Council), consisting of the Secretary of the Treasury, Chair, the U.S. Secretary of State, the Secretary of Commerce, the Secretary of Homeland Security, the Chair of the Board of Governors of the Federal Reserve System, the Chair of the Board of Directors of the Export-Import Bank of Washington, the head of the Trade Representatives Office, and during such period as the MENACA Economic Cooperation Administration shall continue to exist, the Administrator for MENACA Economic Cooperation.

## Section 7. PUBLIC ADVISORY BOARD

(a) A Public Advisory Board, hereinafter referred to as the Board, shall advise and consult with the Administrator with respect to general or basic policy matters arising in connection with the Administrator's discharge of his or her responsibilities. The Board shall consist of the Administrator, who shall be Chair, and shall not exceed twelve additional members to be appointed by the President, by and with the advice and consent of the Senate, and who shall be selected from among citizens of the United States of broad and varied experience in matters affecting the public interest. Officers and employees of the United States who, as such, regularly receive compensation for current services shall be ineligible to serve on the Board.

The Board shall meet at least once a month and at other times upon the call of the Administrator or when three or more members of the Board request the Administrator to call a meeting. Not more than a majority of two of the members shall be appointed to the Board from the same political party.

*A Public Advisory Board is needed to advise and consult with the Administrator with respect to general or basic policy matters. The creation of such a board is desirable both from the standpoint of making available to the Administrator the benefit of the advice and experience of private citizens representing broad public interests and also from the standpoint of assuring the fullest practicable degree of public information concerning the programs and operations under this recovery plan. Board members shall represent business, labor, agriculture, the professions, and other areas affecting the public interest.*

Members of the Board are to be appointed by the President, with the consent of the Senate.

(b) The Administrator may appoint such other advisory committees as he or she may determine to be necessary or desirable to effectuate the purposes of this recovery program.

As required by the Administrator, experts and consultants shall be employed by the Administrator.

Section   8.   UNITED   STATES   SPECIAL REPRESENTATIVE ABROAD

There shall be a U.S. Special Representative in the Middle East/North Africa/Central Asia region who shall (a) be appointed by the President, by and with the advice and consent of the Senate, (b) be entitled to receive the same compensation and allowances as a chief of mission, and (c) have the rank of ambassador extraordinary and plenipotentiary.

He or she shall be the representative of the Administrator, and shall also be the chief representative of the United States Government to any organization of participating countries which may be established by such countries to further a joint program for recovery, and shall discharge, on site, such additional responsibilities as may be assigned by the Administrator, with the approval of the President in furtherance of the purposes of this recovery program. He or she shall receive instructions from the Administrator, and such instructions shall be prepared and transmitted to him or her in accordance with procedures agreed to between the Administrator and the Secretary of State in order to assure appropriate coordination.

He or she shall inform the Administrator, the Secretary of State, the chiefs of the U.S. diplomatic missions, and the chiefs of the special missions abroad of his or her activities.

He or she shall consult with the chiefs of all such missions, who shall give him such cooperation as he or she may require for the performance of duties under this title.

*The U.S. representative in the Middle East/North Africa/Central Asia region will play a key role in the accomplishment of the purposes of this recovery program, serving as the chief representative of the U.S. Government to the continuing organization set up by the participating countries.*

He or she will receive instructions from the Administrator, which shall be prepared and transmitted in such a manner as to assure the necessary effective coordination between the Administrator and the Secretary of State.

Activities of the Representative should also be shared with the Senate Foreign Relations Committee Chair, the House Foreign Affairs Committee, the Senate Appropriations Committee, and the House Appropriations Committee.

Section 9. SPECIAL MIDDLE EAST/NORTH AFRICA/CENTRAL ASIA ECONOMIC COOPERATION MISSIONS ABROAD

(a) There shall be established for each participating country, a special mission for economic cooperation under the auspices of a director who shall be responsible for ensuring the performance within such country of operations. The directors shall be appointed by the Administrator, shall receive instructions from the Administrator, and shall report to the Administrator on their duties.

*In order to ensure the proper performance within each of the participating countries of operations, a special mission for economic cooperation within each such country under the direction of a director who is to be appointed by the Administrator shall exist. The special mission representative shall receive instructions from the Administrator, and shall report to him or her on the performance of assigned duties.*

(b) The director of the special mission shall keep the chief of the U.S. diplomatic mission fully and currently informed on matters, including prospective actions, arising within the scope of the operations of the special mission. Additionally, the director of the diplomatic mission shall keep the director of the special mission fully and currently informed on matters relative to the conduct of the duties of the director of the special mission.

*The director of the U.S. diplomatic mission will be responsible for ensuring that the operations of the special mission are consistent with the foreign-policy objectives of the United States. To that end, whenever the director of the U.S. diplomatic mission believes that any action, proposed action, or failure to act on the part of the special mission is inconsistent with such foreign-policy objectives, he or she shall so advise the director of the special mission and the U.S. Special Representative in the region.*

*If differences are not rectified through consultation, the matter shall be referred to the Secretary of State and the Administrator and, finally, to the President.*

## Section 10. PERSONNEL OUTSIDE THE UNITED STATES

No citizen or resident of the United States may be employed, or if already employed, may be assigned to duties by the Secretary of State or the Administrator under this recovery program for a period to exceed three months unless such individual has been investigated as to loyalty and security by the Federal Bureau of Investigation, and a report has been made to the Secretary of State and the Administrator, and until the Secretary of State or the Administrator has certified in writing (and filed copies thereof with the Senate Committee on Foreign Relations and the House Committee on Foreign Affairs) that, after full consideration of such report, he or she believes such individual is loyal to the United States, its Constitution, and form of government, and is not now and has never been a member of any organization advocating contrary views.

This subsection shall not apply in the case of any officer appointed by the President by and with the advice and consent of the Senate.

*In the sensitive area of the Middle East/North Africa/Central Asia, careful screening of candidates is needed both to provide security and ensure allegiance to the United States and to provide participating nations with the confidence that representatives of the United States are "honest brokers" who seek a fair and equitable solution to the myriad of problems in the region. The Federal Bureau of Investigation, by its design and history, is the appropriate venue for background checks on U.S. participants in the program.*

Section 11. NATURE AND METHOD OF ASSISTANCE
(a) The Administrator may, from time to time, furnish assistance to any participating country when he or she deems it to be in furtherance of the purposes of this title, to be included in the terms and conditions set forth in this recovery program, to be consistent with the provisions of this plan, and to be necessary and proper.
(1) Procuring from any source, including Government stocks, which the Administrator determines to be required for the furtherance of the purposes of this recovery program.
(2) Processing, storing, transporting, and repairing any goods or performing any other services with respect to a participating country which the Administrator determines to be required for accomplishing the purposes of this recovery program.
(3) Procuring and furnishing technical information and assistance.

(4) Transferring of any commodity or service, which transfer shall be signified by delivery of the custody and right of possession and use of each commodity, or otherwise making available any such commodity, or rendering a service to a participating country or to any agency or organization representing a participating country.

(5) Allocating of goods or services to specific projects designed to carry out the purposes of this recovery program, which have been submitted to the Administrator by participating countries and have been approved by him or her.

*It will permit the procurement of goods outside of the U.S. that are in short supply in the U.S., thereby relieving shortages in this country, and it will also reduce the inflationary effect of increased demands for certain commodities from U.S. sources.*

(b) In order to facilitate and maximize the use of private channels of trade, subject to adequate safeguards to ensure that all expenditures in connection with such procurement are in accordance with terms and conditions established by the Administrator, he or she may provide for the performance of any of the functions described in subsection (a) of this section,

(1) by establishing accounts against which, under regulations prescribed by the Administrator which include:

(A) letters of commitment constituting    obligations of the U.S.

(B) withdrawals made by participating countries, or agencies or organizations representing participating countries or by other persons or organizations, upon presentation of contracts, invoices, or other documentation specified by the Administrator to assure the use of such withdrawals for purposes approved by the Administrator.

(2) by utilizing the services and facilities of any department, agency, or establishment of Government as the President shall direct, or with the consent of the head of such department, agency, or establishment.

(3) by making, under rules and regulations to be prescribed by the Administrator, guarantees to any person of investment in connection with projects approved by the Administrator and the participating country concerned as furthering the purposes of this recovery program.

*This subsection prescribes the method under which the Administrator may provide the types of assistance authorized.*

Section 12. PROTECTION OF DOMESTIC ECONOMY

The Administrator shall provide for the procurement in the U.S. of commodities under this recovery program in such a way as to (1) minimize the drain upon the resources of the United States and the impact of such procurement upon the domestic economy, and (2) avoid impairing the fulfillment of vital needs of the people of the United States.

*This provision is designed to assure the protection of the domestic economy.*

Section13. BILATERAL AND MULTILATERAL UNDERTAKINGS

(a) The Secretary of State, after consultation with the Administrator, is authorized to conclude, with individual participating countries or any number of such countries or with an organization representing any such countries, agreements in furtherance of the purposes of this recovery program.

The Secretary of State, before an Administrator or Deputy Administrator shall have qualified and taken office, is authorized to negotiate and conclude such temporary agreements in implementation of subsection (b) of this section as he or she may deem necessary in furtherance of the purposes of this recovery program. When an Administrator or Deputy Administrator shall have qualified and taken office, the Secretary of State shall conclude the basic agreements required by subsection (b) of this section only after consultation with the Administrator or Deputy Administrator, as the case may be.

*This section is designed to ensure that (a) in accordance with the declaration of policy, continuity of assistance provided under this recovery program will be dependent upon continuity of cooperation among countries participating in the program, and (b) as a condition precedent to receiving such assistance, each participating country shall make an executive agreement with the United States embodying undertakings essential to the accomplishment of the purposes of this recovery program.*

(b) The provision of assistance under this recovery program results from the multilateral pledges of the participating countries to use all their efforts to accomplish a joint recovery program based upon self-help and mutual cooperation. Assistance is contingent upon continuous effort of the participating countries to accomplish a joint recovery through multilateral undertakings and to establish a continuing organization for this purpose. In addition to continued mutual cooperation of the participating countries in such a program, each such country shall conclude an agreement with the United States government in order for such a country to be eligible to receive assistance under this recovery program. Such agreement shall provide for the adherence of each country to the purposes of this title and shall, where applicable, make appropriate provision, among others, for:

(1) promoting industrial and agricultural production in order to enable the participating country to become independent of extraordinary outside economic assistance;

(2) taking financial and monetary measures necessary to stabilize its currency, establishing or maintaining a valid rate of exchange, balancing its governmental budget as soon as practicable, and generally to restoring or maintaining confidence in its monetary system.

(3) facilitating and stimulating increased interchange of goods and services among the participating countries as well as between MENACA and with other countries and reducing barriers to trade among themselves as well as with other countries;

(4) making efficient and practical use, within the framework of a joint program for recovery, of the resources of such participating country;

(5) publishing in such country and transmitting to the U.S., not less frequently than every calendar quarter after the date of the agreement, full statements of operations under the agreement, including a report of the use of funds, commodities, and services received under this recovery program;

(6) furnishing promptly, upon request of the U.S., any relevant information which would be of assistance to the United States in determining the nature and scope of operations and the use of assistance under this recovery program.

## Section 14. INVOLVEMENT FROM AROUND THE WORLD

The President shall take appropriate steps to encourage all countries throughout the world to make available to participating entities such assistance as they may be able to furnish.

*The United States should not have to provide total aid to participating countries. When feasible, other nations, specifically from the European Union, Japan, Russia and others, should contribute as they are able.*

## Section 15. TERMINATION OF ASSISTANCE

The Administrator, in determining the form and measure of assistance provided under this recovery program to any participating country, shall take into account the extent to which such country is complying with its pledges to other participating countries and with its agreement concluded with the United States.

The Administrator shall terminate the provision of assistance under this recovery program to any participating country whenever he or she determines that (1) such country is not adhering to its agreement, or is diverting from the purposes of this recovery program, or (2) because conditions are no longer consistent with the national interest of the U.S. Termination of assistance to any country shall include the termination of deliveries of all supplies scheduled under the aid program for such country and not yet delivered.

## Section 16. UNITED NATIONS AND THE EUROPEAN UNION

The President is authorized to request the cooperation of or the use of the services and facilities of the United Nations, its organs and specialized agencies, or other international organizations, in particular the European Union, in carrying out the purposes of this recovery program, and may make payments, by advancements or reimbursements, for such purposes, out of funds made available for the purposes of this recovery program.

As deemed necessary, the President shall cause to be transmitted to the Secretary General of the United Nations and to the President of the Commission of the European Union, copies of reports to Congress on the operations conducted under this recovery program.

Any agreements concluded between the U.S. and participating countries, or groups of such countries, in implementation of the purposes of this recovery program, shall be registered with the United Nations if such registration is required by the Charter of the United Nations. Such agreements shall also be registered with the Council of Ministers, Parliament, and Commission of the European Union, and any other governmental bodies as needed.

*The United Nations, the European Union and other countries such as Russia, Japan, etc., are to receive reports and listings of MERP actions. All agreements resulting from this program shall also be presented to the United Nations and to the European Union, and other governments as deemed appropriate.*

Section 17. REPORTS TO CONGRESS

The President from time to time, but not less frequently than once every calendar quarter, and once every year until all operations under this recovery program have been completed, shall transmit to the Congress a report of operations under this recovery program, including the bilateral and multilateral agreements entered into as a result of carrying out the provisions of MERP.

## APPENDIX II

## ABBREVIATED COMMENTARY

## A. DOLLAR REQUIREMENTS OF THE MIDDLE EAST RECOVERY PROGRAM

Estimates of the kinds and quantities of needed commodities that will be required to enable the countries of the Middle East/North Africa/Central Asia to effect economic reconstruction will be necessarily subject to a wide margin of error. The wide margin is due to the multiplicity of assumptions upon which the estimates will be made, including possible changes in prices, and availability of supplies.

## B. REGIONAL FOCUS, NOT NATIONAL

At the very heart of the recovery program lies the hope that the Middle East/North Africa/Central Asia will develop on a regional basis of community and support. Pursuing national self-sufficiency is anathema to MERP. Hopefully, the countries will volunteer actions that make them economically inter-dependent as opposed to economically isolated..

For an objective of voluntary regional development, there clearly can be no pre-set pattern. To have one, and to establish the controls and means of enforcement that would be necessary to bring it into being, would necessitate the use of some of the very kinds of outside pressures to which the United States and other democratic nations are unalterably opposed.

## C. WORK OF A PLANNING CONFERENCE

Prior to presenting a bill for enactment to the Congress, all interested parties (hopefully at the foreign ministry level or higher) of the MENA region (perhaps expanded to include MENACA nations) should be brought together to work out a joint program for their mutual recovery. They then would have to match the commodity and equipment requirements of such a program against their own resources so as to arrive at estimates of needs from non-MENACA sources.

It might be expected that the figures their experts work up can in many cases be questioned, or that they may not leave much to be desired in allowing for regional, as opposed to national development. But, rather, the remarkable fact might be that they are able to agree upon anything at all definitive.

The conferee should arrive at estimates of need as a function of each country's net balance-of-payments position with the United States and arrive at a total figure for all participating   countries. This group will then add up the individual country estimates and present the totals for the entire area. This procedure could result in overstated national requirements where national economic ambition is inflated instead of relating to members of a closely-coordinated economic group.

## D. SCREENING BY UNITED STATES EXPERTS

U.S. experts, formed into committees, will review the information and data presented by participating nations. The recommendations of these committees should serve as the administration's report to be submitted by the Department of State to Congress, together with the administration's proposed draft legislation. Fine tuning will be needed at all times.

## E. BASIC OBLIGATIONS OF PARTICIPATION

First, the nations within the scope of this program will qualify for assistance through graduating steps, joining with other nations  interested in restoration of the Middle East, North Africa, and Central Asia economies. Second, the nations will all sign bilateral agreements with the U. S.

In order to ensure that the recovery program is carried out, the participating countries will pledge themselves to join together and work  towards regional economic integration. This pledge will be undertaken by each country with respect to its own national program, but it will also take into account similar pledges made by the other participating countries.  In particular, each country will undertake to bend all its efforts:

(a) to develop its production to reach predetermined targets;

(b) to make the fullest and most effective use of its existing productive capacity including all available manpower;

(c) to modernize its equipment and transportation, so that labor becomes more  productive, conditions of work are improved, and standards of living of all MENACA citizens are raised;

(d) to apply all necessary measures leading to the rapid achievement of internal financial monetary and economic stability while maintaining in each country a high level of employment;

(e) to cooperate with one another and with like-minded countries in all possible steps to reduce tariffs and other barriers to the expansion of trade between themselves and the rest of the world, in accordance with the rules and regulations of the World Trade Organization;

(f) to progressively remove the obstacles to the free movement of persons within the MENACA region;

(g) to organize and utilize the means by which common resources can be developed in partnership;

(h) to assist in the resettling of Palestinian refugees, and Israeli settlers now in the West Bank and Gaza Strip;

(i) to refrain from any form of aggression, including terrorism and/or biological/chemical attacks against any other nation that applies for and is accepted to receive funding from MERP;

(j) to move in the direction of a more open, civil, free, accountable, and transparent society; and

(k) to desist from any form of economic boycott against other MENACA nations.

# REFERENCES

Acheson, D., (1970), *Present at the Creation: My Years in the State Department*. London: Hamilton.

*AIPAC's Near East Report*, July 1, 2002.

*AIPAC's Near East Report*, September 9, 2002.

Ajami, F. (2006). *The Foreigner's Gift: The Americans, the Arabs, and the Iraqis in Iraq*, New York: Free Press.

Ajami, F. (2005, May-June). *The Autumn of the Autocrats*, New York: Foreign Affairs.

Ajami, F. (2003, January-February). *Iraq and the Arabs' Future*. New York: Foreign Affairs.

Ajami, F. (1997, May-June). *The Arab Inheritance*. New York: Foreign Affairs.

Albright, M. (2003) *Madam Secretary-A Memoir*, New York: Mirimax Books.

Alterman, E. & Green, M. (2004). *The Book on Bush: How George W. (Mis)leads America.*. New York: Viking.

Anderson, J. & May, R.W. (1952). *McCarthy: The Man, the Senator, the "Ism"*. Boston: The Beacon Press.

Anti-Defamation League. (1997). *Towards Final Status: Pending Issues in Israeli-Palestinian Negotiations*. New York: Anti-Defamation League.

Anti-Defamation League (1994). *Beyond the White House Lawn: Current Perspectives on the Arab-Israeli Peace Process*. New York: Anti-Defamation League.

*Arab News*, October 2, 2002.

Aron, R. (1987). *The Imperial Republic: The United States and the World-1945-1973*, Washington: University Press of America.

Astrup, C. & Dessus, S., (2001, March). *Trade Options for the Palestinian Economy: Some Orders of Magnitude.* Washington: The World Bank.

Avineri, S., (2001, December). *A Realistic U.S. Role in the Arab-Israeli Conflict.* Washington: Carnegie Endowment.

Avineri, S., (2001, November 14). *An Arab Marshall Plan.* Jerusalem Post.

Ayers, E.L (2005), *What Caused the Civil War?: Reflections on the South and Southern History,* New York: W.W.Norton.

Badini, Antonio, (2002) *Parlare meno, agire medlio: alcune idee italiane per avvicinare la pace, LIMES,* Rivista Italiana di Geopolitica, Rome, Pare II, Il Papa, L'Europa E Noi, Vol. 2.

Bailey N.A. & Zoakos, C. (Spring 2005), *Middle East Democratization as the Test Case for Future U.S.* Policy, Journal of International Security Affairs, Number 8,

Bar-El, R., & Benhayoun, G., & Menipaz, E. (2000). *Regional Cooperation in a Global Context.* Paris: L'Harmattan. *BBC,* September 12, 2002.

Behrendt, S. & Hanelt, C-P. (eds) (2000). *Bound To Cooperate - Europe and the Middle East.* Gutersloh: Bertelsmann Foundation.

Beilin, Y. (2004). *The Path to Geneva: The Quest for a Permanent Agreement, 1996-2004,* New York: RDV Books.

Ben-Ami, S. (2006). *Scars of War, Wounds of Peace: The Israeli-Arab Tragedy,* New York: Oxford University Press.

Bernstein, B.J. & Matusow, A.J., (1966). *The Truman Administration: A Documentary History.* New York: Harper & Row.

Biddle, S. (2006). *Seeing Bagdad, Thinking Saigon.* New York: Foreign Affairs.

Bland, L., Machado B., Oliver, George (2006). *Insights from the Marshall Plan for Post-Conflict Reconstruction and Stabilization.* George C. Marshall Foundation-Unpublished.

Blumenthal, B. & Wilner, J. (1995). *Building on Peace: Toward Regional Security and Economic Development in the Middle East.* Washington: Washington Institute for Near East Policy.

Bodansky, Y. (2002). *The High Cost of Peace: How Washington's Middle East Policy Left America Vulnerable to Terrorism.* Roseville, CA: Prima Publishing.

Bonds, J.B. (2002). *Bipartisan Strategy: Selling The Marshall Plan.* Westport: Praeger.

Bright, J. (2000). *A History of Israel,* Louisville: Westminster John Knox Press.

Brown, G. (2001). *Tackling Poverty: A Global New Deal-A Marshall Plan for the Developing World.* London: U.K Treasury.

*Building a Successful Palestinian State,* (2005). Santa Monica: Rand Corporation, The Rand Palestinian State Study Team.

Bulmer, E.R., (2001, June). *The Impact of Future Labor Policy Options on the Palestinian Labor Market.* Washington: The World Bank.

Bush, G.W. (2002, June 24). *Speech of President George W. Bush,* The New York Times.

Carter, Jimmy (2006). *Palestine Peace Not Apartheid,* New York, Simon & Schuster.

Central Intelligence Agency. (2001, July). *World Fact Book.* Washington: CIA.

Chace, J. (1998). *Acheson: The Secretary of State Who Created the American World.* New York: Simon & Schuster.

Clark, J.D. & Balaj, B.S. (1994). *The West Bank and Gaza in Transition: The Role of NGOs in the Peace Process.* Washington: The World Bank.

Clinton, B. (2004): *My Life.* New York: Alfred A. Knopf.

Council on Foreign Relations. (1995). *The Casablanca Report.* New York: Council on Foreign Relations.

Covey, J., and M.J.Dziedzic, L.R. Hawley, (2005), *The Quest for Viable Peace: International Intervention and Strategies for Conflict Transformation,* Washington, D.C. U.S. Institute of Peace Press.

Cray, E. (1990). *General of the Army-George C. Marshall: Soldier and Statement.* New York: W.W. Norton & Company.

Christopher, W. (2004, December 30). *Diplomacy That Can't Be Delegated,* The New York Times.

Crossette, B., (2002, July 2). *Study Warns of Stagnation in Arab Societies.* The New York Times.

De Lombaerde, P. (Editor) (2006). *World Report on Regional Integration and Governance 2006: Multilateralism, Regionalism and Bilateralism in Trade and Investment.* (Unpublished, United Nations University).

Dershowitz, A., (2005). *The Case For Peace: How The Arab-Israeli Conflict Can Be Resolved.* Hoboken: John Wiley & Sons.

Deutch, J. (2006, November 16), *Count on Robert Gates,* The International Herald Tribune.

Diwan, I., & Shaban, R.A. (1999). *Development Under Adversity: The Palestinian Economy in Transition.* Washington: The World Bank.

Djerejian, E.P., (Nov.-Dec.2006), *From Conflict Management to Conflict Resolution,* New York, Foreign Affairs, Volume 85, No. 6.

Dobbins, J. et al. (2003). *America's Role in Nation-Building from Germany to Iraq.* Washington, D.C., Rand Corporation.

Donovan, R.J., 1987. *The Second Victory: The Marshall Plan and Postwar Revival of Europe.* Lanham, Md.

Economist, The (2001, June 6). *The Palestinian Right of Return.*

Economist, The (2001, August 5). *Editorial.*

Economist, The (2002, July 6). *Why Arab Countries Have Failed.*

Eichengreen, B.J., (1995), *Europe's Postwar Recovery:* Cambridge: Cambridge University.

El-Agraa, A.M., (1997). *Economic Integration Worldwide.* London: Macmillan Co.

Ellwood, D.W., (1992), *Rebuilding Europe: Western Europe, America, and Postwar Reconstruction.* London: Longman

Faroun, S.K., (1997). *Palestine and the Palestinians.* Boulder: Westview Press.

Ferguson, N., (September/October 2006), *A New War of the World?,* New York: Foreign Affairs.

Financial Times, The, December 12, 2002.

Fisher, S., & Hausman, L.J., & Karasik, A.D., & Schelling, T.C., (1994). *Securing Peace in the Middle East,* Cambridge: The MIT Press.

Fisher, S., & Rodrik, D., & Tuma, E., (1993). *The Economics of Middle East Peace.* Cambridge: The MIT Press.

Fisk, R. (2005), *The Great War for Civilization: The Conquest of the Middle East,* New York: Knopf.

Foreign Assistance Act of 1948, (1948, April 3). *Chapter 169 - Public Law 472.* Washington: 80th Congress.

Friedman, T. L., (2005). *The World is Flat: A Brief History of the Twenty-First Century.* New York: Farrar, Straus and Giroux.

Friedman, T.L., (2004, December 15). *Holding Up Arab Reform,* The New York Times.

Friedman, T.L., (2002, July 3). *Arabs at the Crossroads.* The New York Times.

Friedman, T.L., (1999). *The Lexus and The Olive Tree.* New York: Farrar, Straus and Giroux.

Fromkin, D., (1989). *A Peace to End All Peace.* New York: Henry Holt and Company.

Frye, R..N. (2001). *The Heritage of Central Asia: From Antiquity to the Turkish Expansion.* Princeton: Markus Wiener Publishers.

Fukuyama, F., (2004), *State-Building: Governance and World Order in the 21st Century,* Ithaca, Cornell University Press.

Gillingham, J., (2003), *European Integration, 1950-2003: Superstate or New Market Economy?* Cambridge: Cambridge University Press.

*Globes,* January 26, 2003.

*Globes,* January 20, 2003.

*Globes,* September 25, 2002.

*Globes*, October 7, 2002.

Gordon,M.R. and B. Trainor, (2006), *Cobra II,* New York: Pantheon Books.

Government of Israel. (1997). *Partnerships in Development*. Jerusalem: Government of Israel.

Government of Israel. (1996). *Programs for Regional Cooperation - 1997*. Jerusalem: Government of Israel.

Government of Israel. (1995). *Development Options for Cooperation: The Middle East/ East Mediterranean Region*. Jerusalem: Government of Israel.

Gresser, E., (2002, January). *Draining the Swamp: A Middle East Trade Policy to Win Peace*. Washington: Progressive Policy Institute.

*Ha-aretz*, June 22, 2002, *Editorial*.

*Ha-aretz*, February 23, 2002, *Editorial*.

*Ha-aretz,* September 17, 2002.

*Ha-aretz,* February 22, 2001.

Haass, R.N. (Nov.-Dec.2006), *The New Middle East*, New York, Foreign Affairs,Volume 85, No. 6.

Haass, R.N. (2005), *The Opportunity: America's Moment to Alter History's Course*. New York: Public Affairs.

Hogan, M.J., (1987), *The Marshall Plan: America, Britain, and the Transformation of Western Europe, 1947-1952*. Cambridge: Cambridge University Press.

*International Jerusalem Post (*2003, February 7).

*International Jerusalem Post* (2003, January 31). *Inflation in 2002 reached 6.5 %.*

*International Jerusalem Post* (2003, January 10). *Editorial.*

*International Jerusalem Post (*2002, December 20). *A Bad Past Returns.*

*International Jerusalem Post* (2002, May 31). *Exports to Arab Countries Plunge 39 %.*

*International Jerusalem Post* (2002, January 12). *Editorial.*

*International Jerusalem Post* (2002, July 26).

*International Jerusalem Post (2001, November 15). Editorial.*

*International Jerusalem Post (2000, December 20). Editorial.*

*International Jerusalem Post* (2002, August 9).

International Monetary Fund. (1997). *A Global Integration Strategy for the Mediterranean Countries: Open Trade and Market Reforms.* Washington: International Monetary Fund.

International Monetary Fund. (1996). *The West Bank and the Gaza Strip: Improving Fiscal Management.* Washington: International Monetary Fund.

International Monetary Fund. (1995). *The West Bank and The Gaza Strip: Tariff, Trade, and Customs Administration Issues.* Washington: International Monetary Fund.

*Iraq Study Group Report*, (2006), Baker J. -Hamilton L. Report), New York: Viking.

*Jerusalem Post, The:* See *International Jerusalem Post, The.*

*Jerusalem Report, The* (2002, December 16*). Israel to Claim Billions from Muslim States for 900,000 Jewish Refugees.*

*Jerusalem Report, The* (2002, December 2). *Ticker.*

*Jerusalem Report, The* (2001, December 12). *Editorial.*

*Jerusalem Report, The* (2001, October 20). *Editorial.*

Judt T., (2006). *Postwar: A History of Europe since 1945.* New York: Penguin Books.

Kaplan F. (2004, December 26). *China Expands. Europe Rises, and the United States,* The New York Times.

Kimche, D., (1995). *Sowing the Seeds of Economic Cooperation.* Jerusalem: Institute of the World Jewish Congress - Middle East Economic Strategy Group.

King N., Jr. (2004, December 29). *Bush Plans New Strategy for Middle East,* The Wall Street Journal.

Lawrence, R.Z., (1995). *Towards Free Trade in the Middle East: The Triad and Beyond.* Cambridge: Harvard University Press.

Lederach, J.P., (1997), *Building Peace: Sustainable Reconciliation in Divided Societies,* Washington, D.C., Institute of Peace Press.

Levin, I. (2001). *Locked Doors: The Seizure of Jewish Property in Arab Countries.* Westport: Praeger.

Levin, I. (2000). *Confiscated Wealth: The Fate of Jewish Property in Arab Lands.* Jerusalem: Institute of the World Jewish Congress.

Lewis, B. (2005, May-June). *Freedom and Justice in the Modern Middle East,* New York: Foreign Affairs.

Lewis, B. (2002). *What Went Wrong?: Western Impact and Middle Eastern Response.* New York: Oxford University Press.

Lewis, B. (2001, November 19). *The Revolt of Islam.* The New Yorker.

Lewis, B. (1997). *The Future of the Middle East.* London: Orion.

Machado, B., and Oliver, G., (2006), *The Ramifications of the Marshall Plan for Contemporary Postconflict Transformation,* George C. Marshall Foundation (unpublished).

Makovsky, D. (2005, May-June), *Gaza: Moving Forward by Pulling Back,* New York: Foreign Affairs.

Makovsky, D. (2001, March-April). *Middle East Peace Through Partition.* New York: Foreign Affairs.

Makovsky, D. (1996). *Making Peace with the PLO: The Rabin Government's Road to the Oslo Accord.* Boulder: Westview Press.

Mallaby, S. (2005, May-June), *Saving the World Bank.* New York: Foreign Affairs.

Marshall, George C. Foundation, Grant Proposal to Smith Richardson Foundation, *The Ramifications of the Marshall Plan for Contemporary Post-Conflict Transformation,* funded July 1, 2005.

McCarthy, J. (1952). *The Story of General George Marshall.* Self-published.

McCullough, D., (1992). *Truman.* New York: Simon & Schuster.

Molle, W., (1997). *The Economics of European Integration.* Brookfield: Ashgate Publishers.

Naim, M. (2005, May 4), *Culture is not the Culprit in Arab poverty,* Financial Times (London).

Nasr, V.,(2006), *The Shia Revival: How Conflicts Within Islam Will Shape the Future*, New York, W.W.Norton & Co.

*New York Times, The* (2004, December 23). *Editorial.*

*New York Times, The (2004, December 12), Seven-Year Drought Puts Afghanistan on the Brink.*

*New York Times, The (2004, December 12), Arab and Western Ministers Voice Different Priorities.*

*New York Times, The* (2003, February 11). *Agency Aiding Palestinians is Strapped..*

*New York Times, The* (2003, February 4). *With Rise in Foreign Aid, Plans for a New Way to Give It.*

*New York Times, The* (2003, February 1). *The Brains Behind Bush's War Policy.*

*New York Times, The* (2003, January 11). *A Worldwide Economic Stimulus Plan.*

*New York Times, The* (2002, December 13). *U.S. Delay on Proposal for Mideast Irks Allies.*

*New York Times, The* (2002, November 24). *The Return of America's Postwar Generosity.*

*New York Times, The* (2002, November 21). *Winning the Peace in Afghanistan.*

*New York Times, The* (2002, April 19). Editorial. *Afghanistan's Marshall Plan.*

*New York Times, The* (2001, November 12). *Editorial.*

*New York Times, The* (2002, October 14).

*New York Times, The* (2002, November 12).

Oliver, G. *See* Machado,B. and Oliver.G.

Peres, S. (1993). *The New Middle East.* New York: Henry Holt.

Peters, J. (1996). *Pathways to Peace: The Multilateral Arab-Israeli Peace Talks,* London: The Royal Institute of International Affairs.

*Pharaohs,* (2001, January) London & Cairo. *Editorial.*

Phillips, C., (1966). *The Truman Presidency: The History of a Triumphant Succession* New York: Macmillan Co.

Pillar, P.R. (2006) *Intelligence, Policy, and the War in Iraq,* New York: Foreign Affairs.

Pogue, F.C. (1987). *George C. Marshall: Statesman.* New York: Viking.

Pollard, S., (1974) *European Economic Integration,* 1815-1970. London: Thames and Hudson.

Rashid, Ahmed, (2002), *JIHAD: The Rise of Militant Islam in Central Asia,* New York: Penguin Books.

Rayburn, J. (2006, March-April), *The Last Exit from Iraq: How the British Quit Mesopotamia,* New York: Foreign Affairs.

Reeves, T.C. (1982). *The Life and Times of Joe McCarthy.* New York: Stein and Day.

Rejewan, N. (1999). *Israel's Place in the Middle East.* Gainesville: University of Florida Press.

Robson, P., (1998). (4th Edition). *The Economics of International Integration.* London: Routledge.

Rosenberg, J.M. (2004): *The Essential Dictionary of International Trade*, New York: Barnes & Noble.

Rosenberg, J.M. (2003): *Nation-Building: A Middle East Recovery Program*: Lanham, Md., University Press of America.

Rosenberg, J.M. (1999): *Arafat's Palestinian State and JIPTA: The Best Hope for Lasting Peace in the Middle East*. Stanford: JAI Press.

Rosenberg, J.M. (1997). *Encyclopedia of the Middle East Peace Process and the Middle East/North Africa Economic Community*. Greenwich: JAI Press.

Rosenberg, J.M. (1996). *The Peace Dividend: Creating a Middle East/North Africa Community*. Rabat: Secretariat of MENA Economic Summits.

Rosenberg, J.M. (1995). *Encyclopedia of the North American Free Trade Agreement, the New American Community and Latin-American Trade*. Westport: Greenwood Press.

Rosenberg, J.M. (1992). *The New American Community: A Response to the European and Asian Economic Challenge*. Westport: Praeger.

Rosenberg, J.M. (1991). *The New Europe: An A to Z Compendium on the European Community*. Washington: The Bureau of National Affairs.

Ross, D. (2004): *The Missing Peace-The Inside Story of the Fight for Middle East Peace*, New York: Farrar, Strauss, Giroux.

Rovere, R.H. (1960). *Senator Joe McCarthy*. Cleveland and New York: The World Publishing Company.

Royal Hashemite Court. (1995). *Building a Prosperous Peace: Amman '95, Middle East and North Africa Economic Summit*. Amman: International Press Office.

Rubin, B. (1999). *The Transformation of Palestinian Politics: From Revolution to State-Building.* Cambridge: Harvard University Press.

Safire, W., (2002, April 4), *Sharon on Survival,* The New York Times.

Said, E.W., (2000). *The End of the Peace Process: Oslo and After.* New York: Pantheon Books.

Samir, S., (2000, December). *Jordan-US FTA: The Ant & The Elephant.* Pharaohs.

Savir, U., (1998). *The Process: 1,100 Days That Changed the Middle East.* New York: Random House.

Schofield, C.H. & Schofield, R.N., (1994), *The Middle East and North Africa.* London: Routledge.

Segev, S., (1998). *Crossing the Jordan.* New York: St. Martin's Press.

Sewell, D., (2001, May). *Governance and the Business Environment in the West Bank/Gaza.* Washington: The World Bank.

Sharansky, N., & Dormer, R., (2004), *The Case for Democracy, The Power of Freedom to Overcome Tyranny & Terror,* New York: Public Affairs.

Sharansky, N., (2002, May 12). *A Marshall Plan for the Palestinians,* The New York Times.

Sokolsky, R., & McMillan, J., (2002, February 12). *Foreign Aid in Our Own Defense,* The New York Times.

Stevenson, Jonathan, (2003, February 1). *The Qaeda Vipers in Europe's Bosom,* The New York Times.

Stoler, M.A., (1989), *George C. Marshall: Soldier-Statesman of the American Century.* Boston: Twayne Publishers.

*Telegraph (UK) (2004, December 19) I Will Bring Peace to Middle East, Bush Promises.*

UNCTAD, (2005, July 21), *Report on UNCTAD's Assistance to the Palestinian People*, Geneva: UNCTAD.

UNCTAD, (2002, July 26), *Report on UNCTAD's Assistance to the Palestinian People,* Geneva: UNCTAD.

UNCTAD, (1998). *Palestine Merchandise Trade in the 1990s.* Geneva: UNCTAD.

UNDP, (2003,2004,2005). *Arab Human Development Report.* New York: United Nations.

Wahby, E., (2001, March). *Forging a Deal: EU-Egypt Trade Agreement.* Pharaohs.

*Wall Street Journal, The* (2003, March 10) *U.S. Prepares for Rebuilding Iraq.*

*Wall Street Journal, The* (2002, April 13). *Editorial.*

*Wall Street Journal, The* (2001, November 12). *Editorial.*

Warren, C. (2001). *Chances of a Lifetime,* New York: Scribner.

Warren, C. (1998). *In the Stream of History.* Stanford: Stanford University Press.

*Washington File,* (2002, July 24), *Hearing,* U.S. Department of State, House International Relations Committee.

Washington Institute for Near East Policy, The  (2005) *Security, Reform and Peace: The Three Pillars of U.S. Strategy in the Middle East,* Washington D.C.

Weiss, J., (Spring 2005), *Iraq and Democracy*, Journal of International Security Affairs,
Washington, D.C., Number 8.

Westad O.A., (2005), *The Global Cold War,* Cambridge: Cambridge University Press.

Wexler, I., (1983) *The Marshall Plan Revisited: The European Recovery Program in Economic Perspective*, Westport, Greenwood Press.

White, T.H. (1978), *In Search of History: A Personal Adventure*. New York: Harper & Row.

Wilson, R., (1995). *Economic Development in the Middle East*. London: Routledge.

Winter, Elmer L., (July 2002), *Middle East Economic Development Plan (MEED)*, unpublished.

Woodward, B. (2002). *Bush At War*. New York: Simon & Schuster.

World Bank, The (2002, March 18). *Fifteen Months-Intifada, Closures and Palestinian Economic Crisis*. Washington: The World Bank.

World Bank, The (1999, Third Quarter). *Carrying the World Bank Program into the Next Millenium - West Bank and Gaza Update*. Washington: The World Bank.

World Bank, The (1997). *Getting Connected: Private Participation in Infrastructure in  the Middle East and North Africa*. Washington: The World Bank.

World Bank, The (1995). *Claiming the Future: Choosing Prosperity in the Middle East and North Africa*. Washington: The World Bank.

Zakaria, F. (2001, October 15). *Why Do They Hate Us? - the Politics of Rage*, Newsweek.

# INDEX

# ABOUT THE AUTHOR

Jerry M. Rosenberg, a 2006 Marshall Foundation Fellow, is Founder and Director of the Center for Middle East Business Studies, Professor of International Business at the Rutgers Business School, and member of the faculty of the Division of Global Affairs, Rutgers University, Newark, New Jersey, USA. He has also been a Visiting Professor at the University of British Columbia (Canada), Middlesex Polytechnic University (England), Ben-Gurion University (Israel), University of Iceland (Iceland), John Cabot University (Italy), Ecole Superieure Commerce Marseille-Provence (France), Bifrost Business School (Iceland), Maastricht School of Management (The Netherlands), University of Aberdeen (Scotland), and has lectured at the University of Pavia (Italy), the University of Pisa (Italy), the London School of Economic and Political Sciences (England), Hebrew University (Israel), and Al-Akawan University (Morocco).

He received his B.S. degree from The City College of New York, an M.A. from Ohio State University, Certificate from the Conservatoire Nationale des Arts et Metiers (National Institute of Science, Technology and Management in Paris), and Ph.D. from New York University.

As a Fulbright-French Government scholarship winner, at the age of 23, he was introduced to the world of international affairs while living in Paris.

He has had 33 books published, including nine subsequent new editions. Many of these works have been translated into several languages, including Japanese, Russian, Czech/Slovak, Chinese, and Spanish.

An "expert" speaker at all four Middle East/North Africa Economic Summits (Casablanca, Amman, Cairo, and Doha), he has drawn from 20 years of experience in writing and researching on regional economic integration dealing with the European Union, NAFTA and Latin-American Trade. He has made numerous trips to North Africa, the Middle East, and Central Asia to collect pertinent data and to interview many of their leaders.

Dr. Rosenberg first presented a model for a potential community of regional nations at the Casablanca- 1994 and October 1995 Amman Middle East/North Africa Economic Summits. The Executive Secretariat of the Middle East/North Africa Summits commissioned Rosenberg's *The Peace Dividend: Creating a Middle East/North Africa Community;* it was printed and distributed it at the Cairo Economic Conference in 1996. His *Encyclopedia of the Middle East Peace Process and the Middle East/ North Africa Economic Community* was completed in time for the Doha, Qatar, opening plenary in November 1997. *Arafat's Palestinian State and JIPTA: The Best Hope for Lasting Peace in the Middle East,* was published in 1999, and *Nation-Building: A Middle East Program* in 2003. He has presented his model for regional economic integration in the North Africa, the Middle East, and Central Asia to numerous government and private-sector organizations, including briefings at the U.S. State Department, and The World Bank.

In February 2006, he was one of several specialists invited by the U.S. Department of State and the Marshall Foundation to discuss "Lessons of the Marshall Plan for Middle East Conflict."